THE PIE BOOK

THE PIE BOOK

CAROLINE BRETHERTON

with Jane Bamforth

LONDON, NEW YORK, MELBOURNE,
MUNICH, AND DELHI

Photography William Reavell
Recipe Editor Kathy Steer

DK UK
Editor Alison Shaw
Project Art Editor Kathryn Wilding
Design Assistant Jade Wheaton
Managing Editor Dawn Henderson
Managing Art Editor Christine Keilty
Senior Jackets Creative Nicola Powling
Jacket Design Assistant Rosie Levine
Pre-Production Producer Andrew Hilliard,
George Nimmo
Senior Producer Jen Lockwood
Creative Technical Support Sonia Charbonnier
Publisher Peggy Vance

DK INDIA
Senior Editor Chitra Subramanyam
Editor Ligi John
Assistant Editor Neha Samuel
Senior Art Editor Anchal Kaushal
Art Editors Vandna Sonkariya,
Isha Nagar, Pankaj Bhatia
Managing Editor Glenda Fernandes
Managing Art Editor Navidita Thapa
DTP Manager Sunil Sharma
DTP Operator Satish Chandra Gaur

10 9 8 7 6 5 4 3 2 1
001–187843–Feb/13

First published in Great Britain in 2013 by
Dorling Kindersley Limited,
80 Strand, London WC2R 0RL
Penguin Group (UK)

A CIP catalogue record for this book
is available from the British Library.

ISBN: 978-1-4093-2112-5

Colour reproduction by Opus Multi Media Services, India
Printed and bound by South China Printing Co. Ltd, China

Discover more at **www.dk.com**

CONTENTS

FOREWORD

It's time that pies and tarts had their moment in the sun. For too long these versatile dishes have been neglected, thought by many to be old-fashioned and heavy. However, there are as many different types of pies and tarts as you have the imagination to create, from heart-warming winter dishes such as suet-crusted Steak and Kidney Pie to the delicate, multi-layered puff pastry confections that are Summer Fruit Millefeuilles.

As well as there being a pie for all occasions, there are also pies for every type of cook. Whether you are just starting out on the road to culinary expertise, or whether you have been travelling down it for years, you will find recipes in this book to excite and stimulate you.

Many home cooks are unnecessarily put off making pastry – they often think it is more difficult than it actually is. Pastry-making traditionally needs cool hands (pastry hands, my grandmother used to call them) and a cool, logical head. Follow a few simple rules and it's hard to go wrong: pastry should be handled as little as possible, to stop it becoming dry and overworked. It should be chilled or rested before use, as it helps the glutens in the flour to relax, and stops the cooked pastry shrinking away from the tin. Most pies and tarts turn out better if blind-baked first, and try to bake pastry in metal tins – the metal conducts heat far better and quicker, which helps to stop that common problem – the soggy bottom!

There are a few shortcuts that can help you to make the perfect pastry. I often make my pastry in a food processor as this saves both time and effort. If you are worried about over-mixing the pastry, try just using the food processor to rub together the fat and flour, then continue by hand. There are also many ready-made products on the market that are indistinguishable from home-made pastry. If time is short, there is nothing wrong with taking a shortcut and using a good-quality ready-made pastry. The important thing is to produce a pie that looks and tastes delicious.

Caroline

INTRODUCTION

The Pie Book draws together recipes for pies and tarts from all over the world. From the lightest, most delicate layered fruit strudels to the heartiest steak pies, all types of the most delicious and diverse recipes are gathered together in one place. Pies and tarts can be as varied as the pastry and fillings they contain, and here there are recipes for every different type of pastry imaginable. Potato- or crumble-topped pies also feature, and some recipes use bread or cobbler dough as a delicious base or a tempting topping.

In *The Pie Book* you will find an enormous variety of pies and tarts – from the classic en croûtes, made with beef and salmon, to the more unusual pastillas of North Africa stuffed with a heady mixture of game, herbs, and spices.

If you're in the mood for baking a sweet pie, there is a multitude of choices. You'll find classic American pies, such as Pumpkin Pie, as well as British recipes like Yorkshire Curd Tart and an updated take on a traditional Treacle Tart. This book is **truly international**, featuring "pie-like" dishes such as the Italian *Torta della Nonna*, a simple, ricotta based tart, or the crispy *Baklava* of the Middle East, stuffed with nuts and spices and dripping with a honey syrup.

Also included is an array of mini pies and hand pies, galettes, turnovers, tartlets, and pasties. These fun, individual pies are loved by adults and children alike, whatever the occasion. They can be put together in a flash, and eaten hot or cold, making them ideal to take on a picnic, pop in a lunchbox, or serve at a party.

Despite the wealth of choice in *The Pie Book*, it is simple to follow. The illustrated **Recipe Choosers** guide you towards a particular dish by listing each recipe by pie type, so you can pick between **Cobblers and Crumbles** or **Double-crust Pies,** and everything in between, to match your mood and occasion beautifully.

The recipes in each chapter are **organized by key ingredient**, such as chicken, spinach, or apple, to help you decide what you want to cook. Each recipe is presented clearly and simply in a few method steps, accompanied by helpful "at-a-glance" icons which tell you the serving size, prep and cook times, and freezing information. Fabulous photography and clear instructions throughout will help you to produce mouth-watering results every time.

For those who really want to master the art of pastry making in all its forms, the **In Praise of Pastry** chapter contains precise, detailed step by step instructions for perfect pastry. Whether it's a time-consuming strudel dough or a handy quick puff pastry recipe, the visual step by steps are there to guide you at every stage.

So whether you want to whip up a quick midweek supper and are seeking fresh inspiration, or wanting to succeed in making the perfect apple pie, there is something for everyone in this book. From novice home cooks to experienced chefs, there is a mixture of both old favourites and new classics for all.

I hope that *The Pie Book* will become a much-loved and well-trusted reference book for all types of pies and tarts for years to come.

TOP-CRUST PIES

A top crust is particularly suited to those pies that require little more than a lid of home-made or shop-bought pastry, and where the filling is already at least partially cooked or needs little cooking time.

RABBIT AND SWEETCORN PIE WITH A HERB CRUST
COOK 1¾ HRS
page 65

SAVOURY

STEAK AND ALE PIE
COOK 2¼ HRS
page 32

HERBY STEAK AND VEGETABLE PIE
COOK 1½ HRS
page 36

BEEF AND STILTON PIE
COOK 50 MINS–1 HR
page 40

FRUITY LAMB PIE
COOK 1¼ HRS
page 46

PORK AND LEEK PIE
COOK 1 HR 10 MINS
page 56

VENISON PIE
COOK 2–2¾ HRS
page 67

PUFF-CRUSTED GAME SOUP
COOK 1 HR 20 MINS
page 71

CHICKEN PIE
COOK 40–45 MINS
page 76

COQ AU VIN PIE
COOK 55 MINS–1 HR 5 MINS
page 79

CHICKEN AND SWEETCORN PIE
COOK 1 HR
page 83

SPANISH CHICKEN PIE
COOK 45–50 MINS
page 91

CHICKEN POT PIES
COOK 40 MINS
page 74

SWEET

STEAK AND WILD MUSHROOM PIE
COOK 2½–3 HRS
page 30

DOUBLE-CRUST PIES

A double crust suits pies that have rich, thick juices that can be soaked up by the bottom layer of pastry. These pies need a slightly longer cooking time to crisp up both the base and the pie lid.

CHERRY LATTICE PIE
COOK 40–45 MINS
page 274

SAVOURY

STEAK AND KIDNEY DOUBLE-CRUST PIE
COOK 2¾–3¼ HRS
page 33

LAMB AND POTATO PIE
COOK 1 HR 20 MINS
page 48

SAUSAGE, BACON, AND EGG PIE
COOK 50 MINS
page 51

PORK AND APPLE PICNIC PIE
COOK 1 HR
page 55

AUVERGNE TOURTE
COOK 1¼ HRS
page 59

CHICKEN AND HAM RAISED PIE
COOK 1½ HRS
page 77

CHICKEN PIE WITH CHEESE
COOK 35–40 MINS
page 82

CHICKEN AND HEART OF PALM PIE
COOK 35–40 MINS
page 85

KALAKUKKO
COOK 6½ HRS
page 142

STARGAZY PIE
COOK 40–50 MINS
page 153

CHEESE AND ONION PIE
COOK 40 MINS
page 178

FLAMICHE
COOK 40–45 MINS
page 208

CHESTNUT AND MUSHROOM PIE
COOK 35–40 MINS
page 210

SWEET

CROSTATA DI MARMELLATA
COOK 50 MINS
page 258

APPLE PIE
COOK 50–55 MINS
page 218

PEAR PIE WITH WALNUT PASTRY
COOK 35–40 MINS
page 231

PEACH PIE
COOK 40–45 MINS
page 246

RHUBARB AND STRAWBERRY PIE
COOK 50–55 MINS
page 261

CHERRY PIE
COOK 50 MINS–1 HR
page 270

CROSTATA DI RICOTTA
COOK 1–1¼ HRS
page 316

GALETTE DES ROIS
COOK 30 MINS
page 325

COBBLERS AND CRUMBLES

A cobbler topping resembles a cross between a scone and a dumpling. It suits hearty, autumnal stews and desserts. A crumble topping is quick and easy to make and traditionally works well to top sweet fruit fillings.

BEEF, FENNEL, AND MUSHROOM COBBLER
COOK 2½ HRS
page 35

SAVOURY

BEEF AND RED WINE COBBLER
COOK 2½–3½ HRS
page 37

CHICKEN COBBLER
COOK 2¼ HRS
page 89

FISH CRUMBLE
COOK 35–40 MINS
page 143

SWEET

OATY BLACKBERRY AND APPLE CRUMBLE
COOK 45 MINS
page 225

APPLE AND BLACKBERRY COBBLER WITH CINNAMON
COOK 30 MINS
page 229

APPLE BROWN BETTY
COOK 35–45 MINS
page 230

PLUM AND CINNAMON COBBLER
COOK 30 MINS
page 240

PLUM CRUMBLE
COOK 30–40 MINS
page 242

PEACH COBBLER
COOK 30–35 MINS
page 244

RHUBARB SMULPAJ
COOK 30 MINS
page 264

BLUEBERRY COBBLER
COOK 30 MINS
page 267

CHERRY CRUMBLE
COOK 35–40 MINS
page 272

INDIVIDUAL PIES AND TARTS

Whether you're feeding a crowd or making a picnic, individual tarts and pies are the way to go. Folded turnovers or pasties make ideal portable food, and tartlets are a pretty addition to any tea table.

SWEET POTATO, RED ONION, AND THYME GALETTES WITH CHILLI
COOK 50 MINS
page 192

SAVOURY

CORNISH PASTIES
COOK 40–45 MINS
page 38

FORFAR BRIDIES
COOK 20–25 MINS
page 41

SPICY BEEF HAND PIES
COOK 50 MINS
page 43

SAUSAGE ROLLS
COOK 10–12 MINS
page 52

MINI PORK PIES
COOK 1 HR
page 57

INDIVIDUAL QUAIL PASTILLA
COOK 55 MINS
page 68

CHINESE BARBECUE DUCK PUFFS
COOK 50 MINS
page 70

CHICKEN PASTIES
COOK 35–40 MINS
page 90

SMOKED CHICKEN AND ROCKET FILO PARCELS
COOK 20 MINS
page 92

ROAST CHICKEN HAND PIES
COOK 40 MINS
page 81

INDIVIDUAL CURRIED MUSSEL PIES
COOK 40–45 MINS
page 156

CONTINUED ....▶

SMOKED TROUT TARTLETS
COOK 30 MINS
page 148

RASPBERRY TARTLETS WITH CRÈME PÂTISSIÈRE
COOK 10 MINS
page 257

SWEET

QUICHES AND SAVOURY TARTS

A savoury quiche is traditionally deeper than a tart, and has a higher ratio of eggs to cream in the filling. Both are ideal when you want to serve a more substantial dish for a light lunch or buffet.

SALMON AND SPINACH QUICHE
COOK 1 HR 10 MINS–1¼ HRS
page 138

QUICHE LORRAINE
COOK 50 MINS–1 HR
page 58

ONION AND ROQUEFORT QUICHE
COOK 1½ HRS
page 181

SPINACH AND GOAT'S CHEESE QUICHE
COOK 55 MINS–1 HR
page 185

ASPARAGUS CREAM CHEESE QUICHE
COOK 35 MINS
page 203

BROCCOLI AND MUSHROOM QUICHE
COOK 50 MINS–1 HR
page 207

LEEK QUICHE
COOK 1–1½ HRS
page 209

SAVOURY TARTS

CREOLE SAUSAGE AND TOMATO TART
COOK 1 HR 10 MINS
page 50

SPINACH, GOAT'S CHEESE, AND PANCETTA TART
COOK 40–45 MINS
page 60

CELERIAC AND SMOKED BACON SOUFFLÉ PIE
COOK 50 MINS
page 61

SWEET TARTS

The starting point for a sweet tart is a good shortcrust case, made from either savoury or sweet pastry. The case can then hold a whole variety of fillings, with or without a custard to bind them.

NORMANDY PEAR TART
COOK 35–45 MINS
page 233

TARTE AUX POMMES
COOK 1¼ HRS
page 222

APPLE TOURTE WITH NUTS AND RAISINS
COOK 30–35 MINS
page 226

PEAR AND ALMOND TART
COOK 50 MINS
page 235

AUTUMN FRUIT TART
COOK 1 HR
PAGE 238

BAVARIAN PLUM TART
COOK 50–55 MINS
PAGE 241

NORMANDY PEACH TART
COOK 35–45 MINS
page 243

ALMOND AND PEACH TART
COOK 30 MINS
page 247

EXOTIC FRUIT TART
COOK 35 MINS
page 248

APRICOT TART
COOK 50 MINS–1 HR
page 251

ALMOND AND RASPBERRY LATTICE TART
COOK 50 MINS–1 HR
page 253

RASPBERRY CREAM CHEESE TART
COOK 35–45 MINS
page 254

RHUBARB AND CUSTARD TART
COOK 1 HR 35 MINS
page 262

DOUBLE CHOCOLATE RASPBERRY TART
COOK 5–10 MINS
page 296

CONTINUED....➡

TARTE AU CITRON

BLUEBERRY CREAM CHEESE TART

EN CROÛTES AND LAYERED PIES

Light, delicate pastries such as puff pastry or rich shortcrusts make good vehicles for en croûtes or layered pies. For a quick dessert, sandwich buttery puff pastry layers together with cream and fruit.

HERBY FETA FILO PIE
COOK 1 HR
page 198

SAVOURY

SALMON EN CROÛTE
COOK 30 MINS
page 140

TARTE TATINS

Named after two French sisters who earned a living by baking their father's favourite apple tart, this is a true French classic. Other fruit works well too, or use vegetables to give this dish a savoury twist.

BEETROOT TARTE TATIN
COOK 35–45 MINS
page 176

SAVOURY

CARAMELIZED SHALLOT TARTE TATIN
COOK 45 MINS
page 180

SWEET

APPLE TARTE TATIN
COOK 35–50 MINS
page 224

PEAR TARTE TATIN
COOK 45–55 MINS
page 236

CARAMELIZED MANGO TARTLETS
COOK 30 MINS
page 249

CARAMEL BANANA TART
COOK 30–35 MINS
page 285

POTATO-TOPPED PIES

Potato toppings can be used with any type of vegetable, fish, or meat filling. An ideal way to use up leftover stews, the topping can be varied with the addition of fresh herbs, grated cheese, or mustard.

FISHERMAN'S PIE
COOK 50 MINS– 1 HR
page 135

MEAT PIES AND TARTS

A perfect dish for autumnal entertaining, this delicious steak pie is both homely and extravagant. If you can't find fresh wild mushrooms, use dried, or even dark chestnut mushrooms instead.

STEAK AND WILD MUSHROOM PIE

 **SERVES 4–6**   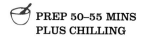 **PREP 50–55 MINS PLUS CHILLING**   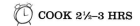 **COOK 2½–3 HRS**    **FREEZE UP TO 1 MONTH**

EQUIPMENT
2 litre (3½ pint) pie dish,
pie funnel

INGREDIENTS

FOR THE FILLING
500g (1lb 2oz) mixed wild mushrooms,
fresh, or 75g (2½oz) dried wild
mushrooms, soaked for 30 minutes
and drained
35g (1oz) plain flour
salt and freshly ground black pepper
1kg (2¼lb) braising steak,
cut into 2.5cm (1in) cubes
4 shallots, finely chopped
900ml (1½ pints) beef stock
or water, plus extra if needed
leaves from 6 sprigs of parsley,
finely chopped

FOR THE PASTRY
(For visual step by step instructions
see puff pastry pp110–113)
250g (9oz) plain flour,
plus extra for dusting
½ tsp fine salt
175g (6oz) unsalted butter, diced
1 egg, beaten, to glaze

1 Preheat the oven to 180°C (350°F/Gas 4). Slice the mushrooms. Make the filling by seasoning the flour with salt and black pepper. Toss the steak in it to coat.

2 Put the meat, mushrooms, and shallots in a casserole. Add the stock and heat, stirring well. Bring to the boil, stirring constantly. Cover and cook in the oven for 2–2¼ hours until tender.

3 To make the pastry, sift the flour and salt into a bowl. Rub in one-third of the butter with your fingertips until the mixture resembles breadcrumbs. Add 100ml (3½fl oz) water and bring it together to form a dough. Chill for 15 minutes.

4 Roll out the dough on a lightly floured surface to a 15 x 38cm (6 x 15in) rectangle. Dot the rest of the butter over two-thirds. Fold the unbuttered side over half the buttered side. Fold the dough again so the butter is completely enclosed in layers of dough. Turn it over and roll over the edges to seal. Wrap in cling film and chill for 15 minutes. Roll to 15 x 45cm (6 x 18in), fold in thirds, make a quarter turn. Seal. Chill for 15 minutes. Repeat three more times, chilling for 15 minutes between each turn.

5 Add the parsley to the meat and season. Spoon it into the dish. Increase the heat to 220°C (425°F/Gas 7). Roll out the dough on a floured surface. Cut a strip from the edge. Dampen the rim of the dish and press the strip onto it. Put the rolled-out dough over the pie and press firmly to seal. Brush with the beaten egg. Make a hole in the top and add a pie funnel to allow steam to escape. Chill for 15 minutes. Bake for 25–35 minutes until golden brown. If browning too quickly, cover with foil. The filling can be made 2–3 days ahead.

This hearty pie is a treasured winter classic. The use of brown ale not only imparts a rich flavour, but also tenderizes the meat as it cooks. Serve with the gravy and lots of mashed potato.

STEAK AND ALE PIE

 **SERVES 4**

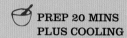 **PREP 20 MINS PLUS COOLING**

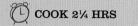 **COOK 2¼ HRS**

 **FREEZE UP TO 1 MONTH**

EQUIPMENT
1.7 litre (3 pint) pie dish

INGREDIENTS

FOR THE FILLING
3 tbsp plain flour
salt and freshly ground black pepper
675g (1½lb) lean braising steak, cut into 2cm (¾in) pieces
3 tbsp sunflower oil
1 large onion, chopped
1 garlic clove, crushed
115g (4oz) button mushrooms, halved
175ml (6fl oz) beef stock
175ml (6fl oz) brown ale
1 bay leaf
½ tsp dried thyme
1 tbsp Worcestershire sauce
1 tbsp tomato purée

FOR THE PASTRY
350g (12oz) ready-made puff pastry (or to make your own, see pp110–113)
flour, for dusting
1 egg, beaten, or milk, to glaze

1 To make the filling, season the flour to taste with salt and black pepper. Toss the beef in the flour, shaking off any excess. Heat 2 tablespoons of the sunflower oil in a large non-stick frying pan and fry the steak in batches over a high heat until browned on all sides. Transfer to a large saucepan.

2 Add the remaining sunflower oil to the pan and fry the onion over a medium heat for 5 minutes. Add the garlic and mushrooms and cook for 3–4 minutes until starting to brown, stirring frequently.

3 Transfer the onion and mushrooms to the saucepan with the stock, ale, bay leaf, thyme, Worcestershire sauce, and tomato purée. Bring to the boil, reduce the heat, cover, and simmer gently for 1½ hours, or until the meat is tender.

4 With a slotted spoon, transfer the meat and vegetables to the pie dish. Reserve 150ml (5fl oz) of the gravy and pour the rest over the meat mixture. Cool.

5 Preheat the oven to 200°C (400°F/Gas 6). Roll out the pastry on a lightly floured surface to a thickness of 3mm (⅛in), and 5cm (2in) larger than the dish. Cut a 2cm (¾in) strip, brush the dish rim with water, and place the strip on the rim. Brush with water. Place the pastry over the dish, press the edges together to seal, trim off the excess pastry, and crimp.

6 Decorate the top of the pie with the pastry trimmings, then brush the pastry with the beaten egg or milk, and cut a slit in the middle to allow steam to escape. Bake for 25 minutes, or until puffed and golden. Serve the pie hot with the reserved gravy. The filling can be made up to 24 hours ahead and kept, covered, in the refrigerator.

Although most pies tend to be single-crusted, a good old-fashioned pie like this steak and kidney one should always have a double crust to soak up the deliciously meaty, dark gravy.

STEAK AND KIDNEY DOUBLE-CRUST PIE

 SERVES 4   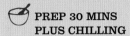 PREP 30 MINS PLUS CHILLING   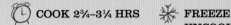 COOK 2¾–3¼ HRS   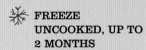 FREEZE UNCOOKED, UP TO 2 MONTHS

1 Heat 2 tablespoons of the olive oil in a saucepan and fry the onions for 5 minutes until soft, but not brown. Add the mushrooms and fry for 3–4 minutes. Remove the vegetables with a slotted spoon. Toss the steak in 2 tablespoons of seasoned flour. Heat the remaining oil in the pan over a high heat and fry the meat in batches until browned. Remove the meat, as it cooks, and add it to the vegetables. Return the meat and vegetables to the pan, cover with the stock, season, and add the thyme. Bring to the boil, reduce the heat to low, cover, and cook for 2–2½ hours until tender.

2 To make the pastry, rub the flour and suet together until the mixture resembles breadcrumbs. Add the salt and enough cold water to form a soft dough. Wrap in cling film and chill for 30 minutes.

3 Mash 2 tablespoons of plain flour into the butter. Uncover the stew and increase the heat. When it boils, stir in the paste a little at a time. Reduce the heat and cook for 30 minutes until thick. Add the kidneys. Preheat the oven to 180°C (350°F/Gas 4).

4 Roll out the pastry on a lightly floured surface to a 20 x 40cm (8 x 16in) rectangle, 3–5mm (⅛–¼in) thick. Place the dish onto a short edge of the pastry and cut a circle around it for the lid. Grease the dish, trim the remaining pastry, and use to line the dish, allowing the sides to overhang. Fill with the filling and brush the edges with egg. Cover with the lid and seal. Brush with egg; cut 2 slits in the top. Bake for 40–45 minutes until golden brown. Cool for 5 minutes and eat the same day.

EQUIPMENT
18cm (7in) pie dish

INGREDIENTS

FOR THE FILLING
4 tbsp olive oil, plus extra for greasing
2 onions, finely chopped
100g (3½oz) button mushrooms, wiped, halved or quartered, if necessary
600g (1lb 5oz) stewing steak, such as chuck, cut into 3cm (1¼in) chunks
4 tbsp plain flour
sea salt and freshly ground black pepper
600ml (1 pint) beef stock
a large sprig of thyme
30g (1oz) unsalted butter, softened
4 fresh lamb's kidneys, about 200g (7oz), trimmed, central core cut out, and cut into chunks

FOR THE PASTRY
(For visual step by step instructions see suet crust pastry pp106–107)
300g (10oz) self-raising flour, plus extra for dusting
150g (5½oz) beef or vegetable suet
½ tsp salt
1 egg, beaten, to glaze

Most cobblers rise like scones on baking, however if you use plain flour they take on a different texture, resulting in a thinner, crisper cobbler topping. This topping will work well with any rich stew.

BEEF, FENNEL, AND MUSHROOM COBBLER

 SERVES 8　　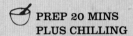 PREP 20 MINS PLUS CHILLING　　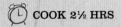 COOK 2½ HRS　　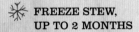 FREEZE STEW, UP TO 2 MONTHS

1 Preheat the oven to 180°C (350°F/Gas 4). Season the meat well, place in a large bowl, and toss with the flour and paprika so the pieces are evenly coated.

2 Heat half the olive oil in the pan, add the meat, and cook over a medium heat, stirring frequently, for 8–10 minutes until evenly browned. Brown the meat in batches as there will be too much to cook altogether. Remove with a slotted spoon and set aside.

3 Heat the remaining oil in the pan. Add the onions and cook for 6–8 minutes until soft. Season well. Add the fennel and cook for 6 minutes until beginning to soften slightly. Add the wine, increase the heat, and simmer for 1–2 minutes until the alcohol evaporates. Return the meat to the pan, pour in the stock, and bring to the boil. Cover with a lid and bake for 1 hour.

4 To make the topping, rub the flour, cornmeal, a pinch of salt, and the butter together with your fingertips until the mixture resembles breadcrumbs. Stir through enough milk to form a soft dough. Chill for 20 minutes, then roll out the dough on a floured surface and cut out 16 circles with the pastry cutter.

5 When the beef has been cooking for 1 hour, melt the butter in a frying pan. Add the mushrooms and oregano, and cook for 5 minutes, or until soft. Stir into the beef and fennel and cook for a further 30 minutes. Increase the oven temperature to 200°C (400°F/Gas 6). Top the stew with the cobbler circles, overlapping them so there are few gaps where the filling can be seen. Brush them with the egg and bake for 30–40 minutes until golden brown. Rest for 5 minutes before serving.

EQUIPMENT
large cast-iron pan, 6cm (2½in) round cutter

INGREDIENTS

FOR THE FILLING
1kg (2¼lb) stewing beef,
　cut into bite-sized pieces
salt and freshly ground black pepper
1 tbsp plain flour
2 tsp mild paprika
3 tbsp olive oil
2 onions, finely sliced
3 fennel bulbs, trimmed
　and cut into eighths
150ml (5fl oz) dry white wine
1.2 litres (2 pints) hot beef stock
　or vegetable stock
a knob of butter
450g (1lb) chestnut mushrooms, quartered
a pinch of dried oregano

FOR THE COBBLER TOPPING
(For visual step by step instructions
　see cobbler dough pp118–119)
150g (5½oz) each plain flour and cornmeal,
　plus extra for dusting
50g (1¾oz) butter
90ml (3fl oz) milk
1 egg yolk, beaten, to glaze

This classic pie is a good midweek stand-by when time is short. If you're serving a stew, make double quantities and serve half another day with this light, buttery crust for a quick and tasty meal.

HERBY STEAK AND VEGETABLE PIE

 **SERVES 4** 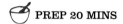 **PREP 20 MINS** 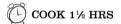 **COOK 1½ HRS**  **FREEZE UP TO 1 MONTH**

EQUIPMENT
1.2 litre (2 pint) pie dish

INGREDIENTS

FOR THE FILLING
1 potato, peeled and cut into bite-sized pieces
2 carrots, peeled and cut into bite-sized pieces
1 parsnip, peeled and cut into bite-sized pieces
salt and freshly ground black pepper
675g (1½lb) braising steak, chopped into bite-sized pieces
2 tbsp olive oil
1 onion, finely chopped
1 tbsp plain flour
1 tbsp Worcestershire sauce
300ml (10fl oz) beef stock
150ml (5fl oz) red wine
2 tbsp finely chopped rosemary leaves
1 bay leaf

FOR THE PASTRY
300g (10oz) ready-made puff pastry
(or to make your own, see pp110–113)
flour, for dusting
1 egg, lightly beaten, to glaze

1 Boil the potato, carrots, and parsnip chunks in a saucepan of salted water for 15 minutes until soft. Drain and set aside. Put the meat in a large, non-stick frying pan with 1 tablespoon of the olive oil, and cook over a high heat for 5–8 minutes until browned all over. Remove with a slotted spoon and set aside.

2 Heat the remaining oil in the frying pan over a low heat. Add the onion and a pinch of salt, and sweat gently for about 5 minutes until soft and translucent. Stir in the flour, and continue to cook for a further 2 minutes. Increase the heat a little, and add the Worcestershire sauce, stock, wine, rosemary, and bay leaf. Bring to the boil, reduce the heat slightly, and return the meat to the pan. Cover and simmer gently over a low heat for about 30 minutes, stirring occasionally. Stir through the cooked vegetables and season well with salt and black pepper.

3 Meanwhile, preheat the oven to 200°C (400°F/Gas 6). Remove the bay leaf from the meat and spoon it into the pie dish. Roll out the pastry on a floured surface so that it is about 5cm (2in) larger all around than the top of the dish. Cut out a strip of pastry about 2.5cm (1in) in from the edge to make a collar. Dampen the edge of the dish with a little water, fit the pastry strip all the way around, and press down firmly.

4 Brush the pastry collar with a little of the beaten egg, then top with the pastry lid. Trim away the excess pastry, then using your finger and thumb, pinch the edges of the pastry together to seal. Brush the top of the pie with beaten egg, then cut 2 slits to allow steam to escape. Bake for 30 minutes, or until puffed up and golden brown. Serve hot.

A twist on a classic Boeuf Bourguignon, this hearty dish is topped with circles of dough flavoured with horseradish. If you find horseradish too strong, try using your favourite mustard instead.

BEEF AND RED WINE COBBLER

 SERVES 4   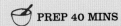 **PREP 40 MINS**   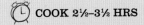 **COOK 2½–3½ HRS**   **FREEZE STEW, UP TO 2 MONTHS**

1 Heat 2 tablespoons of olive oil in the casserole and fry the onions and celery for 5 minutes until soft but not brown. Add the mushrooms and fry for 3–4 minutes until they begin to colour in places. Remove the vegetables with a slotted spoon and set aside.

2 Toss the steak in 2 tablespoons seasoned flour. Heat the remaining oil in the casserole and fry the meat, a few pieces at a time, until well browned on all sides. Take care not to overcrowd the pan, or the meat will begin to steam rather than brown. Remove the meat as it cooks, and add it to the vegetables.

3 Return the meat and vegetables to the casserole, and cover with the wine. Crumble over the stock cube, add 300ml (10fl oz) boiling water, the bouquet garni, sugar, and parsnips. Season and bring to the boil. Reduce the heat to its lowest setting, cover, and cook for 2–2½ hours until the meat is tender. Check it from time to time, adding a little water if it is drying out.

4 Preheat the oven to 200°C (400°F/Gas 6). To make the cobbler topping, sift together the flour, baking powder, and salt. Rub in the butter with your fingertips until the mixture resembles fine breadcrumbs. Add the parsley. Whisk the horseradish and milk, and mix with the dry ingredients to form a soft dough. Roll out the dough on a floured surface to 2cm (¾in) thick. Using the round cutter, cut out circles. Re-roll the offcuts and re-cut until the dough is used up. When the stew is cooked, remove the bouquet garni and top it with the dough discs, overlapping them slightly.

5 Brush the tops with egg and bake for 30–40 minutes until puffed up and golden. Rest for 5 minutes before serving.

EQUIPMENT
large ovenproof casserole,
round cutter

INGREDIENTS

FOR THE FILLING
4 tbsp olive oil
2 onions, finely chopped
2 celery sticks, finely diced
150g (5½oz) baby chestnut
  mushrooms, wiped
600g (1lb 5oz) stewing steak,
  such as shin or chuck,
  cut into 3cm (1¼in) chunks
2 tbsp plain flour
sea salt and freshly ground black pepper
500ml (16fl oz) red wine
1 beef stock cube
1 bouquet garni
1 tbsp sugar
2 parsnips, cut into 2cm (¾in) chunks

FOR THE COBBLER TOPPING
(For visual step by step instructions
  see cobbler dough pp118–119)
300g (10oz) self-raising flour,
  plus extra for dusting
1 tsp baking powder
½ tsp salt
125g (4½oz) unsalted butter,
  chilled and diced
1 tbsp finely chopped parsley
3 tbsp horseradish sauce
  or horseradish cream
2–4 tbsp milk
1 egg, beaten, to glaze

These tasty meat and potato hand pies were originally created as a portable meal for field workers to carry with them. The thick-pleated crust was used as a handle for dirty hands, and discarded after use.

CORNISH PASTIES

 MAKES 4   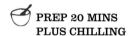 PREP 20 MINS PLUS CHILLING   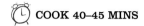 COOK 40–45 MINS    FREEZE UP TO 1 MONTH

EQUIPMENT
baking tray

INGREDIENTS

FOR THE PASTRY
(For visual step by step instructions
see shortcrust pastry p104)
100g (3½oz) lard, chilled and diced
50g (1¾oz) unsalted butter,
chilled and diced
300g (10oz) plain flour,
plus extra for dusting
½ tsp salt
1 egg, beaten, to glaze

FOR THE FILLING
250g (9oz) beef skirt, trimmed and
cut into 1cm (½in) cubes
80g (2¾oz) swede, peeled and
cut into 5mm (¼in) cubes
100g (3½oz) waxy potatoes, peeled
and cut into 5mm (¼in) cubes
1 large onion, finely chopped
splash of Worcestershire sauce
1 tsp plain flour
sea salt and freshly ground black pepper

1 To make the pastry, rub the lard and butter into the flour until the mixture resembles fine breadcrumbs. Add the salt and enough cold water to bring the mixture together into a soft dough. On a lightly floured surface, knead the dough briefly then wrap in cling film and chill in the refrigerator for 30 minutes.

2 Preheat the oven to 190°C (375°F/Gas 5). Mix all the filling ingredients together and season well with salt and black pepper.

3 Roll out the pastry on a well-floured surface to 5mm (¼in) thick. Using a side plate, or saucer, cut 4 circles from the dough. Re-roll the offcuts. Fold the circles in half, then flatten them out, leaving a slight mark down the centre. Pile one-quarter of the filling into each circle, leaving a 2cm (¾in) border all around.

4 Brush the border of the pastry with a little beaten egg. Pull both edges up over the filling and press together to seal. Crimp the sealed edge with your fingers to form a decorative ridge along the top. Brush a little beaten egg all over the finished pasties.

5 Bake in the middle of the oven for 40–45 minutes until golden brown. Set the pasties aside to cool for at least 15 minutes before eating warm or cold. These will keep in the refrigerator for 2 days.

A classic flavour combination of beef and Stilton is used in this rich, tasty pie. Make the puff pastry for a luxurious topping, otherwise use ready-made puff pastry for a speedier result.

BEEF AND STILTON PIE

 SERVES 2    PREP 20 MINS    COOK 50 MINS – 1 HR   FREEZE UP TO 1 MONTH

EQUIPMENT
1.2 litre (2 pint) pie dish

INGREDIENTS

FOR THE FILLING
1 tbsp olive oil
a knob of butter
2 onions, roughly chopped
350g (12oz) leftover roast beef, sliced
150ml (5fl oz) hot beef stock
salt and freshly ground black pepper
125g (4½oz) blue cheese, such as Stilton

FOR THE PASTRY
250g (9oz) ready-made puff pastry
(or to make your own, see pp110–113)
plain flour, for dusting
1 egg, lightly beaten, to glaze

1 Preheat the oven to 200°C (400°F/Gas 6). To make the filling, heat the olive oil and butter in a saucepan over a low heat. Add the onions and sweat very gently for 5–8 minutes until soft and translucent.

2 Add the leftover beef to the onions and pour over the stock. Bring to the boil, then reduce the heat slightly, and simmer for about 10 minutes. Season with salt and black pepper. Set aside to cool slightly, then spoon the mixture into the pie dish, and crumble over the blue cheese.

3 Roll out the pastry on a lightly floured surface until it is a little larger than the pie dish. Dampen the edge of the dish with a little water, then cut out a strip of pastry about 2.5cm (1in) from the edge to make a collar. Dampen the edge of the pie dish with a little water, fit the pastry strip all the way around, and press down firmly. Brush the collar with a little beaten egg and top with the pastry lid. Trim away the excess pastry, then using your finger and thumb, pinch the edges of the pastry together to seal.

4 Brush the top of the pie with the beaten egg to glaze, cut a slit in the top to allow the steam to escape, and bake for 30–40 minutes until golden and puffed. Serve the pie hot.

Originating in Scotland, these delectable hand pies are a regional alternative to the Cornish Pasty. The simple steak and onion filling is complemented by the richness of traditional lard-based pastry.

FORFAR BRIDIES

 MAKES 4   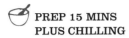 PREP 15 MINS PLUS CHILLING    COOK 20–25 MINS    FREEZE UP TO 1 MONTH

1 To make the pastry, rub the lard into the 2 types of flour until the mixture resembles breadcrumbs. Add the salt and enough cold water to form a soft dough. Bring the dough together, wrap, and chill for 30 minutes. Preheat the oven to 200°C (400°F/Gas 6).

2 Mix the beef, onion, Worcestershire sauce, and salt and black pepper together, then set aside. Roll out the pastry on a floured surface to 5mm (¼in) thick. Using a side plate or saucer, cut 4 circles out of the pastry. You may need to re-roll the offcuts to get all 4. If the pastry cracks on rolling, gather it together and start again; the re-rolling will make it more robust. Fold the circles in half, trim the sides so that they are more rectangular in shape, then flatten them out again.

3 Pile one-quarter of the filling onto one-half of each pastry circle, leaving a 2cm (¾in) border. Brush the border with a little beaten egg. Now fold the pastry over and crimp the edges together. Brush the finished bridies with a little beaten egg, and cut a slit in the top of each one to allow the steam to escape.

4 Bake for 20–25 minutes until golden brown. Set aside to cool for at least 10 minutes before eating. The bridies will keep in the refrigerator for 2 days.

EQUIPMENT
baking tray

INGREDIENTS

FOR THE PASTRY
(For visual step by step instructions see shortcrust pastry p104)
150g (5½oz) lard, chilled and diced
200g (7oz) self-raising flour, plus extra for dusting
100g (3½oz) plain flour
½ tsp salt
1 egg, beaten, to glaze

FOR THE FILLING
300g (10oz) finely chopped beef skirt, or beef steak
1 onion, finely chopped
splash of Worcestershire sauce
sea salt and freshly ground black pepper

Otherwise known as Beef Wellington, this impressive dish is perfect for entertaining. Cooking the puff pastry first, before laying the seared beef on top, helps to keep the pastry crisp.

BOEUF EN CROÛTE

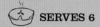 SERVES 6   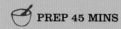 PREP 45 MINS   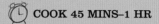 COOK 45 MINS–1 HR

EQUIPMENT
baking tray

INGREDIENTS

FOR THE FILLING
1kg (2¼lb) fillet of beef, cut from the thick end of the fillet, trimmed of fat
salt and freshly ground black pepper
2 tbsp sunflower oil
45g (1½oz) butter
2 shallots, finely chopped
1 garlic clove, crushed
250g (9oz) wild mushrooms, finely chopped
1 tbsp brandy or Madeira

FOR THE PASTRY
500g (1lb 2oz) ready-made puff pastry (or to make your own, see pp110–113)
plain flour, for dusting
1 egg, beaten, to glaze

1 Preheat the oven to 220°C (425°F/Gas 7). Season the meat with salt and black pepper. Heat the sunflower oil in a large frying pan and fry the beef until browned all over. Place the beef in a roasting tin and roast for 10 minutes. Remove and set aside to cool.

2 Melt the butter in a saucepan. Fry the shallots and garlic for 2–3 minutes, stirring, until softened. Add the mushrooms, and cook, stirring constantly, for 4–5 minutes until the juices evaporate. Add the brandy. Let it bubble for 30 seconds. Set aside to cool.

3 Roll out one-third of the pastry on a floured surface to a rectangle, 5cm (2in) larger than the beef. Place on a baking tray, prick with a fork, then bake for 12–15 minutes until crisp. Cool. Spread one-third of the mushroom mix on the centre of the cooked pastry. Make the en croûte (see below). Brush the egg over the uncooked pastry case. Slit the top to allow steam to escape. Bake 30 minutes for rare and 45 minutes for well done. If the pastry starts to brown too much, cover loosely with foil. Rest for 10 minutes before serving.

Making the en croûte

1 Place the beef on top of the cooked pastry and spread the remaining mushroom mixture over the meat.

2 Roll out the remaining pastry and place it over the beef, tucking in the edges.

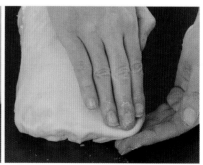

3 Brush the beaten egg around the edges, and press down the raw pastry to seal.

These spicy little parcels are little more than an exotic adaptation of a Cornish Pasty, or a British version of a samosa and are perfect for any occasion. They are best served warm with a mixed salad.

SPICY BEEF HAND PIES

 MAKES 8   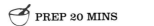 PREP 20 MINS    COOK 50 MINS    FREEZE UP TO 1 MONTH

1 Preheat the oven to 200°C (400°F/Gas 6). Heat 1 tablespoon of the olive oil in a large frying pan over a medium-high heat. Add the steak and brown for about 3 minutes on each side to seal. Remove from the pan and set aside.

2 Heat the remaining oil in the same pan over a low heat. Add the onions and a pinch of salt, and sweat for about 5 minutes until soft and translucent. Add the garlic, chillies, ginger, coriander, and cumin and cook, stirring, for about 2 minutes until fragrant. Tip in the mushrooms, red pepper, and tomatoes and season with the cayenne pepper. Continue cooking over a low heat for 5 minutes until the mushrooms soften and begin to release their juices.

3 Slice the reserved steak into strips, and return to the pan along with 2 tablespoons water. Cook for about 2 minutes until the mixture is thick and moist, but not too runny.

4 Roll out the pastry on a floured surface, and cut into eight 18cm (7in) squares. Dampen each square around the edges with a little water. Divide the meat and onion filling into 8 equal portions, and spoon each one into the middle of a square. Bring together the opposite corners of each pastry square to form a parcel, pinching together to seal. Brush all over with the beaten egg and bake on the baking tray for 20–30 minutes until golden. Serve hot. The pies can be made a day ahead. Fill the pastry and make into parcels, then keep in the refrigerator until needed. Brush with the beaten egg, and bake as above.

EQUIPMENT
baking tray

INGREDIENTS

FOR THE FILLING
2 tbsp olive oil
500g (1lb 2oz) rump steak
2 red onions, finely chopped
salt
2 garlic cloves, grated
   or finely chopped
2–3 medium-hot green chillies,
   deseeded and finely chopped
7.5cm (3in) piece of root ginger,
   finely chopped
1½ tsp coriander seeds, crushed
1½ tsp cumin seeds, crushed
150g (5½oz) mushrooms,
   finely chopped
1 red pepper, finely chopped
2 tomatoes, skinned, deseeded,
   and finely chopped
½ tsp cayenne pepper

FOR THE PASTRY
600g (1lb 5oz) ready-made shortcrust pastry
   (or to make your own, see p104)
plain flour, for dusting
1 egg, lightly beaten, to glaze

This classic French pie is rather like a continental version of the British Cottage Pie. Originally designed to use up leftover roast beef, it is more commonly prepared using fresh minced beef.

FRENCH BEEF AND HERB POTATO PIE

 SERVES 6   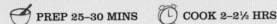 **PREP 25–30 MINS**   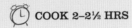 **COOK 2–2½ HRS**

1 Finely chop 2 garlic cloves. Heat one-third of the olive oil in a sauté or frying pan. Add the onion and cook for 3–5 minutes, stirring, until soft but not brown. Add the chopped garlic, minced beef, salt, black pepper, and tomatoes. Reduce the heat and cook gently, stirring occasionally, for 10–12 minutes, until the meat is brown. Stir in the stock and wine. Simmer over a very low heat for 25–30 minutes, stirring occasionally, until most of the liquid has evaporated, but the meat is still moist. Do not cook the meat too fast or it will be tough.

2 To make the topping, place the potatoes in a saucepan with plenty of cold water and add salt. Cover and bring to the boil. Reduce the heat and simmer for 15–20 minutes, until tender when pierced with a knife. Blitz the basil, parsley leaves, the rest of the garlic with the remaining oil in a food processor to form a purée, scraping the side of the bowl occasionally.

3 Drain the potatoes, return them to the pan and mash. Add the herb purée. Scald the milk in another pan. Gradually beat the milk into the potatoes over a medium heat, and stir for 2–3 minutes, until the potatoes just hold a shape. Season to taste.

4 Preheat the oven to 190°C (375°F/Gas 5). Grease the baking dish with oil. Taste the meat for seasoning, then spoon it, with any of its liquid, into the dish. Spoon an even layer of the potatoes over the filling and smooth the top with the back of a spoon. Make a scalloped pattern on the potatoes. Bake until the top is golden brown, the edges bubbling with gravy, and the tip of a skewer inserted in the centre for 30 seconds is hot to the touch when withdrawn; it should take 35–40 minutes. Cut the pie into 6 portions and serve.

EQUIPMENT
large shallow baking dish

INGREDIENTS

FOR THE FILLING
4 garlic cloves, peeled
75ml (2½fl oz) olive oil,
   plus extra for greasing
1 large onion, diced
1kg (2¼lb) minced beef
salt and freshly ground black pepper
400g can chopped tomatoes
250ml (9fl oz) beef stock
125ml (4fl oz) dry white wine

FOR THE TOPPING
1kg (2¼lb) potatoes, peeled
   and cut into 2–3 pieces
salt and freshly ground black pepper
1 bunch of basil, leaves only
1 bunch of parsley, leaves only
250ml (9fl oz) milk,
   plus extra if needed

The addition of pine nuts, dried apricots, and Middle Eastern spices turns this lamb pie into something special. Serve with a green salad garnished with finely sliced red onions and black olives.

FRUITY LAMB PIE

 SERVES 4    PREP 15 MINS   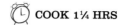 COOK 1¼ HRS    FREEZE UP TO 1 MONTH

EQUIPMENT
1.2 litre (2 pint) pie dish

INGREDIENTS

FOR THE FILLING
1–2 tbsp olive oil
1 onion, finely chopped
salt and freshly ground black pepper
2 garlic cloves, grated or finely chopped
350g (12oz) lamb leg steaks,
cut into bite-sized pieces
1 tsp ground turmeric
½ tsp ground allspice
1 tsp ground coriander
1 tsp ground cumin
2 tbsp plain flour, plus extra for dusting
900ml (1½ pints) hot lamb stock
50g (1¾oz) pine nuts
50g (1¾oz) dried apricots, roughly chopped
50g (1¾oz) raisins

FOR THE PASTRY
300g (10oz) ready-made shortcrust pastry
(or to make your own, see p104)
1 egg, lightly beaten, to glaze

variation

FRUITY BEEF PIE
As an alternative, use stewing beef instead of the lamb. Use beef stock instead of the lamb stock, and simmer the beef for a further 30 minutes before spooning it into the pie dish.

1 Heat 1 tablespoon of the olive oil in a large saucepan over a low heat. Add the onion and a pinch of salt, and sweat gently for about 5 minutes until soft and translucent. Add the garlic then increase the heat to medium, and add a little extra olive oil if needed. Tip in the lamb, and sprinkle over the spices. Cook, stirring occasionally, for 6–8 minutes until the lamb is browned all over.

2 Remove from the heat, and stir in the flour and 1 tablespoon of the stock. Return to the heat, and pour in the remaining stock. Add the pine nuts, apricots, and raisins and season well with salt and black pepper. Bring to the boil, reduce the heat to low, and simmer gently, stirring occasionally so that the mixture doesn't stick, for about 20 minutes, or until the sauce has thickened.

3 Meanwhile, preheat the oven to 200°C (400°F/ Gas 6). Spoon the meat filling into the pie dish. Roll out the pastry on a floured surface so that it is about 5cm (2in) larger than the top of the pie dish. Cut out a strip of pastry about 2.5cm (1in) in from the edge to make a collar. Dampen the edge of the pie dish with a little water, fit the pastry strip all the way around, and press down firmly. Brush the pastry collar with a little of the beaten egg, then top with the pastry lid. Trim away the excess pastry, then using your finger and thumb, pinch the edges of the pastry together to seal. Decorate the top with any leftover pastry, if liked.

4 Brush the top of the pie with the remaining beaten egg, then cut 2 slits in the top to allow steam to escape. Bake for 30–40 minutes until cooked and golden brown all over. Serve hot.

Traditionally made with bone-in lamb chops, this hearty dish can also be made with diced lamb. Although unusual, the addition of anchovies adds a piquancy, but by no means leaves a fishy taste.

LANCASHIRE HOTPOT

 SERVES 8 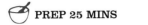 PREP 25 MINS  COOK 2½ HRS

1 Preheat the oven to 180°C (350°F/Gas 4). Heat a drizzle of the olive oil in a large frying pan, add the lamb chops, and cook over a medium heat for 2 minutes on each side until lightly browned. You might need to do this in two batches if your pan is not that big.

2 Put a layer of the potatoes in the bottom of the dish, lay the chops on top, and season well with salt and black pepper. Heat the remaining oil in the frying pan, add the onions, and cook over a low heat, stirring frequently, for 10 minutes, or until beginning to soften. Stir in the anchovies. Spoon a layer of the onion mixture on top of the chops, then add the rest of the sliced potatoes and the onion mixture in alternating layers, finishing with a layer of sliced potatoes.

3 Pour in enough of the stock to come nearly up to the top of the potatoes. Dot the potatoes with butter, cover the dish tightly with foil, then bake for 2 hours, or until the potatoes are meltingly soft and the stock has been absorbed. Remove the foil for the last 20 minutes of cooking. Serve with pickled red cabbage.

EQUIPMENT
2.3 litre (4 pint) flameproof dish

INGREDIENTS

2 tbsp olive oil
8 large lamb chops, each about
  200g (7oz) in weight
900g (2lb) potatoes,
  cut into 5mm (¼in) slices
salt and freshly ground black pepper
4 onions, sliced
8 salted anchovies, finely chopped
600ml (1 pint) hot vegetable stock
a knob of butter

A perfect Monday night supper to follow Sunday's leftover roast lamb – a very simple pie to put together if you use shop-bought pastry. The key flavours are brightened with fresh rosemary.

LAMB AND POTATO PIE

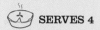 SERVES 4   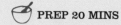 PREP 20 MINS   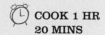 COOK 1 HR 20 MINS

EQUIPMENT
18cm (7in) round pie tin

INGREDIENTS

FOR THE FILLING
450g (1lb) potatoes, peeled and quartered
salt and freshly ground black pepper
1 tbsp olive oil
1 onion, finely chopped
handful of rosemary sprigs,
leaves picked and chopped
350g (12oz) leftover roast lamb,
roughly shredded or sliced
1 tbsp plain flour, plus extra for dusting
300ml (10fl oz) hot vegetable stock
2–3 tsp mint sauce

FOR THE PASTRY
250g (9oz) ready-made shortcrust pastry
(or to make your own, see p104)
1 egg, lightly beaten, to glaze

1 Preheat the oven to 200°C (400°F/Gas 6). Cook the potatoes in a saucepan of boiling salted water for 15 minutes until soft, then drain and set aside.

2 Heat the olive oil in another large pan over a low heat. Add the onion and sweat gently for about 5 minutes until soft and translucent. Stir through the rosemary and add the leftover lamb. Season well with salt and black pepper.

3 Tip in the flour and stir through, then pour in the stock. Keep stirring for about 10 minutes over a medium heat until the liquid begins to thicken, then add the reserved potatoes and stir in the mint sauce. Simmer for a further 10 minutes, then cool slightly.

4 Divide the pastry into 2 pieces, one a little larger than the other. Roll out the larger piece into a large circle on a floured surface and use to line the pie tin, allowing the pastry to hang over the edge. Roll out the other piece to make the pastry lid.

5 Spoon the lamb mixture into the pastry case, then place the pastry lid on top. Using your finger and thumb, pinch the edges of the pastry together to seal, and trim away the excess. Brush the top evenly with a little beaten egg and bake for 40–50 minutes until the pastry is cooked and golden. Set aside to cool in the tin for at least 15 minutes before serving.

There are many recipes for Shepherd's Pie, but the classic, creamy potato topping is a must. Add a little mustard, horseradish, or even Worcestershire sauce to the mash to give it an individual twist.

SHEPHERD'S PIE

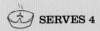 **SERVES 4**   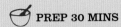 **PREP 30 MINS**   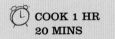 **COOK 1 HR 20 MINS**   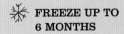 **FREEZE UP TO 6 MONTHS**

1 Cook the potatoes in a large saucepan of boiling salted water for 15 minutes, or until soft. Drain, return to the pan, and mash well. Add the butter and mash again until creamy. Season with salt and black pepper, then set aside.

2 Meanwhile, heat the olive oil in a large heavy-based pan over a medium heat. Add the onions and carrots and cook for 5 minutes, or until the onions are starting to soften. Add the lamb and cook, stirring constantly, for 10 minutes, or until no longer pink. Add the garlic and oregano and cook for 1 minute. Stir in the tomatoes and bring to the boil. Preheat the oven to 180°C (350°F/Gas 4).

3 Add the peas to the pan, and season well with salt and black pepper. Bring to the boil, then reduce the heat and simmer for 20 minutes, stirring occasionally.

4 Pour a layer of the lamb and vegetable filling into a large dish, or the individual serving dishes, and top with the set-aside mashed potato. Bake for 25 minutes or until brown on top and piping hot.

EQUIPMENT
large ovenproof dish,
or 4 individual serving dishes

INGREDIENTS

FOR THE TOPPING
500g (1lb 2oz) floury potatoes
salt and freshly ground black pepper
a knob of butter

FOR THE FILLING
3 tbsp olive oil
1 large onion, diced
2 large carrots, diced
500g (1lb 2oz) lamb mince
3 garlic cloves, chopped
1½ tsp dried oregano
2 x 400g tins chopped tomatoes
125g (4½oz) frozen peas

When you have little more than a packet of sausages and some tomatoes in the house, this is a fantastic alternative to sausage and mash. Of course, fresh sausagemeat can also be used.

CREOLE SAUSAGE AND TOMATO TART

 SERVES 4   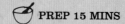 PREP 15 MINS   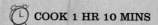 COOK 1 HR 10 MINS

EQUIPMENT
20cm (8in) square pie dish or fluted tart tin, baking beans

INGREDIENTS

FOR THE PASTRY
225g (8oz) ready-made shortcrust pastry (or to make your own, see p104)
plain flour, for dusting
1 egg, lightly beaten

FOR THE FILLING
½ tbsp olive oil
1 onion, finely chopped
salt and freshly ground black pepper
2 stalks celery, sliced
1 green pepper, finely sliced
½ tsp paprika
½ tsp cayenne pepper
½ tsp dried thyme
1 tsp dried oregano
400g (14oz) good-quality pork sausages, skinned
4 tomatoes, sliced

1 Preheat the oven to 200°C (400°F/Gas 6). Roll out the pastry on a floured surface and use to line the pie dish or tart tin. Trim away any excess pastry, line the pastry case with greaseproof paper, and fill with baking beans. Bake for 15–20 minutes until the edges are golden. Remove the beans and paper, brush the bottom of the pastry with a little beaten egg, and return to the oven for 2–3 minutes to crisp. Remove from the oven, and set aside. Reduce the oven temperature to 180°C (350°F/Gas 4).

2 Meanwhile, for the filling, heat the olive oil in a large frying pan over a low heat. Add the onion and a pinch of salt, and sweat gently for about 5 minutes until soft and translucent. Add the celery and green pepper and cook for a further 5 minutes. Add the paprika, cayenne, thyme, oregano, and ¼ teaspoon black pepper, and season well with salt. Add the sausagemeat, breaking it up with a fork or the back of a spatula. Cook, stirring regularly, over a low-medium heat for about 10 minutes until no longer pink. Set aside to cool, then mix in the remaining egg.

3 Spoon the sausage mixture into the pastry case, then layer the tomatoes over the top. Bake for about 20 minutes until lightly golden. Set aside to cool for about 10 minutes, then slice in the dish or tin. Serve with a crisp green salad.

The unusual addition of a little ketchup in the pastry here gives the crust extra flavour. This family-sized pie is perfect for those times when you want to prepare a special picnic or garden meal.

SAUSAGE, BACON, AND EGG PIE

 SERVES 6–8   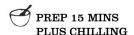 PREP 15 MINS PLUS CHILLING   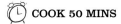 COOK 50 MINS

1 To make the pastry, place the flour and butter in a food processor and pulse until the mixture resembles breadcrumbs. To make by hand, rub the butter into the flour with your fingertips until the mixture resembles breadcrumbs. Season with salt and black pepper, then add the ketchup and 5–6 tablespoons cold water, and pulse or mix again, until it comes together in a ball. Wrap the dough and chill in the refrigerator for 30 minutes.

2 Preheat the oven to 200°C (400°F/Gas 6). Roll out half of the pastry fairly thinly on a lightly floured surface and use to line the pie dish.

3 To make the filling, mix the sausagemeat with the onion, nutmeg, mace, and mustard. Season to taste and spread evenly over the bottom of the pie crust. Place the bacon over the sausagemeat in lines and crack the eggs over the bacon, leaving them intact if possible, as it looks nice when slicing the pie.

4 Roll out the remaining pastry and use to cover the pie, then pinch the edges with your thumb and forefinger to seal. Lightly score a criss-cross pattern on top and brush with a little milk.

5 Bake the pie for 20 minutes, then reduce the heat to 180°C (350°F/Gas 4), and bake for a further 30 minutes. Cool before serving. You can make the pastry case the day before and chill until ready to use.

EQUIPMENT
20cm (8in) ovenproof pie dish,
3.5cm (1½in) deep

INGREDIENTS

FOR THE PASTRY
(For visual step by step instructions see shortcrust pastry p104)
350g (12oz) plain flour,
  plus extra for dusting
175g (6oz) butter
salt and freshly ground black pepper
1½ tbsp tomato ketchup

FOR THE FILLING
450g (1lb) sausagemeat
  or good-quality pork sausages,
  casings removed
½ onion, finely chopped
a pinch of nutmeg
a pinch of mace
1 tbsp wholegrain mustard
6 streaky, rindless bacon bashers
4 eggs
milk, to glaze

Making your own Sausage Rolls (especially using ready-made puff pastry) is surprisingly easy. They can be prepared in advance then frozen, uncooked, making them perfect for entertaining.

SAUSAGE ROLLS

 MAKES 24

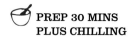 PREP 30 MINS
PLUS CHILLING

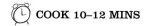 COOK 10–12 MINS

 FREEZE
UNCOOKED, UP TO
3 MONTHS

EQUIPMENT
baking tray

INGREDIENTS

FOR THE PASTRY
400g (14oz) ready-made puff pastry
(or to make your own, see pp110–113)
plain flour, for dusting
1 egg, beaten, to glaze

FOR THE FILLING
675g (1½lb) sausagemeat
1 small onion, finely chopped
1 tbsp chopped thyme
1 tbsp grated lemon zest
1 tsp Dijon mustard
1 egg yolk
salt and freshly ground black pepper

1 Preheat the oven to 200°C (400°F/Gas 6). Line a baking tray with greaseproof paper and chill.

2 Place the puff pastry on a lightly floured surface and cut in half lengthways. Roll out each piece to form a 30 x 15cm (12 x 6in) rectangle, then cover with cling film, and chill in the refrigerator.

3 Meanwhile, combine the sausagemeat with the onion, thyme, lemon zest, mustard, and egg yolk, and season with salt and black pepper.

4 Lay the pastry on a floured surface. Form the sausage mixture into 2 thinly rolled tubes and place in the centre of each piece of pastry. Brush the inside of the pastry with the beaten egg, then roll the pastry over and press to seal. Cut each roll into 12 pieces.

5 Place the rolls on the chilled tray, cut 2 snips in the top of each with scissors, then brush with beaten egg. Bake for 10–12 minutes, or until the pastry is golden and flaky. Serve warm or transfer to a wire rack to cool completely before serving. These sausage rolls are good with a spicy mustard dipping sauce.

In their native Greece, filo pies are made with a mixture of wild bitter greens, but any greens work well, if they have a slightly bitter flavour. Use spring greens or spinach instead of kale, if preferred.

FILO PIE WITH SPICY KALE AND SAUSAGE

 SERVES 6   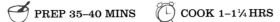 PREP 35–40 MINS   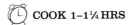 COOK 1–1¼ HRS    FREEZE UNCOOKED, UP TO 2 MONTHS

1 Heat 30g (1oz) of the butter in a sauté pan and cook the sausagemeat, stirring, until it is crumbly and brown. Transfer to a bowl with a slotted spoon, leaving the fat behind. Add the onions to the pan and cook until soft. Add the kale, cover, and cook until the kale is wilted. Uncover and cook for 5 minutes, stirring, until the moisture has evaporated. Return the sausagemeat to the pan with the allspice and stir into the kale. Season. Set aside to cool completely. Stir in the eggs.

2 Preheat the oven to 180°C (350°F/Gas 4). Melt the remaining butter in a saucepan and brush the tin with a little butter. Lay a folded damp tea towel on the work surface. Unroll the filo onto the towel. Using the tin as a guide, cut through the pastry sheets to leave a 7.5cm (3in) border around the tin where possible. Cover the sheets with a second folded damp towel.

3 Place 1 filo sheet on top of a third damp towel and brush with butter. Transfer to the cake tin, pressing it well into the side. Butter another filo sheet and put it in the tin at a right angle to the first. Continue buttering and layering until half the filo is used, arranging alternate layers at right angles.

4 Spoon the filling into the case. Butter another sheet of filo and cover the filling. Top with the remaining filo, brushing each, including the top one, with butter. Fold the overhanging filo over the top and drizzle with butter. Bake for 45–55 minutes until golden brown. Set aside to cool slightly, then serve hot or at room temperature. The pie can be made ahead up to the point of baking, wrapped in cling film, and chilled for 2 days.

EQUIPMENT
28cm (11in) springform cake tin

INGREDIENTS

FOR THE FILLING
30g (1oz) unsalted butter
250g (9oz) sausagemeat
3 onions, finely chopped
750g (1lb 10oz) kale, washed, trimmed, and shredded
½ tsp ground allspice
sea salt and freshly ground black pepper
2 eggs, beaten

FOR THE PASTRY
500g (1lb 2oz) filo pastry
175g (6oz) unsalted butter

This picnic pie makes a fabulous centrepiece for a summer buffet.
Making it the old-fashioned way using lard in the pastry, helps
keep the crust fresh for days, but sturdy enough to hold the filling.

PORK AND APPLE PICNIC PIE

 SERVES 8   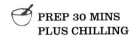 PREP 30 MINS   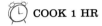 COOK 1 HR
                                   PLUS CHILLING

1 To make the pastry, rub the flour, lard, and salt
together until the mixture resembles breadcrumbs.
Add 6–8 tablespoons cold water, a little at a time, and
bring together to form a dough. Add a little extra
water, if needed. Wrap and chill for 30 minutes.

2 For the filling, heat the olive oil in a frying pan and
fry the onion and pancetta for 5 minutes until soft
but not brown, then set aside to cool. Mix the minced
pork, apples, apple juice, nutmeg, herbs, and lots
of salt and black pepper together in a large bowl with
your hands. Finally, mix in the cooled onion mixture.

3 Preheat the oven to 190°C (375°F/Gas 5). Roll out
the pastry on a well-floured surface into a large
circle about 7mm (¼in) thick, and use it to line the
tin, making sure it overlaps the sides. Trim all but
1cm (½in) of the overhanging pastry. Use your fingers
to push the pastry down into the corners of the tin.

4 Pile the filling into the tart case pressing it down
firmly. Roll out the remaining piece of pastry to
make a circle large enough to cover the pie. Brush the
edges with a little of the egg mixture, place the top on
the pie, and press down firmly to seal. Crimp the edges.
Brush the top with the remaining egg and poke 2 small
holes in the top of the pie with a chopstick or skewer.

5 Place the pie on a baking tray and bake for 1
hour until golden brown. Set the pie aside to cool
completely before serving. The pie can be stored in
the refrigerator, well wrapped, for up to 3 days.

EQUIPMENT
22cm (9in) deep-sided (3cm)
loose-bottomed fluted tart tin

INGREDIENTS

FOR THE PASTRY
(For visual step by step
  instructions see p104)
400g (14oz) plain flour,
  plus extra for dusting
150g (5½oz) lard
1 tsp salt

FOR THE FILLING
1 tbsp olive oil
1 onion, finely chopped
100g (3½oz) pancetta,
  finely chopped
500g (1lb 2oz) minced pork
2 dessert apples, peeled,
  cored, and grated
2 tbsp apple juice
¼ tsp nutmeg, grated
1 tbsp sage or flat-leaf parsley,
  finely chopped
salt and freshly ground black pepper
1 egg yolk, beaten with
  1 tsp cold water, to glaze

A meaty pie with a crisp, buttery pastry top is always a welcome sight at the kitchen table. Using apple juice here sweetens and mellows the tasty filling to create a real winter classic.

PORK AND LEEK PIE

 **SERVES 4**   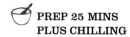 **PREP 25 MINS PLUS CHILLING**   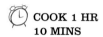 **COOK 1 HR 10 MINS**    **FREEZE UP TO 1 MONTH**

EQUIPMENT
18cm (7in) round pie dish

INGREDIENTS

FOR THE FILLING
2 tbsp vegetable oil
450g (1lb) lean boneless pork steaks, cut into 2.5cm (1in) cubes
2 leeks, thickly sliced
150g (5½oz) mushrooms, halved
1 tsp thyme leaves
150ml (5fl oz) chicken stock
1 tbsp cornflour, mixed with 1 tbsp water
250ml (9fl oz) apple juice
2 tbsp tomato purée
salt and freshly ground black pepper

FOR THE PASTRY
plain flour, for dusting
250g (9oz) ready-made shortcrust pastry
(or to make your own, see p104)
1 egg, beaten, to glaze

1 Heat the vegetable oil in a frying pan, add the pork and fry until browned, then remove from the pan and set aside. Add the leeks, mushrooms and thyme to the pan and fry for 5 minutes. Add the stock, cornflour, apple juice, and tomato purée, and bring to the boil, stirring until thickened. Return the pork to the pan, season to taste, and simmer for 25 minutes.

2 Transfer the pork and vegetables to the pie dish, reserving the sauce. On a lightly floured surface, roll out the pastry and use to cover the dish, decorating the top with the pastry trimmings. Cut a slit in the top of the pie to allow the steam to escape, then brush all over with the beaten egg. Chill for 30 minutes.

3 Preheat the oven to 200°C (400°F/Gas 6). Bake the pie for 35 minutes, or until the pastry is golden, then serve with the reserved sauce.

There is something very satisfying about making your own Pork Pies, and it is not as difficult as it seems. Work fast with the hot-water crust pastry, as it hardens quickly on cooling.

MINI PORK PIES

 MAKES 12   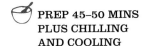 PREP 45–50 MINS PLUS CHILLING AND COOLING    COOK 1 HR

1 Preheat the oven to 200°C (400°F/Gas 6). Whiz the pork, bacon, herbs, seasoning, and spices in a food processor until the meat is chopped, but not mushy. Or, dice the meat into 5mm (¼in) pieces and mix in the other ingredients.

2 To make the pastry, place the flour and salt in a large bowl and make a well. Measure 150ml (5fl oz) boiling water into a jug, add the lard, and stir until the fat has melted. Pour into the well and mix with a wooden spoon. Use your hands to bring the mixture together into a soft dough. Be careful as it will be hot. Wrap one-quarter of the dough in a clean tea towel and put in a warm place.

3 Work quickly as the pastry hardens as it cools. Roll the pastry out on a well-floured surface to 5mm (¼in) thick. Cut 12 circles big enough to line the tray, allowing the pastry to overlap the edges slightly. Pack the filling into each case and brush the edges with egg.

4 Roll out the set-aside pastry and cut out 12 lids. Top the filling with the lids and press down to seal. Brush with egg. Make a hole in the top of each pie if filling with jelly, or cut 2 slits to allow the steam to escape. Bake for 30 minutes, then reduce the heat to 160°C (325°F/Gas 3) and cook for a further 30 minutes until golden brown. Cool in the tray for 10 minutes before turning out. Serve hot or cool and fill with jelly.

5 For the jelly, heat the stock and add the gelatine, stirring until it dissolves. Cool. Once the liquid starts to thicken, use the funnel to pour it into each pie, a little at a time. Each pie will need 2–3 tablespoons of liquid. Chill overnight before eating. The pies will keep for 3 days in an airtight container in the refrigerator.

EQUIPMENT
12-hole muffin tray,
small funnel (optional)

INGREDIENTS

FOR THE FILLING
200g (7oz) pork belly, trimmed of fat and skin, and cubed
200g (7oz) pork shoulder, trimmed and cubed
50g (1¾oz) unsmoked back or streaky bacon, trimmed and diced
10 sage leaves, finely chopped
sea salt and freshly ground black pepper
¼ tsp nutmeg
¼ tsp allspice

FOR THE PASTRY
(For visual step by step instructions see hot-water crust pastry pp108–109)
400g (14oz) plain flour, plus extra for dusting
½ tsp fine salt
150g (5½oz) lard or beef dripping, diced
1 egg, beaten, to glaze

FOR THE JELLY (OPTIONAL)
250ml (9fl oz) chicken stock
2 sheets of leaf gelatine, cut into pieces, and soaked in cold water for 5 minutes

A well-made Quiche Lorraine is undoubtedly one of the finest dishes to serve, either hot or cold on any occasion. Take the time to make your own rich shortcrust pastry for this – it deserves it.

QUICHE LORRAINE

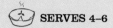 SERVES 4–6   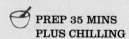 PREP 35 MINS PLUS CHILLING   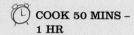 COOK 50 MINS – 1 HR    FREEZE UP TO 1 MONTH

EQUIPMENT
23 x 4cm (9 x 1½in) deep pie dish, baking beans

INGREDIENTS

FOR THE PASTRY
(For visual step by step instructions see shortcrust pastry p104)
225g (8oz) plain flour, plus extra for dusting
115g (4oz) butter, diced
1 egg yolk

FOR THE FILLING
200g (7oz) bacon lardons
1 onion, finely chopped
75g (2½oz) Gruyère cheese, grated
4 large eggs, lightly beaten
150ml (5fl oz) double cream
150ml (5fl oz) milk
freshly ground black pepper

1 To make the pastry, place the flour and butter in a food processor and blend until the mixture resembles fine breadcrumbs. Add the egg yolk, and 3–4 tablespoons of chilled water to make a smooth dough. On a floured surface, knead the dough briefly. To make the pastry by hand, rub the butter into the flour with your fingertips until the mixture resembles breadcrumbs. Add the egg yolk and chilled water and mix to form a dough. Cover with cling film and chill for 30 minutes.

2 Preheat the oven to 190°C (375°F/Gas 5). Roll out the pastry on a lightly floured surface and use to line the tin, pressing the dough into the sides. Prick the bottom of the pastry with a fork, then line with greaseproof paper and baking beans. Bake for 12 minutes, then remove the paper and beans, and bake for a further 10 minutes, or until lightly golden.

3 Meanwhile, heat a large frying pan and dry-fry the bacon lardons for 3–4 minutes. Add the onion, fry for a further 2–3 minutes, then spread the onions and bacon over the pastry case. Add the cheese.

4 Whisk together the eggs, cream, milk, and black pepper, and pour into the pastry case. Place the tin on a baking tray and bake for 25–30 minutes until golden and just set. Set aside to set, then slice and serve. Cook up to 48 hours in advance, cool, then chill. Reheat at 160°C (325°F/Gas 3) for 15–20 minutes.

This warming, winter pie comes from the Auvergne region in France, and is the ideal dish to prepare when it's cold outside. It tastes just as good served cold the following day.

AUVERGNE TOURTE

 SERVES 8   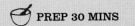 PREP 30 MINS   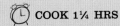 COOK 1¼ HRS

1 Melt the butter in a large saucepan. Add the onion and cook over a medium heat for 10 minutes. Add the garlic and bacon lardons and cook for a further 5 minutes until the onion is soft, but not brown.

2 Preheat the oven to 180°C (350°F/Gas 4). Roll out the puff pastry on a floured surface and, using the pie tin as a template, cut out a circle large enough to top the pie from one side. Use the rest of the pastry to line the tin, leaving a 1cm (½in) overhang around the edges. Re-roll the pastry if necessary after chilling the top.

3 Brush the inside of the pastry case, including the edges, with the egg wash. Set the remaining egg wash aside.

4 Layer the pastry case with one-third of the finely sliced potatoes. Cover them with half the onion and bacon mixture and half the grated cheese. Scatter over half the parsley and season with salt and black pepper.

5 Repeat the procedure and finish with a final layer of potatoes. Whisk together the cream and the egg yolk, and pour it over the pie filling.

6 Top the pie with the pre-cut circle of pastry, pressing it down around the edges to seal. Crimp the edges. Brush the top of the pie with the remaining egg wash and cut 2 small slits in the top to allow steam to escape. Place the pie on a baking tray and bake for 1 hour until well cooked, puffed up, and golden brown. Set aside to rest for 15–20 minutes before serving.

EQUIPMENT
23cm (9in) deep dish pie tin (metal) with sloping sides

INGREDIENTS

FOR THE FILLING
30g (1oz) butter
1 large onion, finely sliced
1 garlic clove, finely chopped
100g (3½oz) bacon lardons
650g (1lb 6oz) waxy new potatoes, peeled and finely sliced
100g (3½oz) Cantal cheese, grated or Wensleydale or mild Cheddar
1 heaped tbsp finely chopped flat-leaf parsley
salt and freshly ground black pepper
200ml (7fl oz) single cream
1 egg yolk

FOR THE PASTRY
500g (1lb 2oz) ready-made puff pastry (or to make your own, see pp110–113)
plain flour, for dusting
1 egg yolk, beaten with 1 tbsp cold water, to glaze

A traditional blind-baked pastry case can be filled with a myriad of different ingredients to create a delicious home-made tart. Omit the pancetta if you are cooking for vegetarians.

SPINACH, GOAT'S CHEESE, AND PANCETTA TART

 SERVES 6–8　　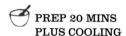 PREP 20 MINS PLUS COOLING　　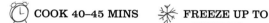 COOK 40–45 MINS　　 FREEZE UP TO 2 MONTHS

EQUIPMENT
22cm (9in) loose-bottomed tart tin, baking beans

INGREDIENTS

FOR THE FILLING
1 tbsp olive oil
150g (5½oz) pancetta, diced
150g (5½oz) baby spinach, washed
100g (3½oz) goat's cheese
sea salt and freshly ground black pepper
300ml (10fl oz) double cream
2 eggs

FOR THE PASTRY CASE
ready-made shortcrust pastry case
(or to make your own,
see p104 and pp122–123)

1　Heat the olive oil in a frying pan and fry the pancetta for 5 minutes, or until golden brown. Add the spinach and cook for a few minutes until it wilts. Drain off any water before using the filling and set aside to cool.

2　Spread the cooled spinach and pancetta mixture over the bottom of the pastry case. Cube or crumble the goat's cheese, and spread it over the spinach. Season with a little salt (the pancetta is salty) and black pepper.

3　Whisk the cream and eggs together in a jug. Place the pastry case on a baking tray and, with the oven door open, rest it half on, half off the middle oven shelf. Hold the tray with one hand and with the other pour the cream and egg mixture into the tart, then slide it into the oven.

4　Bake for 30–35 minutes until puffed up and golden. Set aside to cool for 10 minutes, and remove the tart from the tin. It is best eaten warm from the oven but can be served cold. The pastry case can be made 2 days ahead, wrapped in cling film, and chilled in the refrigerator until needed. The tart can be chilled overnight and gently reheated in a medium oven.

This pastry is an unusual combination of wholemeal flour, cheese, and caraway seeds, which complements the earthy celeriac and the salty bacon well. Serve with mash and greens for a warming dinner.

CELERIAC AND SMOKED BACON SOUFFLÉ PIE

 SERVES 4

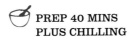 PREP 40 MINS PLUS CHILLING

 COOK 50 MINS

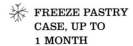 FREEZE PASTRY CASE, UP TO 1 MONTH

1 To make the pastry, mix the flour and salt in a large bowl. Add the caraway seeds, then rub in the butter with your fingertips until the mixture resembles breadcrumbs. Stir in the cheese. Mix 3 tablespoons cold water with the egg yolk and stir into the flour mixture to form a firm dough, adding more water if necessary. On a lightly floured surface, knead the dough gently, then wrap in cling film and chill for 30 minutes. Reserve the egg white for the filling.

2 Cook the celeriac in a saucepan of lightly salted boiling water until tender. Drain and return to the pan and dry out briefly over a gentle heat. Mash with the butter and milk.

3 Dry-fry the bacon until cooked, but not crisp. Add to the celeriac with any fat in the pan. Beat in the egg yolks and chopped chives and season well.

4 Preheat the oven to 200°C (400°F/Gas 6). Roll out the pastry on a floured surface and use to line the tin. Line with greaseproof paper and baking beans. Bake for 10 minutes. Remove the foil or paper and beans and cook for a further 5 minutes to dry out. Remove from the oven.

5 Whisk all 3 egg whites until stiff. Add 1 tablespoon of the whites to the celeriac mixture to slacken slightly, then fold in the remainder with a metal spoon. Spoon into the pastry case and bake for 25 minutes until risen, just set, and golden. Serve hot.

EQUIPMENT
20cm (8in) flan tin, baking beans

INGREDIENTS

FOR THE PASTRY
(For visual step by step instructions see shortcrust pastry p104)
175g (6oz) wholemeal or spelt flour, plus extra for dusting
a good pinch of salt
1 tbsp caraway seeds
75g (2½oz) butter, chilled and diced
85g (3oz) farmhouse Cheddar cheese, grated
1 egg, separated

FOR THE FILLING
1 celeriac, about 450g (1lb), peeled and cut into chunks
salt and freshly ground black pepper
60g (2oz) butter
4 tbsp milk
4 streaky bacon rashers, diced
2 eggs, separated
2 tbsp chives, chopped

The base of this traditional German tart is made from a classic pizza dough, rather than the usual pastry, and topped with sweet, melting onions, soured cream and caraway seeds.

ONION AND SOUR CREAM TART

 **SERVES 8**

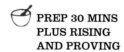 **PREP 30 MINS PLUS RISING AND PROVING**

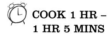 **COOK 1 HR – 1 HR 5 MINS**

EQUIPMENT
26 x 32cm (10 x 13in) baking tray with raised edges

INGREDIENTS

FOR THE TART BASE
3 tbsp olive oil, plus extra for greasing
4 tsp dried yeast, dissolved in 225ml (7½fl oz) warm water
400g (14oz) strong white bread flour, plus extra for dusting
1 tsp salt

FOR THE FILLING
50g (1¾oz) unsalted butter
2 tbsp olive oil
600g (1lb 5oz) onions, finely sliced
½ tsp caraway seeds
sea salt and freshly ground black pepper
150ml (5fl oz) soured cream
150ml (5fl oz) crème fraîche
3 eggs
1 tbsp plain flour
75g (2½oz) smoked streaky bacon, chopped

1 Add the olive oil to the dissolved yeast. Sift the flour and salt into a large bowl. Make a well in the middle and pour in the liquid ingredients, stirring constantly. Use your hands to bring the mixture together to form a soft dough. On a well-floured surface, knead the dough for 10 minutes until soft and elastic.

2 Place the dough in a large, lightly oiled bowl, cover with cling film, and set aside to rise in a warm place for 1–2 hours until doubled in size.

3 For the filling, heat the butter and olive oil in a large, heavy saucepan. Add the onions and caraway seeds, and season well. Cover and cook gently for 20 minutes until they are soft, but not brown. Uncover and cook for 5 minutes until any excess water evaporates.

4 In a separate bowl, whisk together the soured cream, crème fraîche, eggs, and plain flour, and season well. Mix in the cooked onions and set aside to cool.

5 When the dough has risen, turn it out onto a floured surface and push it down gently with your knuckles to knock it back. Lightly grease the baking tray. Roll the dough out to the size of the tray and line it, making sure the pie has an upturned edge. Cover with lightly oiled cling film, and set aside to rise in a warm place for 30 minutes, until puffy in places.

6 Preheat the oven to 200°C (400°F/Gas 6). Gently push down the dough, (if it has risen too much), around the edges of the tray. Spread the filling out over the base, and sprinkle the bacon on top. Bake on the top shelf of the oven for 35–40 minutes until golden brown. Cool for 5 minutes before serving. Serve warm or cold. This dish can be covered and chilled overnight.

The rich buttery crust is filled with salty bacon and creamy Brie to produce a mouth-watering tart, suitable for a summer lunch or a picnic. Use other semi-dried tomatoes if you can't find sunblush ones.

BRIE AND BACON TART

 SERVES 6–8    PREP 15 MINS   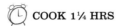 COOK 1¼ HRS    FREEZE UP TO 1 MONTH

1 Preheat the oven to 200°C (400°F/Gas 6). Roll out the pastry on a floured surface and use to line the tart tin, allowing the pastry to hang over the edges. Trim off the excess pastry, then line the pastry case with greaseproof paper and fill with baking beans. Bake for 20 minutes, or until the edges are golden. Remove the beans and paper, brush the bottom of the case with a little beaten egg, and return to the oven for 1–2 minutes to crisp. Set aside. Reduce the oven temperature to 180°C (350°F/Gas 4).

2 Heat the olive oil in a large frying pan over a low heat. Add the onion and a pinch of salt, and sweat gently for about 5 minutes until soft and translucent. Increase the heat slightly, add the bacon, and cook for 5–8 minutes until crisp and golden. Remove from the heat, and stir through the sunblush tomatoes.

3 Spoon the onion and bacon mixture into the pastry case. Top evenly with the Brie strips, and sprinkle with the chives.

4 Mix the cream and the 2 eggs together in a bowl. Add the garlic, and season well with salt and black pepper. Carefully pour over the tart filling. Bake for 30–40 minutes until set, puffed, and lightly golden. Serve with a crisp green salad.

EQUIPMENT
18 x 30cm (7 x 12in) rectangular loose-bottomed fluted tart tin, baking beans

INGREDIENTS

FOR THE PASTRY
300g (10oz) ready-made shortcrust pastry (or to make your own, see p104)
plain flour, for dusting
1 egg, lightly beaten, to glaze

FOR THE FILLING
1 tbsp olive oil
1 onion, finely chopped
salt and freshly ground black pepper
125g (4½oz) thick bacon rashers, chopped into bite-sized pieces
8 sunblush tomatoes
125g (4½oz) Brie cheese, sliced into long strips
a small handful of chives, finely chopped
200ml (7fl oz) double cream
2 eggs
2 garlic cloves, grated or finely chopped

Mixing chopped fresh herbs into the pastry is an easy way of varying the flavours of a dish to complement the pie filling. Use farmed rabbit if possible here, as wild rabbit needs a long, slow cooking time.

RABBIT AND SWEETCORN PIE WITH A HERB CRUST

 SERVES 4   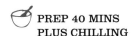 **PREP 40 MINS PLUS CHILLING**    **COOK 1¾ HRS**    **FREEZE UP TO 1 MONTH**

1 To make the pastry, sift 225g (8oz) flour and ¼ teaspoon salt into a bowl. Add 60g (2oz) of the butter and rub it in with your fingertips. Stir in the herbs. Add the remaining butter and 8 tablespoons iced water and mix with a round-bladed knife to form a lumpy dough. On a floured surface, knead the dough, then roll out to an oblong. Fold the bottom-third up and the top-third down over it and press the edges with the rolling pin. Quarter-turn the dough then roll, fold, and turn twice more. Wrap and chill for 30 minutes.

2 For the filling, put the rabbit in a saucepan with the lardons and all the vegetables. Add the stock, bay leaf, and season with salt and black pepper. Bring to the boil, reduce the heat, part-cover, and simmer gently for about 1 hour until the rabbit is tender. Lift out the rabbit. Remove the meat and cut into pieces. Put in the pie dish on a baking tray and discard the bay leaf.

3 Blend the sherry with remaining 4 tablespoons flour and 1 tablespoon water. Stir into the vegetables and stock, then bring to the boil, stirring. Add the cream and season. Stir into the rabbit. Cool.

4 Preheat the oven to 220°C (425°F/Gas 7). Roll and fold the pastry once more then roll out to slightly bigger than the pie dish. Cut off a strip all round. Dampen the rim of the dish and lay the strip on top. Dampen the strip and lay the pastry on top. Press the edges together to seal. Trim, knock up, and flute with the back of a knife. Make leaves out of the trimmings and arrange on top. Cut a slit in the top and glaze with cream. Bake for 30 minutes until golden. Serve hot.

EQUIPMENT
1.7 litre (3 pint) pie dish

INGREDIENTS

FOR THE PASTRY
345g (12oz) flour, plus extra for dusting
salt and freshly ground black pepper
175g (6oz) butter, chilled and diced
2 tbsp chopped parsley
1 tbsp chopped thyme

FOR THE FILLING
1 oven-ready rabbit, jointed
60g (2oz) smoked bacon lardons
1 onion, chopped
2 carrots, sliced
1 potato, diced
4 tomatoes, skinned and chopped
kernels from 2 sweetcorn cobs
600ml (1 pint) chicken stock
1 bay leaf
3 tbsp dry sherry
4 tbsp double cream, plus extra to glaze

variation

HERB CRUST CHICKEN PIE
Wild rabbit tastes like free-range organic chicken, which you could use instead. Use 175g (6oz) canned or frozen sweetcorn instead of fresh corn, if liked.

An alternative to Beef Wellington, these individual parcels are both rich and luxurious. Perfect for entertaining, they can be prepared ahead up to the baking stage then finished at the last minute.

VENISON WELLINGTONS

 MAKES 4   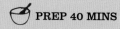 PREP 40 MINS   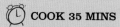 COOK 35 MINS

EQUIPMENT
baking tray

INGREDIENTS

FOR THE FILLING
10g (¼oz) dried wild mushrooms (optional)
2 tbsp olive oil
4 venison loin steaks,
each 120–150g (4–5½oz)
salt and freshly ground black pepper
30g (1oz) unsalted butter
2 shallots, finely chopped
1 garlic clove, finely chopped
200g (7oz) mixed mushrooms, including
wild mushrooms if possible
1 tbsp thyme leaves
1 tbsp brandy or Madeira

FOR THE PASTRY
500g (1lb 2oz) puff pastry
(or to make your own, see pp110–113)
plain flour, for dusting
1 egg, beaten, to glaze

1 Preheat the oven to 200°C (400°F/Gas 6). If using dried mushrooms, put them in a bowl and cover with boiling water. Leave for at least 15 minutes.

2 Heat the olive oil in a frying pan. Season the venison steaks on all sides with salt and black pepper and fry them, two at a time, for 2 minutes each side, until brown all over. Set aside to cool completely.

3 Melt the butter in the same pan. Add the shallots and cook for 5 minutes over a medium heat until soft. Add the garlic and cook for 1–2 minutes.

4 Roughly chop the mushrooms and add them to the pan with the thyme. Season and cook for 5 minutes until they are well softened and any juices have evaporated. Add the brandy and cook over a high heat for 1 minute until it evaporates. Remove and set aside to cool. If using dried mushrooms, drain them, chop roughly, and add to the mushroom mixture.

5 Divide the pastry into 4 equal pieces and roll out rectangles about 5mm (¼in) thick, large enough to wrap around each steak on a floured surface. Pat the steaks dry with kitchen paper.

6 Place one-quarter of the mushroom filling in a rectangle roughly the same shape as the venison steak to one side of the pastry, leaving a clean edge of at least 2cm (¾in). Flatten the mushrooms and put a steak on top. Brush the edges of the pastry with beaten egg and fold the pastry over the meat. Press the edges down firmly to seal and crimp them. Repeat with the remaining steaks and pastry. Cut small slits in the top for the steam to escape, and brush the tops with more beaten egg. Bake the pastries on the baking tray for 20–25 minutes until puffed up and golden. Set aside to cool for 5 minutes before serving.

variation

LAMB WELLINGTONS
Swap the venison for lamb loin steaks. Follow the recipe, but in step 2, fry the lamb for 1 minute each side. In step 3, cook finely chopped leeks in the melted butter, instead of shallots, and omit the brandy in step 4. Cook as directed for 15–20 minutes.

For those on a low-fat diet, venison is a good alternative to beef. A long, slow cooking time is needed to truly tenderize this wonderful, gamey meat. If time is short, prepare the filling the day before.

VENISON PIE

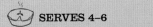 SERVES 4–6   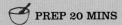 PREP 20 MINS   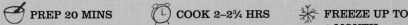 COOK 2–2¾ HRS   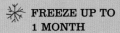 FREEZE UP TO 1 MONTH

1 Heat half the olive oil in a medium, heavy-based pan and gently fry the shallots, celery, and carrot for 3 minutes. Add the garlic and cook for 2–3 minutes. Remove with a slotted spoon and set aside.

2 Place the flour, nutmeg, and allspice in a large plastic food bag, season well, and add the cubed meat. Firmly hold the top of the bag to seal it, and shake it to coat the meat in the seasoned flour.

3 Add the remaining olive oil to the pan and brown the meat in 3 batches over a medium heat, removing each batch to a plate lined with kitchen paper.

4 Add the port and stir well to deglaze the bottom of the pan. Add the cranberry sauce, orange zest and juice, stock, and bay leaf to the pan, season and stir.

5 Return the vegetables and venison to the pan, stir well, and bring to the boil. Cover, reduce the heat, and simmer for 1½–2 hours or until the venison is tender. Remove the bay leaf.

6 Preheat the oven to 200°C (400°C/Gas 6). With a slotted spoon, transfer the cooked venison and vegetables to the pie dish. Bring the remaining cooking liquid in the pan to the boil and cook over a high heat for 5 minutes to reduce. Pour the reduced sauce over the meat in the dish.

7 Cut 2cm (¾in) wide strips from the edge of the pastry to fit round the rim of the pie dish. Brush the edge of the dish with water and place the strips on the rim. Cover the pie with the remaining pastry, trim, and press to seal. Brush with beaten egg and cut a slit in the top to allow steam to escape. Bake on a baking tray for 15–20 minutes until browned.

EQUIPMENT
23cm (9in) pie dish

INGREDIENTS

FOR THE FILLING
2 tbsp olive oil
4 shallots, halved
2 celery sticks, finely chopped
1 carrot, finely chopped
2 garlic cloves, finely chopped
2 tbsp plain flour
½ tsp freshly grated nutmeg
½ tsp ground allspice
salt and freshly ground black pepper
675g (1½lb) shoulder of venison,
  cut into bite-sized chunks
150ml (5fl oz) port
4 tbsp cranberry sauce
zest and juice of 1 orange
150ml (5fl oz) fresh beef stock
1 bay leaf

FOR THE PASTRY
215g (7½oz) sheet ready-rolled
  puff pastry (or to make your own,
  see pp110–113)
1 egg, beaten, to glaze

These fragrant parcels are a variation of the classic Moroccan pastilla, which is made with baby pigeon. It may look lengthy, but make the filling the day before, and then they are quick to finish.

INDIVIDUAL QUAIL PASTILLA

 MAKES 4   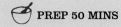 PREP 50 MINS   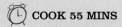 COOK 55 MINS

EQUIPMENT
baking tray

INGREDIENTS

FOR THE FILLING
4 prepared quails or pigeons
750ml (1¼ pints) good-quality chicken stock
1 cinnamon stick, broken in half
1 red chilli, halved and deseeded
1 red onion, quartered
2 garlic cloves, peeled
2cm (¾in) piece of ginger, thickly sliced
30g (1oz) flaked almonds, toasted and chopped
2 tbsp coriander, chopped
½ tsp ground cinnamon
freshly ground black pepper

FOR THE PASTRY
5 sheets ready-made filo pastry
plain flour, for dusting
3 tbsp olive oil

1 Place the quail in a saucepan. Add the stock, cinnamon stick, chilli, onion, garlic, and ginger, and bring to the boil. Reduce the heat and simmer for 30 minutes until the quails are cooked. Strain the contents of the pan, reserving the liquid. Remove the quail, onion, and garlic and cool. Put the reserved liquid into the cleaned-out pan and simmer until it barely covers the bottom. Pull the meat off the bones in bite-size shreds. Roughly chop the onions and garlic and add them to the meat. Combine the meat mixture, almonds, and spices and season. Add the cooking liquid, so that the mixture is moist, but not too wet.

2 Preheat the oven to 200°C (400°F/Gas 6). Lay the filo out on a floured surface and cut them into quarters. Make a pastilla (see below). Repeat 3 more times to make 4 pastry bases. Divide the filling between the bases, heaping it in a circle in the centre. Fold the edges in one at a time in a clockwise direction to cover the filling. Bake on the baking tray for 20–25 minutes until golden and crisp. Cool slightly before serving.

Making a pastilla

1 Brush 1 piece of filo with olive oil. Place a second piece at right angles across it, and brush with the oil.

2 Put a third piece diagonally across pastry, brush with oil. Put a fourth piece diagonally other way and oil.

3 Brush 1 final piece with oil and fold in half. Trim to make a square, use to make a base in centre of pastry.

There are times in autumn when pigeons are plump and plentiful. If you live near a supplier, stock up on them and use the breasts for this wonderful dish. The carcasses can be reserved for stock.

PIGEON BREASTS EN CROÛTE

 MAKES 4   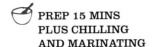 PREP 15 MINS
                                    PLUS CHILLING
                                    AND MARINATING   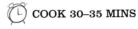 COOK 30–35 MINS

1 Mix the red wine, balsamic vinegar, zest and juice of 1 orange in a shallow non-metallic dish. Add the pigeon breasts and season well. Coat evenly with the marinade, cover, and chill for at least 8 hours.

2 Remove the pigeon from the marinade and season with salt and black pepper. Heat the olive oil in a saucepan and fry the shallots, lardons, and mushrooms over a medium heat for 3–4 minutes, or until golden. Set aside. Preheat the oven to 200°C (400°F/Gas 6). Line the baking trays with baking parchment.

3 Cut each pastry sheet into 4, to give 8 x 11.5 x 18.5cm (5 x 7in) rectangles. Divide the shallot mixture between 4 of the pastry rectangles, leaving a 5cm (2in) border all around. Place 2 pigeon breasts on top of the shallot mixture in the centre of each pastry rectangle. Brush the edges with water and top with the remaining rectangles. Press the pastry edges down firmly to seal, transfer to the baking trays, and snip the top with scissors to make a hole for steam to escape. Brush each parcel with the beaten egg and bake for 25–30 minutes.

EQUIPMENT
2 baking trays

INGREDIENTS

FOR THE FILLING
4 tbsp red wine
2 tbsp balsamic vinegar
grated zest and juice of 1 orange
8 pigeon breasts
salt and freshly ground black pepper
1 tbsp olive oil
2 shallots, sliced
100g (3½oz) dry-cure bacon lardons
50g (1¾oz) chestnut mushrooms,
  finely sliced

FOR THE PASTRY
2 x 320g (10¾oz) sheets ready-rolled
  puff pastry, each 23 x 37cm (or to
  make your own, see pp110–113)
1 egg, beaten to glaze

These bite-sized puffs were inspired by a favourite dim sum dish of my family – Honey Puffs. Trying to recreate them at home, I came up with this surprisingly simple, yet delicious recipe.

CHINESE BARBECUE DUCK PUFFS

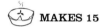 MAKES 15   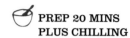 PREP 20 MINS PLUS CHILLING   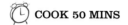 COOK 50 MINS    FREEZE UP TO 2 MONTHS

EQUIPMENT
baking tray, 8cm (3¼in)
fluted round cutter

INGREDIENTS

FOR THE PASTRY
(For visual step by step instructions
see quick puff pastry pp112–113)
200g (7oz) plain flour,
plus extra for dusting
a pinch of salt
100g (3½oz) butter, frozen for 30 minutes
1 egg yolk, beaten, plus 1 egg,
beaten, to glaze
1 tbsp sesame seeds (optional)

FOR THE FILLING
1 tbsp sunflower oil
4 large spring onions,
trimmed and finely sliced
1 garlic clove, crushed
½ Chinese barbecue-roasted duck
giving 200g (7oz) duck meat,
or 200g (7oz) Chinese-roasted pork
1 tsp finely grated ginger
1 tbsp oyster sauce
1 tbsp Peking duck or hoisin sauce
1 tsp cornflour

1 To make the pastry, put the flour and salt into a large bowl. Grate the butter into the flour, coating the grater with a little flour first to stop the butter sticking. Work the butter and flour together with your hands, add the beaten egg yolk and 2 tablespoons cold water, and bring the mixture together to form a dough. Wrap in cling film and chill for 30 minutes.

2 For the filling, finely chop the meat. If not using ready-prepared duck, marinate 2 duck legs in 1 tablespoon hoisin sauce mixed with 1 tablespoon soy sauce for 30 minutes, then preheat the oven to 200°C (400°F/Gas 6) and roast for 30 minutes until cooked. Cool and pull off the meat before shredding it.

3 Heat the sunflower oil in a saucepan and fry the spring onions and garlic for 2–3 minutes until soft but not brown, then add the duck meat, ginger, oyster, and hoisin sauces. Mix the cornflour with 4 tablespoons cold water and add to the pan. Cook briefly until thick, shiny, and any excess liquid has evaporated. Cool.

4 Preheat the oven to 200°C (400°F/Gas 6). Roll out the pastry on a well-floured surface and cut out 15 x 8cm (3¼in) circles with the round cutter. Brush the edges with beaten egg. Place a heaped teaspoon of the filling into the centre of the circles, then use your hands to crimp the edges and seal the pastries.

5 Place the pastries on the baking tray and brush with beaten egg, and a sprinkle of sesame seeds, if using. Bake for 20 minutes until shiny and golden brown. Set aside to cool for at least 5 minutes before serving. The filling can be chilled for up to 3 days. The pastry can be made and chilled overnight The puffs can be frozen; defrost and reheat well.

Adding a puff-pastry lid to a hearty soup is a simple yet effective way of turning a starter-sized dish into a main course. Serve with a crusty country bread for mopping up all the juices.

PUFF-CRUSTED GAME SOUP

 **SERVES 4**   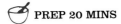 **PREP 20 MINS**   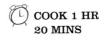 **COOK 1 HR 20 MINS**   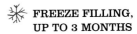 **FREEZE FILLING, UP TO 3 MONTHS**

1 Melt the butter in a saucepan and fry the meat and onion for 5 minutes, stirring, until browned.

2 Blend in the flour and cook for 1 minute. Remove from the heat, gradually stir in the stock, add the redcurrant jelly, and bring to the boil, stirring. Add the mushrooms, sage, port, and some salt and black pepper. Return to the boil, then reduce the heat, cover, and simmer very gently for 1 hour, stirring occasionally until rich and really tender. Taste and adjust the seasoning if necessary.

3 Meanwhile, preheat the oven to 220°C (425°F/Gas 7). Cut 4 circles from the pastry slightly larger than the soup cups and brush with a little beaten egg. Stand the soup cups on a baking tray. Brush the edges with a little more beaten egg. Ladle in the soup. Top with the circles of pastry, pressing down lightly with a fork around the edge to secure. Cut a small slit in the top of each pie lid to allow steam to escape. Bake for about 15 minutes or until puffy, crisp, and golden brown. Set aside to cool for 3–5 minutes before serving.

EQUIPMENT
deep ovenproof soup cups

INGREDIENTS

FOR THE FILLING
a large knob of butter
175g (6oz) diced game meat, cut into small pieces
1 red onion, chopped
2 tbsp plain flour
900ml (1½ pints) beef stock
1 tbsp redcurrant jelly
3 chestnut mushrooms, halved and sliced
1 tbsp sage, chopped
4 tbsp ruby port
salt and freshly ground black pepper

FOR THE PASTRY
1 sheet ready-rolled puff pastry (or to make your own, see pp110–113)
1 egg, beaten, to glaze

POULTRY PIES AND TARTS

When you need a simple yet sophisticated dish for entertaining, these individual pies are just the thing. Most fillings could be presented like this, just cut the lids to fit and bake until puffed up and golden.

CHICKEN POT PIES

 MAKES 6

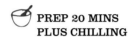 **PREP 20 MINS PLUS CHILLING**

 **COOK 40 MINS**

 **FREEZE UP TO 1 MONTH**

EQUIPMENT
6 x 7.5cm (3in) round pie dishes, 7.5cm (3in) round cutter

INGREDIENTS

FOR THE PASTRY
(For visual step by step instructions see shortcrust pastry p104)
350g (12oz) plain flour, plus extra for dusting
175g (6oz) butter, diced
½ tsp salt
1 egg, beaten, to glaze

FOR THE FILLING
1 litre (1¾ pints) chicken stock
3 carrots, sliced
750g (1lb 10oz) large potatoes, diced
3 celery sticks, thinly sliced
175g (6oz) peas
500g (1lb 2oz) cooked, skinless, boneless chicken
60g (2oz) unsalted butter
1 onion, chopped
30g (1oz) plain flour
175ml (6fl oz) double cream
whole nutmeg, for grating
sea salt and freshly ground black pepper
leaves from 1 small bunch of parsley, chopped

1 Preheat the oven to 200°C (400°F/Gas 6). To make the pastry, rub the flour and butter together until the mixture resembles breadcrumbs. Add the salt and enough cold water to bring the mixture together to form a soft dough. Wrap in cling film and chill in the refrigerator for 30 minutes.

2 For the filling, boil the stock in a large saucepan. Add the carrots, potatoes, and celery, and simmer for 3 minutes. Add the peas and simmer for a further 5 minutes until all the vegetables are tender. Drain, reserving the stock. Cut the chicken into slivers and put in a bowl. Add the vegetables.

3 Melt the butter in a small pan over a medium heat. Add the onion and cook for 3–5 minutes until softened but not browned. Sprinkle the flour over the onions and cook for 1–2 minutes, stirring. Add 500ml (16fl oz) of the stock and heat, whisking, until the sauce comes to the boil and thickens. Reduce the heat and simmer for 2 minutes, then add the cream and a grating of nutmeg, then season. Pour the sauce over the chicken and vegetables, add the parsley, and mix gently. Divide the filling evenly among the dishes.

4 Roll the pastry out on a well-floured surface to 5mm (¼in) thick. Cut out 6 rounds using the cutter. Brush the edge of each pie dish with water and place the pastry lids on top, pressing down firmly to secure in place. Place the pies on a baking tray and brush with the beaten egg. Cut a slit in the top of each pie and bake for 15–20 minutes. The filling can be prepared 1 day ahead, covered, and stored in the refrigerator.

This rich, creamy Chicken Pie is topped with a glossy, golden brown pastry lid that should shatter to the touch. Use home-made or shop-bought puff pastry for a family-pleasing, speedy midweek supper.

CHICKEN PIE

 SERVES 4 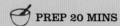 PREP 20 MINS 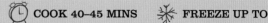 COOK 40–45 MINS 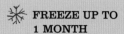 FREEZE UP TO 1 MONTH

EQUIPMENT
18cm (7in) pie dish

INGREDIENTS

FOR THE FILLING
3 tbsp olive oil
1 onion, finely chopped
50g (1¾oz) pancetta, diced
2 leeks, about 200g (7oz),
cut into 1cm (½in) slices
150g (5½oz) button mushrooms, wiped,
halved or quartered if necessary
2 large chicken breasts, about 400g (14oz),
cut into 2.5cm (1in) chunks
1 heaped tbsp chopped thyme
1 heaped tbsp chopped flat-leaf parsley
1 tbsp plain flour
300ml (10fl oz) single cream
1 tbsp Dijon mustard
salt and freshly ground black pepper

FOR THE PASTRY
250g (9oz) ready-made puff pastry
(or to make your own, see pp110–113)
1 egg, beaten, to glaze
flour, for dusting

1 Preheat the oven to 200°C (400°F/Gas 6). Heat 2 tablespoons of the olive oil in a saucepan, add the onion and fry for 5 minutes until softened, but not brown. Add the pancetta and cook for 2 minutes. Add the leeks and button mushrooms and cook for a further 3–5 minutes until the pancetta is crisp.

2 Add the remaining olive oil to the pan and add the chicken and herbs. Fry over a high heat for 3–4 minutes until coloured on all sides. Sprinkle the flour over the pie filling and stir it in well. Pour over the cream, add the mustard and seasoning and bring to the boil, stirring constantly. The mixture should thicken as it heats. Reduce the heat to low and cook for a further 5 minutes until the liquid has reduced. Transfer the filling to the pie dish.

3 Roll out the pastry on a floured surface to a circle bigger than the pie dish and 3–5mm (⅛–¼in) thick. Cut a circle to fit the pie. Roll some of the trimmings out into long strips. Brush the rim of the dish with a little of the beaten egg and press the pastry strips around the rim. Brush the edging with more beaten egg and top with the pastry lid. Press down to seal the lid, then trim away any excess pastry.

4 Brush the top of the pie with beaten egg, then cut 2 slits in the top to allow steam to escape. Bake for 20–25 minutes until golden brown. Set aside to rest for 5 minutes before serving.

A home-made raised pie is wonderful, and this one is large enough to make a perfect buffet centrepiece. Make the pie ahead of time and chill for up to three days, but be sure to serve it at room temperature.

CHICKEN AND HAM RAISED PIE

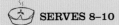 SERVES 8–10 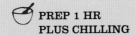 PREP 1 HR PLUS CHILLING 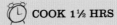 COOK 1½ HRS

1 To make the pastry, sift the flour and 2 teaspoons of salt into a bowl. Rub in the fat until the mix resembles breadcrumbs. Make a well, add 150ml (5fl oz) water, and cut in with a knife to form coarse breadcrumbs. Form a dough and knead until smooth. Wrap and chill for 30 minutes.

2 Cook 6 eggs in a saucepan of water for 7 minutes. Drain, cool, and peel. Cut 2 of the breasts and the pork into chunks. Mince coarsely, place in a bowl, and add lemon, herbs, nutmeg, and seasoning. Whisk 2 eggs, add to the minced meat, and beat until it pulls away from the sides. Cut the reserved chicken and ham into 2cm (¾in) cubes, and stir into the filling.

3 Preheat the oven to 200°C (400°F/Gas 6). Grease the tin. Shape three-quarters of the dough into a ball. Make the pie (see below). Make a hole in the lid and insert a foil roll for a chimney. Cut out leaves from the leftover pastry, decorate, glaze, and bake for 1 hour. Reduce the heat to 180°C (350°F/Gas 4) and bake for 30 minutes.

EQUIPMENT
20–23cm (8–9in) springform cake tin

INGREDIENTS

FOR THE PASTRY
500g (1lb 2oz) plain flour,
   plus extra for dusting
salt and freshly ground black pepper
75g (2½oz) butter, chilled and diced,
   plus extra for greasing
75g (2½oz) lard, chilled and diced

FOR THE FILLING
9 eggs
4 skinless, boneless chicken breasts,
   total weight 750g (1lb 10oz)
375g (13oz) lean boneless pork
finely grated zest of ½ lemon
1 tsp each dried thyme and sage
a large pinch of ground nutmeg
375g (13oz) cooked lean ham

Constructing the pie

1 Roll out dough to size of tin, with a 2cm (¾in) overhang. Spread over half the filling; put the eggs on top.

2 Push in eggs; cover with the mix. Fold over dough overhang. Beat last egg with salt; use to brush edges.

3 Roll out the remaining dough 5mm (¼in) thick. Lay on top, press to seal, and trim.

This Greek-inspired pie is both pretty to look at and delicious to eat. Using filo pastry like this means you don't have to worry too much about a perfect finish – the more crumpled the better!

CRISPY CHICKEN AND SPINACH PIE

 **SERVES 6**　　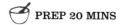 **PREP 20 MINS**　　 **COOK 35–40 MINS**　　 **FREEZE UP TO 1 MONTH**

EQUIPMENT
20cm (8in) loose-bottomed cake tin

INGREDIENTS

FOR THE FILLING
250g (9oz) spinach
2 garlic cloves, finely chopped
100g (3½oz) feta cheese,
roughly chopped
½ tsp freshly grated nutmeg
200g (7oz) cooked chicken, shredded
75g (2½oz) drained Peppadew
peppers, roughly chopped
2 eggs, beaten
salt and freshly ground black pepper

FOR THE PASTRY
6 sheets ready-made filo pastry
50g (1¾oz) butter, melted

1 Place the spinach in a colander and pour boiling water, from the kettle over it, to wilt it. Set aside to cool and drain.

2 Place the garlic, cheese, nutmeg, chicken, peppers, and eggs in a large bowl, season well, and stir to combine. Squeeze the liquid from the spinach, chop finely, and add to the bowl. Stir well and set aside. Preheat the oven to 200°C (400°F/Gas 6).

3 Place a sheet of filo pastry in the bottom of the tin, so the edges are hanging over the sides. Brush it generously with butter and place another sheet of pastry across the first, so they form a cross shape in the base. Brush with more butter. Repeat the pastry layers until all the pastry is used up and the bottom of the tin is completely covered.

4 Spoon the filling into the pastry case and carefully pull the overhanging layers of pastry into the centre to cover the filling. Brush the finished pie with the remaining melted butter. Place the tin on a baking tray and bake for 35–40 minutes until the pastry is golden brown and crisp. Remove the outer ring of the tin and slice to serve. Serve hot or cold.

A lovely recipe to cook from scratch, this pie is also a great time-saver. Cook double the amount of chicken, then before you debone it, simply freeze what you don't need for a delicious stew for another day.

COQ AU VIN PIE

 SERVES 4–6   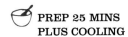 PREP 25 MINS
PLUS COOLING    COOK 55 MINS –
1 HR 5 MINS    FREEZE UP TO
1 MONTH

1 Heat a medium, heavy-based saucepan, add the lardons, and gently fry for 1 minute. Add the shallots and cook for 2 minutes. Add the garlic and mushrooms and cook for a further 1–2 minutes.

2 Add the chicken, wine, bay leaf, and thyme to the pan, bring to the boil, season with salt and black pepper, cover, and simmer gently for 25 minutes or until the chicken is tender and cooked.

3 Place a colander over a large bowl or jug and transfer the contents of the pan into the colander. Set aside for 10 minutes to allow all the juices to drain through and for the chicken to cool a little.

4 Remove the bay leaf from the colander. Place the chicken on a plate and spoon the lardon and mushroom mixture into the pie dish. Remove the meat from the chicken pieces and add to the dish. Sprinkle the parsley over the filling.

5 Return the drained cooking liquid to the pan, bring to the boil and cook over a high heat for 5–10 minutes to reduce and thicken. Pour the reduced sauce over the pie filling.

6 Preheat the oven to 200°C (400°C/Gas 6). Cut enough 2cm (¾in) wide strips from the edge of the pastry to fit around the rim of the pie dish. Brush the edge of the dish with water and place the strips on the rim. Cover the pie with the remaining pastry, trim, and press firmly to seal. Brush with beaten egg and cut a slit in the top to allow steam to escape. Bake on a baking tray for 20–25 minutes or until browned.

EQUIPMENT
23cm (9in) pie dish

INGREDIENTS

FOR THE FILLING
100g (3½oz) lardons
5 shallots, halved
2 garlic cloves, finely chopped
150g (5½oz) button mushrooms
4 chicken thighs
300ml (10fl oz) red wine
1 bay leaf
leaves from 4 sprigs of fresh thyme
  or ½ tsp dried thyme
salt and freshly ground black pepper
3 tbsp curly parsley, chopped

FOR THE PASTRY
215g (7½oz) sheet ready-rolled puff pastry
  (or to make your own, see pp110–113)
1 egg, beaten, to glaze

Pies are often the recipients of leftovers, brought together with a few added ingredients and a fresh, buttery pastry wrapping. Here Sunday's leftovers become Monday's supper.

ROAST CHICKEN HAND PIES

 **MAKES 10**   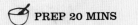 **PREP 20 MINS**   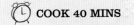 **COOK 40 MINS**   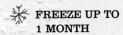 **FREEZE UP TO 1 MONTH**

1 Preheat the oven to 200°C (400°F/Gas 6). Drizzle the pumpkin or squash with olive oil, scatter with the thyme, season with salt and black pepper, and place in a roasting tin. Roast for 15–20 minutes or until just softened and turning golden at the edges. Set aside to cool completely.

2 Mix the shredded chicken, roasted squash, spring onions, and crème fraîche together in a bowl and season well. Roll out the pastry on a well-floured surface into a large sheet about 5mm (¼in) thick. Cut 20 x 10cm (4in) circles out of the pastry, gathering it up and re-rolling it if necessary.

3 Place 10 of the pastry circles onto 2 baking trays, and brush the edges with a little beaten egg. Pile a heaped tablespoon of the filling mixture into the centre of each and flatten it down with the back of the spoon, making sure to leave a 1cm (½in) border around the edge.

4 Top with the remaining 10 circles of pastry. These should be lightly rolled a little larger after cutting, as they will need to cover the mounded filling. Press down around the edges of the pies firmly, crimping the edges if desired to finish. Brush the tops with a little more beaten egg.

5 Use a chopstick to poke a small hole in the centre of each pie and bake for 20 minutes until well puffed up and golden brown. Remove from the oven and set aside to cool on a wire rack before serving warm or cold for a picnic. Chill the pies for up to 2 days. If freezing, reheat before serving.

EQUIPMENT
2 baking trays

INGREDIENTS

FOR THE FILLING
200g (7oz) pumpkin or butternut
  squash, peeled and cut into cubes
olive oil, for drizzling
1 tsp finely chopped thyme
salt and freshly ground black pepper
150g (5½oz) cold roast chicken,
  finely diced or shredded
2 spring onions, trimmed
  and finely sliced
3 tbsp crème fraîche

FOR THE PASTRY
500g (1lb 2oz) ready-made
  puff pastry (or to make
  your own, see pp110–113)
plain flour, for dusting
1 egg yolk, beaten
  with 1 tsp cold water,
  to glaze

A Brazilian favourite, this simple chicken pie uses cream cheese, instead of a more usual flour-based sauce to bring the ingredients together and gives the filling a wonderfully creamy texture.

CHICKEN PIE WITH CHEESE

 SERVES 6   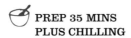 PREP 35 MINS
PLUS CHILLING   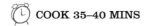 COOK 35–40 MINS    FREEZE UP TO
1 MONTH

EQUIPMENT
23cm (9in) pie dish

INGREDIENTS

FOR THE PASTRY
(For visual step by step
instructions see p104)
250g (9oz) plain flour,
plus extra for dusting
a pinch of salt
100g (3½oz) butter, diced,
plus extra for greasing
2 eggs, beaten, plus 1 egg,
beaten, to glaze
100ml (3½fl oz) double cream

FOR THE FILLING
2 tbsp olive oil
1 large onion, chopped
2 chicken breasts, finely sliced
2 tomatoes, skinned,
deseeded and chopped
100g (3½oz) chestnut
mushrooms, sliced
2 tbsp parsley, chopped
400g (14oz) cream cheese
salt and freshly ground black pepper

1 Grease and flour the pie dish. To make the pastry, rub the flour, salt, and butter together with your fingertips until the mixture resembles breadcrumbs. Add the 2 beaten eggs and cream and bring the mixture together to form a dough. Wrap in cling film and chill in the refrigerator for 1 hour.

2 Meanwhile, for the filling, heat the olive oil in a medium non-stick frying pan and fry the onion until soft. Add the chicken, and cook for 5 minutes. Add the tomatoes and mushrooms, and cook for a further 5 minutes. Remove from the heat, stir in the parsley and cream cheese, and season well with salt and black pepper. Set aside to cool.

3 Preheat the oven to 200°C (400°F/Gas 6). Roll half the pastry out on a floured surface to a circle large enough to line the pie dish. Place the pastry in the dish and trim around the edges. Add the filling and brush all around the edges with a little of the remaining beaten egg.

4 Roll out the remaining dough to a circle large enough to top the pie. Cover the pie with the remaining dough, trim, and press firmly to seal. Brush with the rest of the beaten egg and cut a slit in the top to allow steam to escape. Place on a baking tray and bake for 20–25 minutes until browned. Serve immediately or set aside to cool, and chill in the refrigerator for up to 2 days.

This quick and easy pie makes a tasty teatime treat for children. Most children like sweetcorn, and extra diced vegetables, such as mushrooms, celery, or carrots could also be added to the filling.

CHICKEN AND SWEETCORN PIE

 SERVES 4 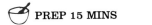 PREP 15 MINS COOK 1 HR

1 Preheat the oven to 200°C (400°F/Gas 6). Heat 1 tablespoon of olive oil in a large frying pan over a medium-high heat. Season the chicken with salt and black pepper. Add to the pan and cook, stirring, for about 10 minutes until golden brown all over. Remove from the pan and set aside.

2 Heat the remaining olive oil in the same pan over a low heat. Add the onion and a pinch of salt and sweat gently for about 5 minutes until soft and translucent. Remove from the heat and stir in the flour and a little of the cream. Return the pan to a low heat and add the remaining cream and the stock, stirring constantly for 5–8 minutes until the mixture thickens. Stir through the sweetcorn and parsley and season well with salt and black pepper.

3 Spoon the mixture into the pie dish or dishes. Roll out the pastry on a floured surface so that it is 5cm (2in) larger all around than the top of the pie dish. Cut a strip of pastry about 2.5cm (1in) in from the edge to make a collar. Dampen the edge of the dish with a little water; fit the pastry strip all the way around, and press down firmly. Brush the pastry collar with a little of the beaten egg, then top with the pastry lid. Pinch the edges together with your fingers to seal.

4 Brush the top with the remaining beaten egg and cut 2 slits in the top to allow steam to escape. Bake for 30–40 minutes until the pastry is puffed and golden. Serve hot.

EQUIPMENT
1.2 litre (2 pint) pie dish
or 4 individual pie dishes

INGREDIENTS

FOR THE FILLING
2 tbsp olive oil
3 skinless chicken breast fillets,
   cut into chunks
salt and freshly ground black pepper
1 onion, finely chopped
1 tbsp plain flour,
   plus extra for dusting
150ml (5fl oz) double cream
300ml (10fl oz) hot vegetable stock
350g (12oz) can sweetcorn kernels, drained
handful of flat-leaf parsley,
   finely chopped

FOR THE PASTRY
300 (10oz) ready-made puff pastry
   (or to make your own, see pp110–113)
1 egg, lightly beaten, to glaze

Entertaining is often easier if you serve individual portions to ensure that there will be enough to go around. This dish has the added advantage of being easy to prepare in advance and bake as needed.

STUFFED CHICKEN BREASTS EN CROÛTE

 MAKES 4   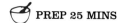 PREP 25 MINS   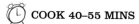 COOK 40–55 MINS    FREEZE UP TO 1 MONTH

EQUIPMENT
2 baking trays

INGREDIENTS

FOR THE FILLING
1 tbsp oil from a jar of sun-dried tomatoes
½ red onion, finely chopped
2 garlic cloves, finely chopped
1 red pepper, finely sliced
salt and freshly ground black pepper
4 sun-dried tomatoes in oil, drained
4 chicken breasts, deskinned and boned
75g (2½oz) mozzarella cheese, sliced into 4
16 basil leaves
8 slices Parma ham

FOR THE PASTRY
2 x 320g (10¾oz) sheets ready-rolled puff pastry, each 23 x 37cm (9 x 15in) (or to make your own, see pp110–113)
1 egg, beaten, to glaze

1 Preheat the oven to 200°C (400°F/Gas 6). Line the baking trays with baking parchment.

2 For the filling, heat the oil in a non-stick frying pan and gently fry the onion for 3 minutes. Add the garlic, red pepper, and plenty of seasoning, and cook for 5 minutes until the peppers are tender. Transfer to a medium high-sided bowl and add the sun-dried tomatoes. Whiz the vegetables using a hand-held electric blender, to form a rough paste.

3 To stuff the chicken breast, make a lengthways split down the side of each chicken breast with a very sharp knife. Place a slice of mozzarella and a quarter of the vegetable mixture into each pocket.

4 Place 4 basil leaves on top of each stuffed breast and season well with salt and black pepper. Wrap 2 slices of Parma ham around each breast, this will help to keep the stuffing in place.

5 Cut each pastry sheet into 4, to give 8 x 11.5 x 18.5cm (4½ x 7in) rectangles. Place a stuffed chicken breast on the centre of a pastry rectangle, brush the edges with water, and top with another rectangle. Press the pastry edges down firmly to seal and transfer to the baking tray. Repeat to wrap the remaining chicken. Brush each parcel with the beaten egg and bake for 35–40 minutes.

A version of the popular Brazilian pie, this pie is unusual in that it uses plain yogurt, rather than water, to bring the pastry together. This gives the finished pastry a more crumbly, flaky texture.

CHICKEN AND HEART OF PALM PIE

 SERVES 6   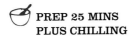 **PREP 25 MINS PLUS CHILLING**    **COOK 35–40 MINS**

1 Grease and flour the pie dish. To make the pastry, rub the flour, salt, and fat together with your fingertips until the mixture resembles breadcrumbs. Add the egg and yogurt and bring the mixture together to form a soft dough. Wrap in cling film and chill in the refrigerator for 1 hour.

2 For the filling, heat the olive oil in a medium non-stick frying pan over a medium heat and fry the onion for 3 minutes. Add the garlic and chicken and fry for 10 minutes. Add the hearts of palm, tomatoes, and cream, season well, and stir to combine. Remove from the heat and set aside.

3 Preheat the oven to 200°C (400°F/Gas 6). Roll out half the pastry on a floured surface to a circle large enough to line the pie dish. Place the pastry in the dish and trim off the excess. Add the filling and brush the edge with a little of the beaten egg.

4 Roll out the remaining pastry to a circle large enough to top the pie, then use to cover the pie. Trim off the excess pastry, then, using your thumbs and forefingers, press firmly to seal. Brush with the remaining beaten egg, then cut a hole in the top to allow steam to escape. Place on a baking tray and bake for 20–25 minutes until brown.

EQUIPMENT
23cm (9in) pie dish

INGREDIENTS

FOR THE PASTRY
(For visual step by step
  instructions see p104)
325g (11oz) plain flour,
  plus extra for dusting
a pinch of salt
100g (3½oz) vegetable fat, diced,
  plus extra for greasing
1 egg, plus 1 extra, beaten, to glaze
100ml (3½fl oz) plain yogurt

FOR THE FILLING
1 tbsp olive oil
1 onion, finely chopped
2 garlic cloves, finely chopped
2 chicken breasts, chopped into
  bite-sized chunks
400g can hearts of palm, chopped
  into bite-sized chunks
2 tomatoes, skinned, deseeded,
  and finely chopped
100ml (3½fl oz) double cream
salt and freshly ground black pepper

This tangy chicken pie is a pleasant change to a traditional pastry-based pie. Gently flavouring the filling with turmeric turns this midweek meal into something special.

VEGETABLE AND CHICKEN PIE

 SERVES 2　　　 PREP 20 MINS　　　 COOK 50 MINS

EQUIPMENT
small ovenproof dish

INGREDIENTS

FOR THE TOPPING
450g (1lb) large potatoes, peeled and cut into large chunks
salt and freshly ground black pepper
a large knob of butter
4–5 tbsp milk

FOR THE FILLING
40g (1½oz) butter
1 red pepper, thinly sliced
1 leek, sliced
¼ tsp ground turmeric
40g (1½oz) plain flour
250ml (9fl oz) milk
200g (7oz) tub crème fraîche
150g (5½oz) green beans, cut into 2cm (¾in) pieces and blanched
225g (8oz) cooked chicken, sliced (or 2–3 chicken thigh fillets, cooked)

1 Preheat the oven to 200°C (400°F/Gas 6). Cook the potatoes in a large saucepan of boiling salted water for 15 minutes, or until tender. Drain, return the potatoes to the pan, and mash with the butter and enough milk to make a thick mash. Season with salt and set aside.

2 For the filling, melt the butter in a large pan. Add the red pepper and leek, and cook for 3–4 minutes until soft. Stir in the turmeric, cook for a minute, then add the flour and cook for a further 2–3 minutes. Pour in the milk slowly, while stirring constantly, and cook for 4–5 minutes until thickened. Add the crème fraîche, green beans, and cooked chicken, and mix well.

3 Season well with salt and black pepper and pour the filling into the dish. Cover with the mashed potato then cook in the oven for 25 minutes until golden and piping hot.

A fantastic dish for entertaining, this dish is prepared in handy, individual servings. Use a good-quality puff pastry and leftover or ready-cooked chicken to achieve an impressive result in minutes.

CHICKEN JALOUSIE

 SERVES 4    PREP 25 MINS   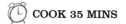 COOK 35 MINS    FREEZE UP TO 1 MONTH

EQUIPMENT
baking tray

INGREDIENTS

FOR THE FILLING
25g (scant 1oz) butter
2 leeks, thinly sliced
1 tsp chopped fresh thyme
or ½ tsp dried thyme
1 tsp plain flour, plus extra for dusting
90ml (3fl oz) chicken stock
1 tsp lemon juice
300g (10oz) skinless boneless
cooked chicken, chopped
salt and freshly ground black pepper

FOR THE PASTRY
plain flour, for dusting
500g (1lb 2oz) puff pastry
(or to make your own, see pp110–113)
1 egg, beaten, to glaze

1 Melt the butter in a saucepan. Add the leeks and cook over a low heat, stirring frequently, for 5 minutes, or until fairly soft. Stir in the thyme, then sprinkle over the flour and stir in. Gradually blend in the stock and bring to the boil, stirring until thickened. Remove from the heat, stir in the lemon juice, and set aside to cool.

2 Preheat the oven to 220°C (425°F/Gas 7). On a lightly floured surface, roll out just under half of the pastry to a 25 x 15cm (10 x 6in) rectangle and lay the pastry on a large dampened baking tray. Roll out the remaining pastry to a 25 x 18cm (10 x 7in) rectangle, lightly dust with flour, then fold in half lengthways. Make cuts 1cm (½in) apart along the folded edge to within 2.5cm (1in) of the outer edge.

3 Stir the chopped chicken into the leek mixture and season generously with salt and black pepper. Spoon evenly over the pastry base, leaving a 2.5cm (1in) border. Dampen the edges of the pastry with water. Place the second piece of pastry on top and press the edges together to seal, then trim off the excess pastry. Brush the top with beaten egg and bake for 25 minutes or until golden brown and crisp. Set aside to cool for 2–3 minutes before serving.

Although often used to top sweet dishes, a cobbler topping can also be used to turn a stew or casserole into a one-pot meal. Add mustard, chopped herbs, or even horseradish to complement the filling.

CHICKEN COBBLER

 SERVES 4   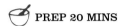 PREP 20 MINS    COOK 2¼ HRS

1 Preheat the oven to 150°C (300°F/Gas 2). Heat 1 tablespoon of the olive oil in the casserole over a medium heat. Add the onion and cook for 3–4 minutes until soft. Season with salt and black pepper, then stir in the garlic and parsnips, and cook for a further 2–3 minutes until the parsnips take on some colour. Remove the vegetables and set aside. Heat the remaining oil in the casserole over a higher heat.

2 Toss the chicken in the flour and cook, skin-side down, for 8–10 minutes, or until golden all over. Pour in the Marsala and bring to the boil, then return the onion and parsnips to the casserole, add the tarragon, and pour over the stock. Bring to the boil, reduce to a simmer, cover with the lid, and put in the oven for 2 hours. Check occasionally that it's not drying out, topping up with a little hot water if needed.

3 To make the cobbler topping, put the sifted flour into a bowl, season, then rub in the butter until the mixture resembles fine breadcrumbs. Stir in the cheese and add the buttermilk to form a dough. Roll out the dough on a lightly floured surface to 2.5cm (1in) thick and cut out 10 x 5cm (2in) diameter circles. For the last 30 minutes of cooking, place them around the edge of the stew and return to the oven, uncovered.

EQUIPMENT
large flameproof casserole

INGREDIENTS

FOR THE FILLING
3 tbsp olive oil
1 onion, finely chopped
salt and freshly ground black pepper
3 garlic cloves, finely chopped
3 parsnips, peeled and sliced
6 chicken thighs, with skin on
1 tbsp plain flour, seasoned with salt
  and black pepper
120ml (4fl oz) Marsala wine, sherry,
  or white wine
a few tarragon leaves
about 450ml (15fl oz) hot chicken stock

FOR THE COBBLER TOPPING
(For visual step by step instructions
  see cobbler dough pp118–119)
125g (4½oz) plain flour, sifted
salt and freshly ground black pepper
50g (1¾oz) butter, softened
25g (scant 1oz) Cheddar cheese, grated
3–4 tbsp buttermilk

A lighter alternative to the beef filling of the Cornish Pasty, these delicious chicken parcels are given an unusual twist with the use of a mixture of sweet potato and the more traditional white potato.

CHICKEN PASTIES

 MAKES 4   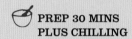 PREP 30 MINS PLUS CHILLING   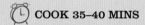 COOK 35–40 MINS

EQUIPMENT
baking tray

INGREDIENTS

FOR THE PASTRY
(For visual step by step instructions see shortcrust pastry p104)
350g (12oz) plain flour, plus extra for dusting
175g (6oz) butter, chilled and diced
2 eggs
oil, for greasing

FOR THE FILLING
115g (4oz) cream cheese
6 spring onions, sliced
2 tbsp parsley, chopped
salt and freshly ground black pepper
2–3 chicken breasts, about 350g (12oz), cut into 2cm (¾in) chunks
1 potato, about 150g (5½oz), cut into 1cm (½in) cubes
1 sweet potato, about 150g (5½oz), cut into 1cm (½in) cubes

1 To make the pastry, sift the flour into a bowl, then rub in the butter with your fingertips until the mixture resembles fine breadcrumbs. In another bowl, beat the eggs and 3 tablespoons cold water together. Set aside 1 tablespoon of the mixture for glazing, then pour the rest over the dry ingredients, and mix to form a dough. Wrap the dough in oiled cling film and chill in the refrigerator for 30 minutes.

2 Meanwhile, for the filling, mix the cream cheese, spring onions, and parsley together in a bowl, and season to taste with salt and black pepper. Stir in the chicken, potato, and sweet potato.

3 Preheat the oven to 200°C (400°F/Gas 6). Divide the pastry into 4 pieces. Roll out each piece on a floured surface and, using a small plate as a guide, cut into a 20cm (8in) circle. Spoon a quarter of the filling into the centre of each circle. Brush the edges with water and bring together to seal, then crimp.

4 Place the pasties on a baking tray and brush with the reserved egg mixture. Cut a slit in the tops and bake for 10 minutes, then reduce the heat to 180°C (350°F/Gas 4) and cook for 25–30 minutes until a thin knife comes out clean when inserted into the centre. Serve the pasties hot or cold.

A quick supper dish is given a Spanish makeover with this delicious pie. Try to find smoked paprika, as it will add a layer of sweet, smoky spice to this dish. Serve with any lightly steamed green vegetable.

SPANISH CHICKEN PIE

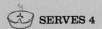 SERVES 4   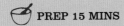 PREP 15 MINS   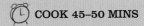 COOK 45–50 MINS    FREEZE UP TO 1 MONTH

1 Heat the olive oil in a medium saucepan, add the chicken strips, and fry for 5 minutes over a medium heat. Remove the chicken from the pan using a slotted spoon and transfer to a plate lined with kitchen paper.

2 Add the red onion to the pan and fry gently for 5 minutes. Add the paprika, garlic, peppers, and chorizo and cook for 5 minutes.

3 Stir in the tomatoes, olives, and rosemary, season well, bring to the boil, then reduce to a simmer. Cook for 15 minutes or until the sauce has thickened. Preheat the oven to 200°C (400°F/Gas 6).

4 Stir the chicken strips into the tomato and chorizo mixture and place in the pie dish.

5 Cut enough 2cm (¾in) wide strips from the edge of the pastry to fit round the rim of the dish. Brush the edge of the dish with water and place the strips on the rim. Cover the pie with the remaining pastry, trim, and press firmly to seal. Brush with the beaten egg and cut a hole in the top to allow the steam to escape. Place on a baking tray and bake for 15–20 minutes until browned.

EQUIPMENT
23cm (9in) pie dish

INGREDIENTS

FOR THE FILLING
1 tbsp olive oil
3 boneless, skinless chicken thighs, cut into strips
1 red onion, finely sliced
1 tsp pimenton dulce (smoked paprika)
2 garlic cloves, finely chopped
½ red pepper, finely sliced
½ yellow pepper, finely sliced
85g (3oz) chorizo, sliced into bite-sized pieces
400g can chopped tomatoes
30g (1oz) pitted green olives
2 tbsp rosemary leaves, chopped
salt and freshly ground black pepper

FOR THE PASTRY
215g (7½oz) ready-rolled puff pastry (or to make your own, see pp110–113)
1 egg, beaten, to glaze

For people who cook a lot, finding a new ingredient is often a great inspiration. This smoked chicken is a great alternative to normal roast chicken, and inspired these tasty little parcels.

SMOKED CHICKEN AND ROCKET FILO PARCELS

 MAKES 12   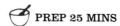 PREP 25 MINS   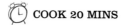 COOK 20 MINS    FREEZE UNCOOKED, UP TO 1 MONTH

EQUIPMENT
baking tray

INGREDIENTS

FOR THE FILLING
225g (8oz) rocket
4 spring onions, finely chopped
115g (4oz) smoked chicken
85g (3oz) crème fraîche
60g (2oz) pine nuts, toasted
2 tbsp red pesto
grated zest of 1 lemon
freshly ground black pepper
30g (1oz) Parmesan cheese, finely grated

FOR THE PASTRY
200g (7oz) filo pastry
60g (2oz) butter, melted

1 Preheat the oven to 180°C (350°F/Gas 4). Line the baking tray with baking parchment. Wash the rocket and remove any tough stalks. Place in a food processor with the spring onions, smoked chicken, and crème fraîche, then process for a slightly chunky texture. The mixture should not be totally smooth. Add the pine nuts, pesto, and lemon zest. Season to taste with freshly ground black pepper.

2 Lay the filo pastry out on a clean surface. Cover with a clean, damp tea towel to stop the pastry drying out. Brush one strip of filo pastry with melted butter, then place another layer on top and brush with more butter. Cut the pastry into 7.5cm (3in) strips, and place 1 heaped teaspoon of the rocket mixture near the top. Take the right corner and fold diagonally to the left to form a triangle over the filling. Fold along the crease of the triangle and repeat until you reach the end of the strip. Brush with butter once finished and scatter with grated Parmesan cheese. Place the parcels on the lined baking tray.

3 Repeat with the rest of the pastry and filling to make 12 parcels. Bake for 20 minutes. Remove from the baking tray and put on a wire rack to cool. The pastry parcels can be made the day before and chilled in the refrigerator until ready to cook.

These lovely little Latin American pastries make great party or picnic food, and are good served hot or cold. Unusually, the pastry is fried rather than baked, giving a deliciously crisp finish to the dish.

CHICKEN AND CHEESE EMPANADAS

 **MAKES 10–12**　　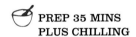 **PREP 35 MINS PLUS CHILLING**　　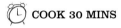 **COOK 30 MINS**

1 To make the pastry, melt the butter in a small saucepan, then add the lemon juice and 100ml (3½fl oz) water. Add the flour and salt, and stir well to make a paste. On a floured surface, knead the dough well, then chill.

2 Meanwhile, for the filling, mince the chicken in a food processor. Heat the olive oil in a frying pan, add the onion, and cook over a medium heat for 5 minutes. Add the minced chicken and cook for a further 5 minutes, stirring occasionally. Add the wine, garlic, tomato purée, cayenne, and finely chopped parsley, and season well with salt and black pepper. Mix well and cook for 10 minutes, then set aside to cool for 5 minutes. Stir in the grated cheeses.

3 Meanwhile, roll out the pastry on a lightly floured surface to 5mm (¼in) thick. Using the cutter, cut out 10–12 circles. Place 1 tablespoon of the chicken and cheese mixture in the middle of each and fold in half. Dampen the edges a little with some cold water, then crimp together with your fingers.

4 Heat the sunflower oil in a deep-sided frying pan until hot, then fry the empanadas in batches over a medium heat, turning them occasionally, for 3–5 minutes, or until golden brown. Serve with aïoli and a tomato and basil salad.

EQUIPMENT
10cm (4in) round cutter

INGREDIENTS

FOR THE PASTRY
100g (3½oz) butter
juice of 1 lemon
225g (8oz) plain flour,
　　plus extra for dusting
salt and freshly ground black pepper

FOR THE FILLING
125g (4½oz) skinless chicken breast
2 tbsp olive oil
1 onion, finely chopped
3 tbsp dry white wine
3 garlic cloves, crushed
1 tbsp tomato purée
1 tsp cayenne pepper
1 tbsp finely chopped flat-leaf parsley
salt and freshly ground black pepper
75g (2½oz) mozzarella cheese, grated
25g (scant 1oz) Parmesan cheese, grated
250ml (9fl oz) sunflower oil

Blind bake a shortcrust case and you have the basis of many, tasty meals. Fill it with new season's asparagus, tender chicken, and fresh tarragon, and you have the taste of summer on a plate.

CHICKEN, ASPARAGUS, AND TARRAGON SUMMER TART

 SERVES 6–8   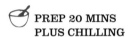 PREP 20 MINS PLUS CHILLING   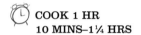 COOK 1 HR 10 MINS–1¼ HRS   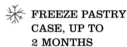 FREEZE PASTRY CASE, UP TO 2 MONTHS

EQUIPMENT
22cm (9in) deep-sided (3cm) loose-bottomed fluted tart tin, baking beans

INGREDIENTS

FOR THE PASTRY
(For visual step by step instructions see shortcrust pastry p104)
200g (7oz) plain flour,
plus extra for dusting
100g (3½oz) unsalted butter, softened
½ tsp salt

FOR THE FILLING
100g (3½oz) asparagus, trimmed and cut into 3cm (1¼in) pieces
salt and freshly ground black pepper
250ml (9fl oz) single cream
2 eggs, plus 1 egg yolk
1 heaped tbsp tarragon, chopped
grated rind of ½ lemon
250g (9oz) cold, cooked chicken

1 To make the pastry, rub the flour, butter, and salt together with your fingertips until the mixture resembles breadcrumbs. Add 4–6 tablespoons cold water, a little at a time, and bring the mixture together to form a soft dough. Add a little extra water if needed. Wrap in cling film and chill for 30 minutes. Preheat the oven to 180°C (350°F/Gas 4).

2 Roll out the pastry on a well-floured surface to a large circle about 5mm (¼in) thick, and use to line the tart tin, making sure it overlaps the sides. Trim all but 1cm (½in) of the overhanging pastry. Prick the bottom with a fork, line with greaseproof paper, and fill with baking beans. Place it on a baking tray and bake for 20–25 minutes until the pastry is lightly cooked. Remove the beans and paper and bake for a further 5 minutes to crisp. Trim off any ragged edges from the pastry case while it is still warm.

3 Blanch the asparagus pieces in a saucepan of boiling salted water for 1 minute then plunge them into a bowl of cold water. Whisk together the cream, eggs, egg yolk, tarragon, and lemon rind, and season.

4 Distribute the chicken and asparagus evenly in the bottom of the tart case, taking care not to pack the filling down too much. Place the tart on a baking tray and carefully pour the cream mixture over the filling.

5 Bake for 40–45 minutes until it is cooked through, and browning in places. Set aside to rest for at least 20 minutes before serving warm or cold. Best eaten the same day, but can be chilled overnight.

Sometimes simple entertaining dishes are what's required, but it's nice to spend a little more time producing something special. These tiny pies are a bit fiddly, but make a wonderful Christmas canapé.

CHICKEN AND VEGETABLE PIELETS

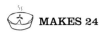 MAKES 24  PREP 15 MINS 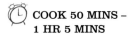 COOK 50 MINS – 1 HR 5 MINS

EQUIPMENT
24-hole mini muffin tin,
6cm (2½in) round cutter

INGREDIENTS

2 tbsp olive oil, plus extra for greasing
50g (1¾oz) butter
1 small carrot, finely chopped
1 celery stick, finely chopped
1 leek, white part only,
finely chopped
1 garlic clove, grated
or finely chopped
200g (7oz) chestnut mushrooms, diced
500g (1lb 2oz) skinless chicken
breast fillet, diced
1 tbsp thyme leaves, chopped
grated zest of 1 lemon
½ glass of dry white wine
250ml (9fl oz) double cream
salt and freshly ground black pepper

FOR THE PASTRY
3 sheets ready-rolled puff pastry
(or to make your own, see pp110–113)
2 eggs, lightly beaten, to glaze

1 Heat the olive oil and butter in a large frying pan over a low heat. Add the carrot and celery, and gently sweat for about 5 minutes until soft. Add the leek and sweat for a further 2–3 minutes until softened. Stir in the garlic and cook for 30 seconds before adding the diced mushrooms. Cook, stirring occasionally, for 5 more minutes.

2 Increase the heat slightly and add the diced chicken, thyme, lemon zest, and white wine. Cook, stirring occasionally, for 15–20 minutes. Pour in the cream, and season with salt and black pepper. Cook for a further 5 minutes until thickened slightly. Remove the pan from the heat and set aside to cool.

3 Preheat the oven to 200°C (400°F/Gas 6). Lightly oil the muffin tin. Cut out 24 x 6cm (2½in) circles from the puff pastry with a round cutter and use to line the holes in the prepared muffin tin. Spoon the chicken mixture into the pastry cases.

4 Cut out 24 x 5cm (2in) circles from the remaining puff pastry and use to cover each of the chicken pies. Gently press the edges together with your fingers to seal. Brush the tops with the beaten eggs and bake for 15–20 minutes until the pastry is golden brown. Serve the pielets hot with a salad of mixed leaves and a dollop or two of tomato relish.

After a festive meal there are sometimes more leftovers than you know what to do with. These little parcels make use of some of those leftovers, and are a good stand-by to serve unexpected guests.

ROAST TURKEY AND CRANBERRY TURNOVERS

 MAKES 4   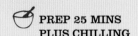 **PREP 25 MINS PLUS CHILLING**   **COOK 25–30 MINS**    **FREEZE UP TO 1 MONTH**

1 To make the pastry, rub the flour and butter together with your fingertips until the mixture resembles breadcrumbs. Add the salt and enough cold water to bring the mixture together to form a soft dough. Wrap in cling film and chill for 30 minutes.

2 For the filling, heat the olive oil in a medium non-stick frying pan. Add the onion and cook over a medium heat for 3 minutes, then add the garlic and cook for a further 2 minutes. Remove from the heat and stir in the crème fraîche, cranberry sauce, turkey, and oregano. Season generously, stir well, and set aside.

3 Preheat the oven to 190°C (375°F/Gas 5). Line the baking trays with baking parchment. Roll out the pastry on a well-floured surface to 5mm (¼in) thick. Using a small plate (about 20cm/8in in diameter) cut out 4 circles from the dough, re-rolling the pastry if necessary. Arrange one-quarter of the filling on half of each circle, leaving a 1cm (½in) border around the edge. Brush the edges with beaten egg, then bring them together to seal and crimp for a decorative finish.

4 Place the turnovers on the prepared baking trays and brush with the remaining beaten egg. Cut a slit in the top of each pastry to allow steam to escape and bake for 20–25 minutes until golden brown.

EQUIPMENT
2 baking trays

INGREDIENTS

FOR THE PASTRY
(For visual step by step instructions
   see shortcrust pastry p104)
300g (10oz) plain flour,
   plus extra for dusting
150g (5½oz) butter, chilled and diced
½ tsp salt
1 egg, beaten, to glaze

FOR THE FILLING
1 tbsp olive oil
1 red onion, finely chopped
2 garlic cloves, finely chopped
100ml (3½fl oz) half-fat crème fraîche
3 tbsp cranberry sauce
200g (7oz) roast turkey,
   roughly chopped
2 tbsp fresh, chopped
   or 1 tsp dried oregano
salt and freshly ground black pepper

Traditionally, both a turkey and a ham are served on or around Christmas day, which can leave you with a lot of meaty leftovers. This simple, classic pie is always a good solution.

TURKEY AND HAM PIE

 **SERVES 4**   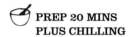 **PREP 20 MINS PLUS CHILLING**    **COOK 35–40 MINS**    **FREEZE UP TO 1 MONTH**

EQUIPMENT
23cm (9in) pie dish

INGREDIENTS

FOR THE FILLING
45g (1½oz) butter
45g (1½oz) plain flour
350–450ml (12–15fl oz) whole milk
1 heaped tsp Dijon mustard
salt and freshly ground black pepper
4 sprigs of thyme, leaves picked
or 1 tsp dried thyme
225g (8oz) cooked turkey, shredded
225g (8oz) cooked ham, shredded

FOR THE PASTRY
215g (7½oz) ready-rolled puff pastry
(or to make your own, see pp110–113)
1 egg, beaten, to glaze

1 Preheat the oven to 200°C (400°F/Gas 6). Melt the butter in a medium saucepan. Stir in the flour and cook for 2–3 minutes over a medium heat, stirring constantly with a wooden spoon, until a smooth paste is formed. Gradually add the milk, stirring constantly, then bring to the boil. Reduce the heat and simmer for 3 minutes to make a white sauce. Stir in the mustard and season well with salt and black pepper.

2 Add the thyme, turkey, and ham to the sauce, season well and stir to combine. Spoon the mixture into the pie dish.

3 Cut enough 2cm (¾in) wide strips from the edge of the pastry to fit round the rim of the pie dish. Brush the edge of the dish with water and place the strips on the rim. Cover the pie with the remaining pastry, trim the edges, and press firmly with your thumb and forefinger to seal. Brush with the beaten egg and cut a slit in the top to allow steam to escape. Chill in the refrigerator for 10 minutes to firm up the pastry.

4 Place the pie on a baking tray and bake for 25–30 minutes or until puffed up and golden brown on top.

This is an interpretation of the classic Moroccan pastilla, but here a large family-sized pie is served, which tastes even better cold the next day. You can make and chill the filling three days ahead.

MIDDLE-EASTERN GUINEA FOWL PIE

 SERVES 4    PREP 1½ HRS   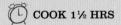 COOK 1½ HRS   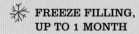 FREEZE FILLING, UP TO 1 MONTH

1 If using a guinea fowl, remove the breasts and set aside to use in another dish. Take the legs and wings off the body and chop the carcass roughly. Put the guinea fowl or chicken legs and the rest of the guinea fowl (if using) in a large saucepan. Add the onions, garlic, ginger, and cinnamon stick and cover with the stock. Bring to the boil, reduce the heat to low and simmer, uncovered, for 45 minutes, until the legs are cooked through. Set aside to cool, then strain through a colander, reserving the liquid. Clean out the pan, add the reserved liquid and bring to a simmer until it barely covers the bottom of the pan.

2 Pull the guinea fowl meat off the bones, leaving it in bite-sized shreds. Remove the onions and garlic, roughly chop, add them to the meat, and return to the pan. Mix in the pomegranate molasses and honey and cook over a medium heat until the mixture looks wet. Add the eggs and coriander and cook for 2 minutes until the mixture comes together. Season and cool.

3 Combine the walnuts, apricots, and cinnamon. Preheat the oven to 190°C (375°F/Gas 5). Brush the bottom of the tin with a little olive oil. Put a layer of filo into the bottom of the tin. Brush with more oil and layer a filo sheet on top, angling it slightly off centre to the first piece. Continue until you have used 6 layers. Spread half the walnut mix over the base. Cover with half the meat. Top with remaining nut mix and finish with meat. Fold any ragged edges over the top, cut the remaining filo in half, and repeat the layering process. Brush with oil. Bake for 30–40 minutes until brown. Cool for 5 minutes; dust with icing sugar, if liked.

EQUIPMENT
20cm (8in) loose-bottomed cake tin

INGREDIENTS

FOR THE FILLING
1 small guinea fowl,
  or 2 large chicken legs
2 onions, quartered
4 garlic cloves, peeled
2cm (¾in) piece of ginger,
  thickly sliced
1 cinnamon stick
1 litre (1¾ pints) good-quality
  chicken stock
2 tbsp pomegranate molasses
1 tbsp runny honey
2 eggs, lightly beaten
2–3 heaped tbsp coriander, chopped
salt and freshly ground black pepper
100g (3½oz) walnut pieces, toasted
  and roughly chopped
50g (1¾oz) dried apricots,
  finely chopped
½ tsp ground cinnamon

FOR THE PASTRY
3 tbsp olive oil
9 sheets ready-made filo pastry
icing sugar (optional)

A sophisticated pairing of wild mushrooms and cream perfectly complements the subtle gamey flavour of the guinea fowl. Serve with greens and plenty of mashed potato for a homely autumnal treat.

CREAMY WILD MUSHROOM AND GUINEA FOWL PIE

 **SERVES 6–8**   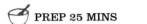 **PREP 25 MINS**   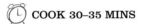 **COOK 30–35 MINS**    **FREEZE UP TO 1 MONTH**

1 Preheat the oven to 200°C (400°C/Gas 6). Place the porcini mushrooms in a small bowl and cover with boiling water. Set aside for 10 minutes, then drain and squeeze any moisture out of the mushrooms.

2 Heat the olive oil in a medium, non-stick frying pan and gently fry the shallots for 3 minutes. Add the garlic and cook for 1–2 minutes.

3 Add the guinea fowl to the pan and cook for 3–4 minutes until lightly browned. Add the chestnut mushrooms, porcini mushrooms, Madeira, thyme, nutmeg, and seasoning and cook gently for 5 minutes. Add the cream, stir well, and transfer to the pie dish.

4 Cut enough 2cm (¾in) wide strips from the edge of the pastry to fit around the rim of the pie dish. Brush the edge of the dish with water and place the strips on the rim. Cover the pie with the remaining pastry, trim off the excess, and press firmly to seal. Brush with the beaten egg and cut a hole in the lid to allow steam to escape. Place on a baking tray and bake for 15–20 minutes until browned.

EQUIPMENT
23cm (9in) pie dish

INGREDIENTS

FOR THE FILLING
25g (scant 1oz) dried porcini mushrooms
1 tbsp olive oil
4 shallots, halved
2 garlic cloves, finely chopped
400g (14oz) guinea fowl breasts, cut into bite-sized pieces
200g (7oz) chestnut mushrooms, halved
2 tbsp Madeira
leaves from 1 bunch fresh thyme or 1 tsp dried thyme
¼ tsp freshly grated nutmeg
salt and freshly ground black pepper
2 tbsp double cream

FOR THE PASTRY
215g (7½oz) sheet ready-rolled puff pastry (or to make your own, see pp110–113)
1 egg, beaten, to glaze

variation

CREAMY WILD MUSHROOM AND CHICKEN PIE

Try using chicken or turkey breast instead of the guinea fowl in step 3, and follow the recipe as directed.

IN PRAISE
OF PASTRY

SHORTCRUST PASTRY

A good shortcrust pastry is light, crisp, and suits all types of pies and tarts. Use the following quantities: 150g (5$\frac{1}{2}$oz) plain flour, 75g (2$\frac{1}{2}$oz) unsalted butter, or follow the quantities in the recipe you are using.

1 Rub the plain flour and the unsalted butter, chilled and diced, together with your fingertips until the mix resembles fine breadcrumbs. Work swiftly, handling the pastry as little as possible to avoid the gluten in the flour heating up. Try working in a cool room. To make a richer pastry, add 1 lightly beaten egg yolk at this stage.

2 Add 3–4 tablespoons cold water and a pinch of salt to the crumbs and bring together to form a soft dough (if you are making a rich shortcrust and have added in an egg yolk at step 1, add just enough water to the crumbs, 1 tablespoon at a time, to form a soft dough). Handle the pastry gently and be careful not to overwork it; just work it until the texture is smooth. Add extra water if it is too dry. Wrap in cling film and chill for 30 minutes. You could substitute the butter for lard or use half lard and half butter for some traditional recipes.

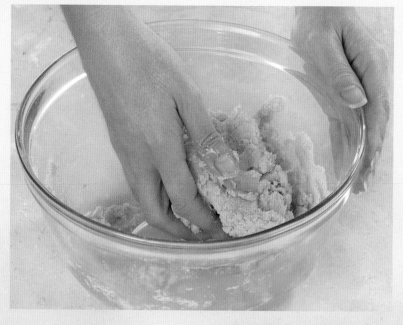

SWEET SHORTCRUST PASTRY

The classic shortcrust pastry (see opposite) can be turned into something sweeter. Just substitute 30g (1oz) of the flour for caster sugar, or follow the quantities in the recipe you are using.

1 Rub the plain flour and the chilled and diced unsalted butter together with your fingertips until the mixture resembles fine breadcrumbs. Work swiftly, handling the pastry as little as possible to avoid the gluten in the flour heating up. Try working in a cool room. Stir in the caster sugar. To make a richer pastry, add 1 lightly beaten egg yolk to the flour mixture.

2 Add 3–4 tablespoons cold water and bring together to form a soft dough (if you are making a rich shortcrust and have added in an egg yolk at step 1, add just enough water to the crumbs, 1 tablespoon at a time, to form a soft dough). Handle the pastry gently and be careful not to overwork it; just work it until the texture is smooth. Add extra water if it is too dry. Wrap in cling film and chill for 30 minutes. If you need to scale up pastry quantities, add extra water instead of more egg.

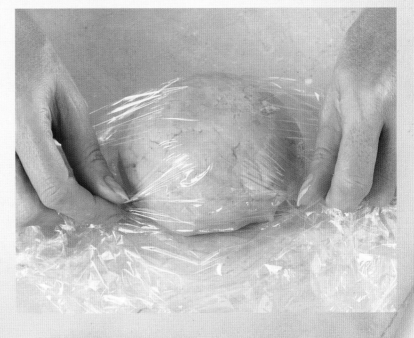

SUET CRUST PASTRY

For this classic pastry, great for a steak and kidney pie, use these quantities: 300g (10oz) self-raising flour, ½ teaspoon of salt, 150g (5½oz) suet, or follow the quantities in the recipe you are using.

1 Sift the self-raising flour into a large bowl and add the salt. Combine these ingredients by mixing briefly with a wooden spoon.

2 Dice the beef or vegetable suet into small 1cm (½in) cubes, then add the diced suet to the flour in the bowl and stir in slightly.

3 Rub the diced suet into the flour with your fingertips until the mixture resembles rough breadcrumbs. Work swiftly, handling the pastry as little as possible to avoid the gluten in the flour heating up. Try working in a cool room.

4 Add 4–6 tablespoons of cold water and mix to start to bring the mixture together, first with a wooden spoon, and then using your hands.

5 Use your fingertips to bring the mixture together to form a soft dough. Handle the pastry gently and be careful not to overwork it; just work it until the texture is smooth. Add more water if the dough is too dry.

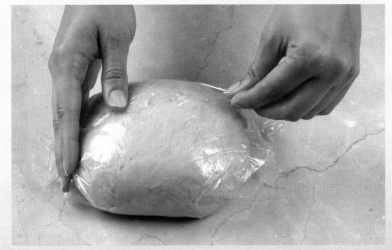

6 Wrap the pastry in cling film and chill in the refrigerator for at least 30 minutes before using.

HOT-WATER CRUST PASTRY

This pastry is best for pork pies. Use 400g (14oz) plain flour, ½ teaspoon of fine salt, 150ml (5fl oz) boiling water, 150g (5½oz) cubed lard, or follow the quantities in the recipe you are using.

1 Sift the flour into a large bowl and add the salt. Using a wooden spoon, mix, and then make a well in the middle of the flour mixture.

2 Measure the boiling water into a jug and add the diced lard. Stir the mixture with a metal spoon until the fat has melted.

3 Carefully pour the hot melted fat mixture into the well in the centre of the flour.

4 Stir the mixture with a wooden
spoon, starting in the well, to
combine all the ingredients,
until it starts to come together.

5 Knead the mixture with
your hands into a soft dough,
being careful because it will be
hot. This pastry must be used
quickly, as it begins to harden
as it cools. Any pastry kept for
tops or lids should be wrapped
in a clean tea towel and kept in
a warm place until needed.

PUFF PASTRY

To make this flaky pastry, which is suitable for a variety of sweet and savoury pies, use 250g (9oz) plain flour, ¹/₂ teaspoon of salt, 175g (6oz) butter, or follow the quantities in the recipe you are using.

1 Sift the plain flour and salt into a bowl. Rub in 60g (2oz) diced butter with your fingertips until it resembles breadcrumbs.

2 Add 100ml (3½fl oz) water and bring it together to form a soft, elastic dough. Wrap in cling film and chill in the refrigerator for 15 minutes.

3 Turn the dough out onto a lightly floured surface and roll out until it is a large rectangular shape, about 3mm (⅛in) in thickness.

4 Dot 115g (4oz) diced butter over the top two-thirds of the dough, then fold the unbuttered side over half the buttered side.

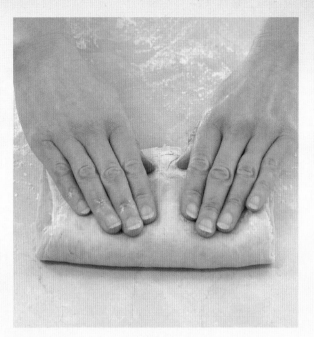

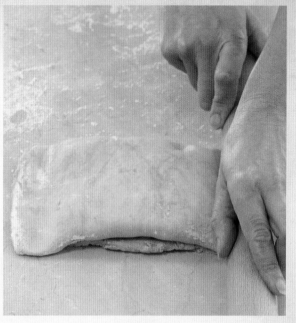

5 Fold the dough over again so the butter is completely enclosed in the layers of dough, then turn the dough over.

6 Roll over the edges of the dough with the rolling pin to seal. Wrap in cling film and chill in the refrigerator for 15 minutes.

7 Lightly re-flour the surface. Repeat the rolling and folding process of step 4, but without adding the butter. Seal, wrap, and chill for 15 minutes.

8 Repeat step 7 three more times, chilling the dough for 15 minutes between each turn. The dough is now ready to use as required.

QUICK PUFF PASTRY

This pastry is much quicker to make than the classic puff pastry. Use 250g (9oz) semi-frozen butter, 250g (9oz) plain flour, 1 teaspoon of salt, or follow the quantities in the recipe you are using.

1 Freeze the butter for 30 minutes. Coarsely grate it into a bowl. Sift over the flour and the salt and rub together until well-combined and crumbly.

2 Pour in 90–100ml (3–3½fl oz) water. Use a fork to start mixing, then use your fingertips to form a rough dough. If it is too dry, add more water.

3 Shape the dough into a ball, then place in a clean plastic bag. Seal the bag and set aside to chill in the refrigerator for 20 minutes.

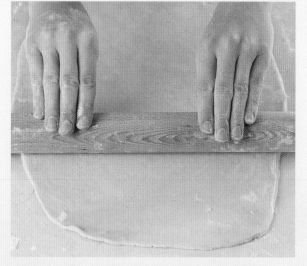

4 Thinly roll out the dough on a lightly floured surface to a long rectangle, short sides, about 25cm (10in). Keep the edges straight and even.

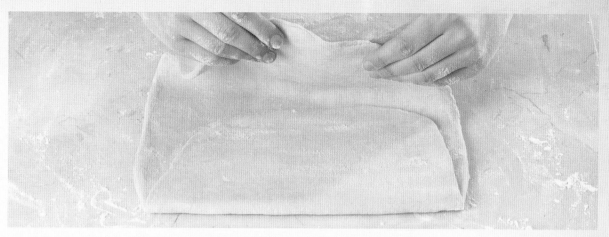

5 Take one-third of the pastry and fold it into the middle of the rectangle, then fold the remaining third over to make 3 layers. The rolling and folding process incorporates air into the pastry, making it puff up on baking.

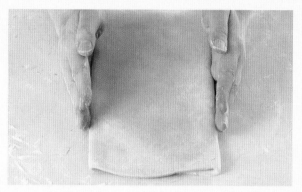

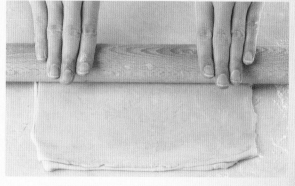

6 Turn the dough over so the joins are easily sealed when it is re-rolled. Give it a quarter turn so that the folded edges are at the sides.

7 Roll out the dough again to a similar size as the original rectangle. Make sure to keep the short sides even in size.

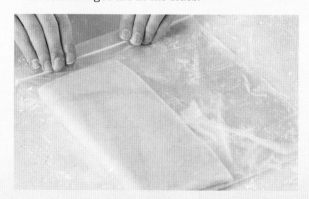

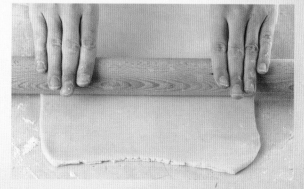

8 Repeat the folding, turning, and rolling. Put the dough back in the plastic bag and chill in the refrigerator for 20 minutes.

9 Roll, fold, and turn the pastry twice more, then chill in the refrigerator for a final 20 minutes. The dough is now ready to use as required.

STRUDEL PASTRY

To make a light, delicate strudel pastry, use: 250g (9oz) plain flour, 1 egg, ¹/₂ teaspoon of lemon juice and a pinch of salt, or follow the quantities in the recipe you are using.

1 Sift the plain flour into a mound onto a clean work surface. Then, using your fingers, make a well in the centre of the flour.

2 Beat the egg with 125ml (4 fl oz) water, lemon juice, and a pinch of salt together in a large bowl, then pour the mixture into the well.

3 Work the ingredients in the well with your fingertips, gradually drawing in the flour to combine into a dough.

4 Knead just enough flour into the other ingredients so that the dough forms a ball; it should be quite soft.

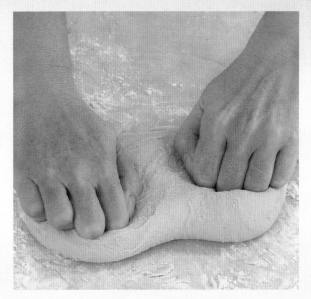

5 On a floured surface, knead the dough for about 10 minutes until it is shiny, smooth and elastic, then shape the dough into a ball.

6 On the floured surface, cover the ball of dough with another large clean bowl, and set aside to rest for 30 minutes.

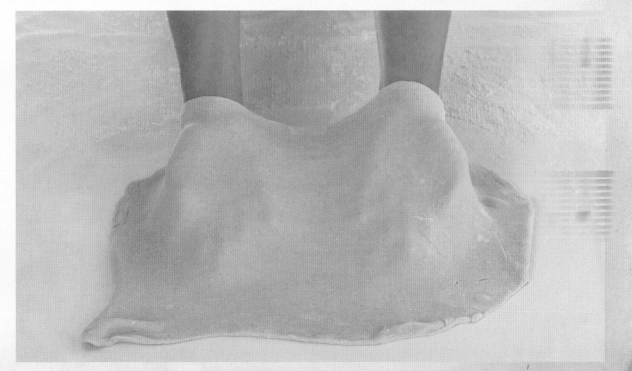

7 Flour your hands and stretch the dough, starting at the centre and working outwards. Continue to work outwards until the dough is as thin as possible; it should be translucent. The dough is now ready to use as required.

WHEAT-FREE SHORTCRUST PASTRY

Ideal for people with a gluten intolerance. Use 225g (8oz) gluten-free plain flour, 1 teaspoon xanthan gum, a pinch of salt, 100g (3½oz) butter, 1 egg, or follow the quantities in the recipe you are using.

1 Sift the flour, xanthan gum, and a pinch of salt into a large bowl and mix together to combine. For sweet pastry, add 2 tablespoons icing sugar with the flour.

2 Add the chilled, diced butter and rub it in with your fingertips until the mixture resembles breadcrumbs. Alternatively, pulse in a food processor.

3 Beat the egg, then add to the mixture and stir it in with a palette knife or a round-bladed table knife until the mixture clumps together.

4 Add 1–2 tablespoons of cold water, gradually, a few drops at a time, mixing after each addition. Repeat until it comes together to form a dough.

5 On a floured surface, knead the dough lightly until smooth. Shape the dough into a ball, then wrap in cling film.

6 Chill the dough in the refrigerator for 10 minutes until firm. This will make rolling out the pastry easier. Use the pastry as required.

COBBLER DOUGH

Use these quantities: 225g (8oz) self-raising flour, 2 tablespoons baking powder, 75g (2½oz) caster sugar, a pinch of salt, 75g (2½oz) butter, 100ml (3½fl oz) buttermilk, 1 egg, or follow the recipe you are using.

1 For a cobbler topping, sift the flour, baking powder, caster sugar (omit for a savoury cobbler), and a pinch of salt into a large bowl.

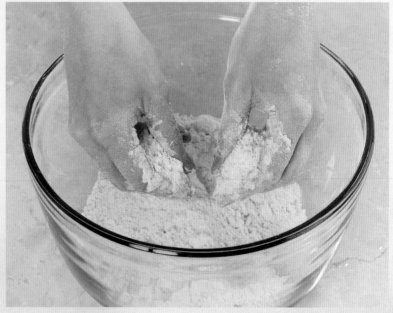

2 Add the chilled and diced unsalted butter and mix with your fingertips until the mixture resembles breadcrumbs.

3 Beat together the buttermilk and egg, then add to the dry ingredients, and mix to form a dough.

4 Put the filling into a baking dish. Place walnut-sized spoonfuls of the dough over the filling; leave space for the mix to spread.

5 Lightly press down on the balls of mixture to help them combine with the filling and bake. If liked, add chopped herbs or spices to the basic mix to complement the filling.

BISCUIT CASE

These simple, sweet cases are an ideal alternative to pastry. Use 250g (9oz) digestive biscuits, 60g (2oz) caster sugar, 125g (4½oz) unsalted butter, or follow the quantities in the recipe you are using.

1 Preheat the oven to 180°C (350°F/Gas 4). Crush the digestive biscuits in a plastic bag with a rolling pin, or use a food processor.

2 Mix the biscuit crumbs and caster sugar with the melted and cooled butter in a large bowl until it resembles wet sand.

3 Pour the biscuit mixture into your chosen tart or cake tin and press it firmly into the bottom and sides of the tin. Make sure the filling is packed as firmly as possible, and that there is a good side to the case so that the filling can be contained, unlike a cheesecake base. Place the tart case on a baking tray and bake for 10 minutes. Set aside to cool. Once cold, store the tart case in the refrigerator until needed.

CRUMBLE TOPPING

To make a traditional sweet crumble topping, use 125g (5oz) plain flour, 85g (3oz) caster sugar, 85g (3oz) unsalted butter, or follow the quantities in the recipe you are using.

1 Sift the flour into a large bowl. Add the caster sugar and mix to combine. Use soft light brown sugar instead of caster, if liked.

2 Dice the cold butter into 1cm (½in) cubes with a sharp knife, then add the diced butter to the flour mixture.

3 Rub the butter into the flour and sugar mixture with your fingertips until the mixture resembles rough breadcrumbs. Do not make the mixture too fine or uniform, as any larger lumps of butter will melt into the crumble topping and give a nicer taste and texture to the finished dish.

LINING A TART TIN

Follow these steps to lining any tart tin perfectly every time.
Use the tart tin as a template before lining it with the pastry,
and take care not to overstretch it or it may shrink when baked.

1 Roll out the pastry on a lightly floured surface
to a large circle, about 3mm (⅛in) thick. Don't
use too much flour as it may make the pastry dry.

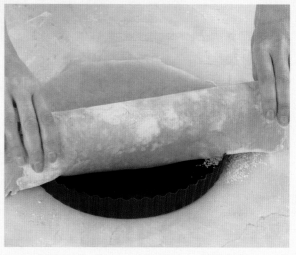

2 Roll the pastry up carefully using the rolling pin,
then unroll it over the tart tin, making sure it
overlaps on all sides.

3 Push the pastry in with your
fingers, gently pressing it into
the base and sides of the tin.
It should overlap the sides by
at least 2cm (¾in).

BAKING BLIND

To achieve a crisp pastry case, bake the unfilled pastry shell either partially or completely before adding the filling, depending on the recipe. Use dried pulses as an alternative to baking beans.

1 Prick the bottom of the pastry all over with a fork to stop it puffing up, and line with a piece of baking parchment or greaseproof paper.

2 Weigh the baking parchment down with baking beans. Place the pastry case on a baking tray – this supports the sides of the pastry until cooked.

3 Bake blind in the centre of a preheated oven for 20–25 minutes until the sides of the pastry are cooked. Remove the beans and paper.

4 Return the case to the oven and bake for 5 more minutes to crisp the bottom. Set aside to cool, trimming the edges with a knife while warm.

DECORATIVE EDGES

There's nothing like a home-made pie or tart. For an individual finishing touch, don't just stop at neatly trimming the edges, try one of these ideas to make your pastry treats look as special as they taste.

Crimped
Pinch the pastry edge with the forefinger and thumb of your right hand, and make even indentations in the top edge with the forefinger of your left hand.

Fork-crimped
A quick and simple finishing touch that also helps to seal the pastry lid – especially useful if the filling is quite wet. Press down all around the edges of the pie using the tines of a fork.

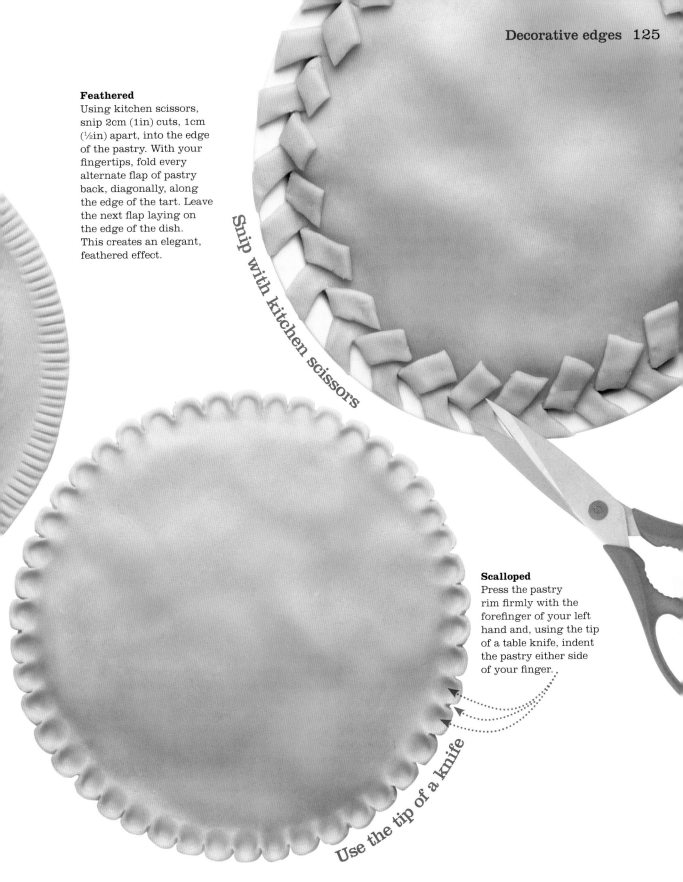

Feathered
Using kitchen scissors, snip 2cm (1in) cuts, 1cm (½in) apart, into the edge of the pastry. With your fingertips, fold every alternate flap of pastry back, diagonally, along the edge of the tart. Leave the next flap laying on the edge of the dish. This creates an elegant, feathered effect.

Snip with kitchen scissors

Scalloped
Press the pastry rim firmly with the forefinger of your left hand and, using the tip of a table knife, indent the pastry either side of your finger.

Use the tip of a knife

Arrowhead
Cut a 2cm (1in) wide strip, from leftover pastry, long enough to go around the edge of the pie. Cut the strip into equal-sized triangles. Moisten the edge of the pie lid with water and position the triangles all the way around, slightly overlapping each other.

Work at an angle to achieve this impressive finish

Fluted
Pinch the pastry edge with the forefinger and thumb of your right hand, and make indentations at a slight angle, in the edge, with the forefinger of your left hand.

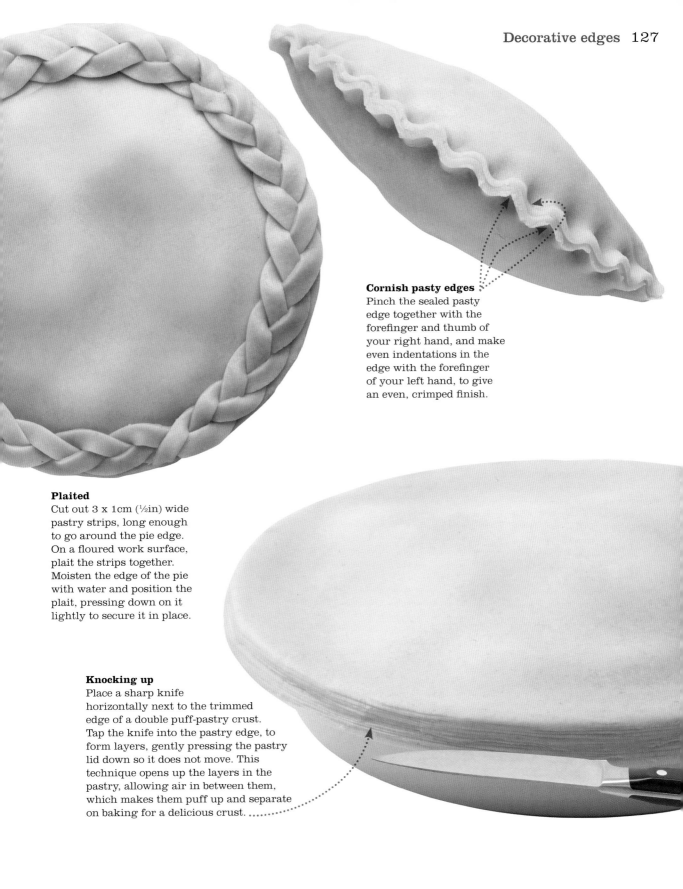

Cornish pasty edges
Pinch the sealed pasty edge together with the forefinger and thumb of your right hand, and make even indentations in the edge with the forefinger of your left hand, to give an even, crimped finish.

Plaited
Cut out 3 x 1cm (½in) wide pastry strips, long enough to go around the pie edge. On a floured work surface, plait the strips together. Moisten the edge of the pie with water and position the plait, pressing down on it lightly to secure it in place.

Knocking up
Place a sharp knife horizontally next to the trimmed edge of a double puff-pastry crust. Tap the knife into the pastry edge, to form layers, gently pressing the pastry lid down so it does not move. This technique opens up the layers in the pastry, allowing air in between them, which makes them puff up and separate on baking for a delicious crust.

DECORATIVE TOPS

The top of a covered pie can be decorated in a variety
of ways with leftover pastry trimmings. You could also
make a feature of the steam-hole in a pie – it looks great
and stops the pastry going soggy.

Decorative shapes
Roll out any leftover pastry
and design your own shapes,
such as leaves, and cut them
out using a sharp knife.
Or use a small cutter in the
shape of a heart, flower,
star, numbers, or letters to
personalize the pie.

Pastry shapes personalize your pie

Twisted ribbon
Cut a 2cm (1in) wide pastry
strip, long enough to go around
the pie. Hold the strip at one end
and twist it from the other end.
Moisten the edge of the pie with
water and secure the pastry strip
in place. Seal the edges together.

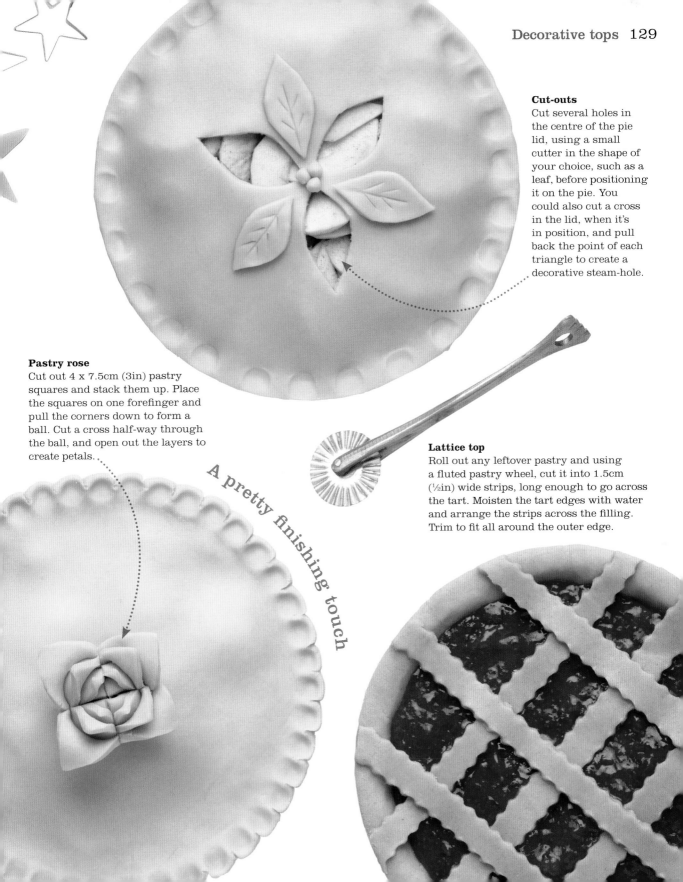

Cut-outs
Cut several holes in the centre of the pie lid, using a small cutter in the shape of your choice, such as a leaf, before positioning it on the pie. You could also cut a cross in the lid, when it's in position, and pull back the point of each triangle to create a decorative steam-hole.

Pastry rose
Cut out 4 x 7.5cm (3in) pastry squares and stack them up. Place the squares on one forefinger and pull the corners down to form a ball. Cut a cross half-way through the ball, and open out the layers to create petals.

A pretty finishing touch

Lattice top
Roll out any leftover pastry and using a fluted pastry wheel, cut it into 1.5cm (½in) wide strips, long enough to go across the tart. Moisten the tart edges with water and arrange the strips across the filling. Trim to fit all around the outer edge.

FISH PIES AND TARTS

This simple dish is quick and easy to make, but always goes down a treat. Substitute the white wine for fish stock when cooking for children and serve with a green vegetable, such as peas.

FISH AND SWEETCORN PIE

 SERVES 4 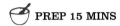 PREP 15 MINS 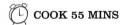 COOK 55 MINS  FREEZE UP TO 1 MONTH

EQUIPMENT
1.2 litre (2 pint) pie dish

INGREDIENTS

FOR THE FILLING
1 tbsp olive oil
1 onion, finely chopped
salt and freshly ground black pepper
6 rashers streaky bacon, finely chopped
1 tsp plain flour
150ml (5fl oz) dry white wine
handful of flat-leaf parsley, finely chopped
150ml (5fl oz) double cream
200g can sweetcorn, drained
675g (1½lb) raw white fish, such as haddock or pollack, cut into chunks

FOR THE PASTRY
300g (10oz) ready-made puff pastry (or to make your own, see pp110–113)
plain flour, for dusting
1 egg, lightly beaten, to glaze

1 Preheat the oven to 200°C (400°F/Gas 6). Heat the olive oil in a large frying pan over a low heat. Add the onion and a pinch of salt, and sweat gently for about 5–10 minutes until soft and translucent. Add the bacon and cook for a further 5 minutes. Remove from the heat, stir in the flour, and add a little of the wine. Return to the heat, pour in the remaining wine, and cook for 5–8 minutes until thickened.

2 Stir through the parsley, cream, and sweetcorn, and spoon the mixture into the pie dish with the fish. Combine gently, and season well with salt and black pepper.

3 Roll out the pastry on a floured surface so it is about 5cm (2in) larger all around than the pie dish. Cut out a strip of pastry about 2.5cm (1in) from the edge to make a collar. Dampen the edge of the pie dish with a little water, fit the pastry strip all the way around, and press down firmly. Brush the collar with a little beaten egg and top with the pastry lid. Trim away the excess pastry, then using your thumb and finger, pinch the edges of the pastry together to seal. Cut 2 slits in the top of the pie to allow steam to escape.

4 Brush the top of the pie all over with the remaining beaten egg and bake for 20–30 minutes until the pastry is puffed and golden. Serve hot.

Here a traditional fish pie mix is topped with a buttery puff-pastry lid. Use any mixture of fresh and smoked fish in the filling, and for variety, add a couple of hard-boiled eggs, cut into quarters.

CLASSIC FISH PIE

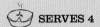 SERVES 4   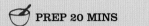 PREP 20 MINS    COOK 20–25 MINS    FREEZE UP TO 1 MONTH

1 Preheat the oven to 200°C (400°F/Gas 6). Poach the salmon and haddock in a saucepan of lightly simmering water for 5 minutes until just cooked. Drain and set aside to cool. Melt the butter in another pan, then remove from the heat and whisk in the flour until a thick paste is formed. Add the milk a little at a time, whisking to avoid any lumps. Season with salt and black pepper, and add the nutmeg. Bring the sauce to the boil, stirring constantly, then reduce the heat and cook for a further 5 minutes, stirring.

2 Flake the fish into a bowl and add the prawns. Spread the spinach over the top and pour the sauce over it. Season to taste. When the spinach is wilted, mix the filling together and transfer to the pie dish.

3 Roll out the pastry on a floured surface to a circle bigger than the pie dish and 3–5mm (⅛–¼in) thick. Cut a circle to fit the pie. Roll some of the trimmings out into long strips. Brush the rim of the dish with beaten egg and press the pastry strips around the rim. Brush the edge with more egg and top with the pastry lid. Press the edges down to seal, then trim away any excess pastry. Brush the top of the pie with the remaining egg and cut 2 slits to allow steam to escape.

4 Bake for 20–25 minutes until golden. Set aside to rest for 5 minutes before serving. Best eaten the same day, the pie can be chilled overnight and reheated.

EQUIPMENT
18cm (7in) pie dish

INGREDIENTS

FOR THE FILLING
300g (10oz) skinless salmon fillet, bones picked
200g (7oz) skinless smoked haddock fillet, bones picked
50g (1¾oz) unsalted butter
5 tbsp plain flour
350ml (12fl oz) milk
salt and freshly ground black pepper
a pinch of freshly grated nutmeg
200g (7oz) prawns
100g (3½oz) baby spinach, washed

FOR THE PASTRY
250g (9oz) ready-made puff pastry (or to make your own, see pp110–113)
plain flour, for dusting
1 egg, beaten, to glaze

Haddock is the fish of choice in this traditional family dish, but you can use your favourite white fish if you like. Serve the pie with steamed broccoli or fresh peas for a healthy midweek supper.

FISHERMAN'S PIE

 SERVES 6 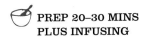 PREP 20–30 MINS PLUS INFUSING  COOK 50 MINS–1 HR

1 Cook the potatoes in a saucepan of boiling, salted water for 15–20 minutes until tender. Drain thoroughly, then put back into the pan and mash. Heat the milk in a small pan, add the butter, salt, and black pepper, and stir until mixed. Pour the mixture into the potatoes, and beat over a medium heat for 2–3 minutes, until fluffy. Taste for seasoning. Set aside.

2 For the filling, pour the milk into a sauté pan, then add the peppercorns, bay leaves, and onion. Bring to the boil, then remove, cover, and leave in a warm place to infuse for about 10 minutes.

3 Add the fish to the milk, cover, and simmer for 5–10 minutes, depending on thickness; it should flake easily when tested with a fork. Transfer the fish to a large plate, using a slotted spoon; reserve the cooking liquid. Let the fish cool, then flake with a fork.

4 Melt the butter in a pan over a medium heat. Whisk in the flour and cook for 30 seconds–1 minute until foaming. Remove from the heat. Pour the fish cooking liquid through a sieve into the butter mixture. Whisk the liquid into the sauce, then return to the heat and cook, whisking, until the sauce boils and thickens. Season and simmer for 2 minutes. Stir in the parsley.

5 Preheat the oven to 180°C (350°F/Gas 4). Melt some butter and use to brush the pie dish. Ladle one-third of the sauce into the bottom of the dish. Spoon the flaked fish on top, in an even layer. Cover with the remaining sauce, then distribute the prawns evenly on top. Sprinkle the chopped eggs over the prawns.

6 Spread the mashed potatoes on top to cover the filling completely. Bake for 20–30 minutes until the topping is brown and the sauce bubbles.

EQUIPMENT
2 litre (3½ pint) pie dish

INGREDIENTS

FOR THE TOPPING
625g (1lb 6oz) potatoes, washed, peeled, and cut into pieces
salt and freshly ground black pepper
4 tbsp milk
60g (2oz) butter

FOR THE FILLING
1 litre (1¾ pints) milk
10 peppercorns
2 bay leaves
1 small onion, peeled and quartered
750g (1lb 10oz) skinned haddock fillets, cut into pieces
90g (3oz) butter, plus extra for greasing
60g (2oz) plain flour
leaves from 5–7 parsley sprigs, chopped
125g (4½oz) prawns, peeled, deveined, and cooked
3 eggs, hard-boiled, coarsely chopped

Slow cooking the onions gives them a gentle, sweet taste–perfect when paired with strong, salty anchovies. If freezing the tart, add the anchovy garnish after it is defrosted.

ONION AND ANCHOVY TART

 **SERVES 4–6**

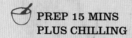 **PREP 15 MINS PLUS CHILLING**

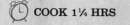 **COOK 1¼ HRS**

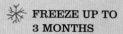 **FREEZE UP TO 3 MONTHS**

EQUIPMENT
20cm (8in) loose-bottomed fluted tart tin, baking beans

INGREDIENTS

FOR THE PASTRY
350g (12oz) ready-made shortcrust pastry (or to make your own, see p104)
plain flour, for dusting

FOR THE FILLING
2 tbsp olive oil
30g (1oz) butter
450g (1lb) onions, thinly sliced
750g (1lb 10oz) curd cheese
115ml (4fl oz) milk
2 large eggs
1 tsp cumin seeds or caraway seeds, crushed (optional)
salt and freshly ground black pepper
60g (2oz) anchovy fillets, halved lengthways

1 Roll out the pastry thinly on a lightly floured surface, and use it to line the tin. Chill for 30 minutes.

2 Heat the olive oil and butter in a saucepan, add the onions, cover, and cook over a gentle heat, stirring occasionally, for 20 minutes, or until the onions are soft, but not browned. Uncover and cook for a further 4–5 minutes until golden. Set aside to cool.

3 Preheat the oven to 200°C (400°F/Gas 6). Line the pastry case with greaseproof paper and fill with baking beans. Bake for 15 minutes, then remove the beans and paper and bake for a further 10 minutes.

4 Reduce the heat to 180°C (350°F/Gas 4). Spoon the onions into the pastry case, spreading them in an even layer. Beat the curd cheese, milk, eggs, and cumin or caraway, if using, together in a bowl. Season to taste with salt and black pepper, then pour into the tart case. Lay the anchovy fillets in a lattice pattern on top and bake for 25 minutes, or until the pastry is golden and the filling is set. Serve warm. The tart can be cooked up to 1 day in advance, covered, and chilled. Reheat in a hot oven for 10 minutes, or until warmed through.

All the tastes of a Mediterranean summer come together in these quick and easy tartlets. If you are short on time, buy ready-made puff pastry. Serve as a starter or light lunch with a green salad.

ANCHOVY, PEPPER, AND THYME TARTLETS

 MAKES 4   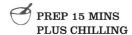 PREP 15 MINS PLUS CHILLING    COOK 25–30 MINS

1 Preheat the oven to 200°C (400°F/Gas 6). Lightly brush or spray the muffin tin with oil.

2 Cut the pastry into 4 squares on a lightly floured surface and use to line the holes in the prepared muffin tin, pushing the pastry down gently into the corners. Chill in the refrigerator for 1 hour.

3 To make the filling, combine the eggs, cream, and Parmesan in a jug, and season to taste with salt and black pepper. Mix well.

4 Place an anchovy in each of the prepared puff pastry cases. Divide and arrange the peppers, thyme, and mozzarella evenly between the 4 cases. Top each tart with a slice of tomato. Pour the egg and cream mixture over the filling, into the cases and grind over a little black pepper. Bake the tarts for 25–30 minutes until golden on top. Serve warm.

EQUIPMENT
4-hole 125ml (4fl oz) muffin tin

INGREDIENTS

FOR THE PASTRY
oil, for greasing
1 sheet ready-rolled puff pastry
   (preferably made with butter)
   (or to make your own, see pp110–113)
plain flour, for dusting

FOR THE FILLING
2 eggs
175ml (6fl oz) cream
2 tbsp freshly grated Parmesan cheese
salt and freshly ground black pepper
4 anchovy fillets in olive oil, drained
½ x 280g jar roasted mixed peppers,
   drained and chopped
leaves from 4 sprigs of thyme
75g (2½ oz) mozzarella cheese, grated
1 plum tomato, sliced into 4 rounds

Baking a pastry case blind helps to ensure that the crust does not go soggy once the filling is introduced and baked. However, spinach produces a lot of water, so be sure to drain it well before use.

SALMON AND SPINACH QUICHE

 **SERVES 6–8**

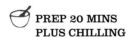 **PREP 20 MINS PLUS CHILLING**

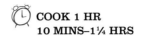 **COOK 1 HR 10 MINS–1¼ HRS**

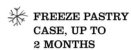 **FREEZE PASTRY CASE, UP TO 2 MONTHS**

EQUIPMENT
22cm (9in) deep-sided, loose-bottomed fluted tart tin, baking beans

INGREDIENTS

FOR THE PASTRY
(For visual step by step instructions see shortcrust pastry p104)
200g (7oz) plain flour,
plus extra for dusting
100g (3½oz) unsalted butter, softened
½ tsp salt

FOR THE FILLING
200g (7oz) baby spinach
2 tbsp olive oil
1 garlic clove, crushed
salt and freshly ground black pepper
100g (3½oz) cooked salmon, broken into pieces
250ml (9fl oz) single cream
2 eggs, plus 1 egg yolk
1 tsp grated lemon rind

1 For the pastry, rub the flour, butter, and salt together with your fingertips until the mixture resembles fine breadcrumbs. Add enough cold water, a little at a time to bring the mixture together to form a soft dough. Add a little more water if the mixture is too dry. Wrap in cling film and chill for 30 minutes.

2 Preheat the oven to 180°C (350°F/Gas 4). Roll out the pastry on a well-floured surface to a large circle about 5mm (¼in) thick and use to line the tart tin, making sure it overlaps the sides, then trim all but 1cm (½in) off the overhanging pastry with a pair of scissors. Push the pastry down into the corners of the tin making sure it clings to the sides well.

3 Prick the bottom of the pastry case with a fork, line with greaseproof paper and fill with baking beans. Place on a baking tray and bake 20–25 minutes until the pastry is lightly cooked. Remove the beans and paper and bake for a further 5 minutes to crisp. Trim off any ragged edges while it is still warm.

4 For the filling, cook the baby spinach in a large saucepan with the olive oil and garlic for 2–3 minutes until soft. Season well. Place the spinach in a sieve and press out any excess water. Set aside to cool.

5 Spread the cooled spinach evenly over the bottom of the tart. Spread the salmon out alongside the spinach. Whisk together the cream, eggs, yolk, lemon rind, and seasoning. Place the tart case on a baking tray and pour the cream mixture over the filling.

6 Bake for 45 minutes until just set. Cool for 30 minutes before eating warm or cold. Best eaten on the day it is made, but can be chilled overnight.

Baking salmon "en croûte" (wrapped in a puff-pastry case before baking), helps keep this delicate fish moist and succulent. The watercress cream also adds a layer of flavour to the finished dish.

SALMON EN CROÛTE

 SERVES 4    PREP 25 MINS   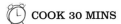 COOK 30 MINS

EQUIPMENT
baking tray

INGREDIENTS

FOR THE FILLING
oil, for greasing
85g (3oz) watercress,
coarse stems removed
115g (4oz) cream cheese
salt and freshly ground black pepper
600g (1lb 5oz) skinless salmon fillet

FOR THE PASTRY
400g (14oz) ready-made puff pastry
(or to make your own, see pp110–113)
plain flour, for dusting
1 egg, beaten, or milk, to glaze

1 Preheat the oven to 200°C (400°F/Gas 6). Lightly grease the baking tray. Chop the watercress very finely, place in a bowl, add the cream cheese, season generously with salt and black pepper, and mix well.

2 Cut the salmon fillet into 2 pieces. Roll out the pastry on a lightly floured surface to 3mm (⅛in) thick. It should be roughly 7.5cm (3in) longer than the salmon pieces and just over twice as wide. Trim the edges straight, then transfer to the baking tray.

3 Place 1 piece of salmon in the middle of the pastry. Spread the top with the watercress cream and place the other piece of salmon on top. Lightly brush the pastry edges with water, then fold the 2 ends over the salmon. Fold in the sides so they overlap slightly and press together to seal. Re-roll the trimmings and use to decorate the top of the pastry, if liked. Brush with beaten egg, and make 2 or 3 holes with a skewer to allow steam to escape.

4 Bake for 30 minutes, or until the pastry is well risen and golden brown. Test if the salmon is cooked by pushing a skewer halfway through the thickest part and leaving for 4–5 seconds; when removed, it should feel hot.

5 Remove from the oven and set aside to cool for 2–3 minutes, then slice and serve. The whole dish can be made up to 12 hours before baking. Cover with cling film and chill until ready to cook.

Fish and fennel is a wonderful pairing. This sophisticated version of a fish pie will become an all-time favourite with friends and family. Use other varieties of fish if you like, such as haddock or pollack.

SALMON, FENNEL, AND WHITE WINE PIE

 SERVES 6   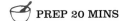 **PREP 20 MINS**   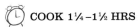 **COOK 1¼–1½ HRS**

1 Preheat the oven to 200°C (400°C/Gas 6). Arrange the fennel slices in the bottom of the ovenproof dish, pour the wine over, season well, and cover tightly with foil. Bake for 35–45 minutes until tender. Pour the cooking liquor out of the dish and set aside, leaving the fennel in the dish. Reduce the oven temperature to 180°C (350°C/Gas 4).

2 Melt the butter in a medium saucepan. Stir in the flour and cook for 2–3 minutes over a medium heat, stirring with a wooden spoon, until a smooth paste is formed. Gradually add the milk and the reserved cooking liquid, stirring constantly, to make a white sauce. Stir in the parsley, dill, and lemon zest and juice, and season well.

3 Place the salmon in the dish with the fennel, then pour the sauce over the top and stir well.

4 Cut a 28 x 20cm rectangle from the pastry. Cut enough 2cm (¾in) wide strips from the remaining pastry to fit around the edges of the filling. Place the strips around the edge of the dish, directly on the filling. Brush the strips with a little of the beaten egg and cover the pie with the pastry rectangle. Brush with the remaining beaten egg and cut a hole in the top to allow steam to escape. Place on a baking tray and bake for 40–45 minutes until browned.

EQUIPMENT
28 x 20 x 5cm (11 x 8 x 2in) ovenproof dish

INGREDIENTS

FOR THE FILLING
1 bulb fennel, about
   250g (9oz), thinly sliced
250ml (9fl oz) dry white wine
salt and freshly ground black pepper
45g (1½oz) butter
45g (1½oz) plain flour
350ml (12fl oz) whole milk
2 tbsp flat-leaf parsley, chopped
2 tbsp dill, chopped
zest of 1 lemon
1 tbsp lemon juice
500g (1lb 2oz) salmon fillet, skinned
   and cut into bite-sized pieces

FOR THE PASTRY
320g (12oz) sheet ready-rolled puff pastry
   (or to make your own, see pp110–113)
1 egg, beaten to glaze

A twist on the traditional Finnish dish of fish, usually made with perch and baked slowly. As perch is difficult to find, salmon is used in this wonderfully unusual recipe.

KALAKUKKO

 **SERVES 6–8**    **PREP 30 MINS**   ⏰ **COOK 6½ HRS**

EQUIPMENT
baking tray

INGREDIENTS

FOR THE PASTRY
(For visual step by step
instructions see p104)
450g (1lb) rye flour,
plus extra for dusting
150g (5½oz) plain flour
½ tbsp salt
50g (1¾oz) butter, diced

FOR THE FILLING
375g (13oz) salmon fillet, skinned
and cut into bite-sized pieces
125g (4½oz) streaky bacon,
cut into bite-sized pieces
salt and freshly ground black pepper
20g (¾oz) butter, melted

1 Preheat the oven to 200°C (400°F/Gas 6). Line a baking sheet with baking parchment. To make the pastry, place the flours and salt in a bowl, then rub in the butter with your fingertips until the mixture resembles breadcrumbs. Gradually add about 300–400ml (10–14fl oz) cold water to make a soft dough. Cut the dough into 2 equal portions.

2 Roll out half the pastry on a lightly floured surface to form a circle about 28cm (11in) in diameter. Place the circle onto a large baking tray lined with baking parchment. Scatter some rye flour in the middle of the pastry, then put alternate layers of salmon and bacon pieces in the centre of the pastry, seasoning with salt and black pepper between the layers, and leaving a 2cm (¾in) border around the edge. Brush the border of the pastry with a little water.

3 Repeat to roll out the remaining pastry, as before. Place the second circle of pastry carefully over the salmon and bacon and press the edges firmly together to seal tightly. Crimp the edges to finish if required.

4 Brush the pie generously with melted butter and bake for 30 minutes, or until it starts to brown. Reduce the oven temperature to 110°C (225°F/Gas ¼).

5 Remove the pie from the oven and carefully transfer it (still on the parchment) onto a large sheet of foil. Wrap it completely in foil, return to the oven, and cook for a further 6 hours.

6 Remove from the oven and cover with a tea towel so that crust doesn't get too hard. To serve, slice the kalakukko like a cake. It can be served hot or cold.

To make a change from the more usual potato-topped fish pies, try topping your fish with this tasty crumble mix. Steamed asparagus or fine beans would be the perfect accompaniment to this special dish.

FISH CRUMBLE

 SERVES 4–6    PREP 30 MINS    COOK 35–40 MINS

1 Preheat the oven to 180°C (350°F/Gas 4). To make the crumble topping, melt the butter in a large non-stick frying pan, add the sliced baby leeks, and gently fry over a low-medium heat for 10 minutes. Remove the pan from the heat.

2 Place the bread, pine nuts, tarragon, and cheese in a food processor, and process until even-sized breadcrumbs form. Transfer to the pan with the cooked leeks, add the oats, mustard, and plenty of salt and black pepper, and stir well. Remove from the heat.

3 For the filling, grease the ovenproof dish and place the salmon, prawns, and scallops in the dish. Pour over the wine and cream, then sprinkle with lemon zest and parsley. Season well with salt and black pepper.

4 Sprinkle the crumble mixture over the top and place the dish on a baking tray. Bake for 25–30 minutes, or until the crumble starts to turn golden brown and the fish is cooked through.

EQUIPMENT
2 litre (3½ pint) ovenproof dish

INGREDIENTS

FOR THE CRUMBLE TOPPING
30g (1oz) butter
6 baby leeks, finely sliced
175g (6oz) fresh white bread,
 roughly torn
45g (1½oz) toasted pine nuts
3 tbsp tarragon leaves
60g (2oz) Grana Padano cheese,
 roughly chopped
60g (2oz) oats
1 tsp English mustard
 or mustard powder
salt and freshly ground black pepper

FOR THE FILLING
butter, for greasing
200g (7oz) salmon fillet, skinned
 and chopped into bite-size pieces
200g (7oz) king prawns, peeled
 and deveined
200g (7oz) scallops, without the coral
120ml (4fl oz) dry white wine
120ml (4fl oz) single cream
zest of 1 lemon
3 tbsp parsley, chopped

This impressive dish is perfect for entertaining. It can be prepared and assembled, covered with cling film, and chilled until needed. Remove it from the refrigerator 15 minutes before baking.

SALMON COULIBIAC

 SERVES 6    PREP 30 MINS    COOK 55 MINS–1 HR

EQUIPMENT
baking tray

INGREDIENTS

FOR THE FILLING
60g (2oz) long-grain white rice
175ml (6fl oz) fish stock
a pinch of turmeric
10g (¼oz) butter
1 shallot, finely chopped
115g (4oz) prawns, peeled,
deveined, and cooked
3 tbsp mixed green herbs,
such as tarragon, dill, chives,
and flat-leaf parsley, chopped
zest of 1 lemon
1 tbsp lemon juice
salt and freshly ground black pepper
50g(1¾oz) wild rocket
400g (14oz) piece of salmon fillet
(approximately 10 x 13 cm/4 x 5½in),
skinned and pin-boned

FOR THE PASTRY
320g (10¾oz) sheet ready-rolled
puff pastry, 23 x 35cm (9 x 14in) each
(or to make your own, see pp110–113)
plain flour, for dusting
1 egg, beaten to glaze

1 Place the rice, fish stock, and turmeric in a small saucepan. Bring to the boil, cover, reduce the heat and simmer for 15 minutes, or until the rice is cooked.

2 Melt the butter in a small pan over a medium heat and fry the shallot for 3–5 minutes until cooked. Preheat the oven to 180°C (350°F/Gas 4) and line the baking tray with baking parchment.

3 Place the prawns, herbs, lemon zest, and juice in a large bowl. Add the cooked rice and shallot, season well, and stir to combine.

4 Cut the pastry in half widthways to get 2 x 23 x 17.5cm (9 x 7in) rectangles. Place one half on the lined baking tray. Roll out the second half of the pastry on a lightly floured surface until it measures 33 x 27.5cm (13 x 11in). Set aside.

5 Place half the rocket on the smaller pastry rectangle, leaving a 5cm (2in) border all around, and top with half the rice mixture. Place the salmon on top and cover with the remaining rice and rocket.

6 Brush the pastry border with beaten egg and place the larger pastry rectangle over the salmon. Press the pastry edges together, seal, and trim to make a neat shape. Brush the pastry with beaten egg and bake for 30–35 minutes until golden brown.

A gougère is a little choux pastry puff traditionally made in the Burgundy region of France. Here they are flavoured with Gruyère cheese and smoked salmon for an elegant canapé or party dish.

CHEESE GOUGÈRES WITH SMOKED SALMON

 MAKES 8   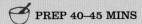 **PREP 40–45 MINS**   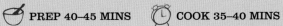 **COOK 35–40 MINS**

1 Preheat the oven to 190°C (375°F/Gas 5). Grease the baking trays. To make the pastry, melt the butter in a saucepan with 250ml (9fl oz) water and ¾ teaspoon of salt. Bring to the boil, then remove the pan from the heat, add the flour, and beat until smooth. Return the pan to the hob and beat over a low heat for 30 seconds to dry.

2 Remove the pan from the heat. Add 4 eggs, 1 at a time, beating well. Beat the fifth egg, and add it gradually. Stir in half the cheese. Place eight 6cm (2½in) mounds of dough on the baking trays. Beat the remaining egg and salt together, and brush over each of the puffs. Sprinkle with the remaining cheese. Bake for 30–35 minutes until firm. Remove, and transfer to a wire rack. Slice the tops and set aside to cool.

3 Wilt the spinach in a pan of boiling, salted water for 1–2 minutes. Drain well and set the spinach aside to cool. When cool, squeeze to remove the water and chop. Melt the butter in a frying pan. Add the onion and cook until soft. Add the garlic, nutmeg, salt and black pepper to taste, and the spinach. Cook, stirring, until all the liquid has evaporated. Add the cream cheese and stir until the mixture is thoroughly combined. Remove from the heat.

4 Add two-thirds of the smoked salmon, pour in the milk, and stir. Mound 2–3 tablespoons of filling into each cheese puff. Arrange the remaining smoked salmon on top. Rest the tops against the side of each filled puff and serve at once.

EQUIPMENT
2 baking trays

INGREDIENTS

FOR THE PASTRY
75g (2½oz) unsalted butter, plus extra for greasing
1¼ tsp salt
150g (5½oz) plain flour, sifted
5 eggs, plus 1 extra, to glaze
125g (4½oz) Gruyère cheese, coarsely grated

FOR THE FILLING
1kg (2¼lb) fresh spinach, trimmed and washed
salt and freshly ground black pepper
30g (1oz) unsalted butter
1 onion, finely chopped
4 garlic cloves, finely chopped
a pinch of ground nutmeg
250g (9oz) cream cheese
175g (6oz) smoked salmon, sliced into strips
4 tbsp milk

Here a traditional mashed potato-topped fish pie is given a grown-up twist with the use of succulent king prawns. The mustard should complement the filling, not overwhelm it, so taste as you go.

SALMON AND PRAWN PIE

 SERVES 6   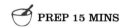 **PREP 15 MINS**    **COOK 35 MINS**

EQUIPMENT
20 x 30cm (8 x 12in) ovenproof dish

INGREDIENTS

FOR THE TOPPING
900g (2lb) potatoes, peeled and quartered
salt and freshly ground black pepper
2 tbsp milk

FOR THE FILLING
350g (12oz) cooked salmon,
flaked into chunks
350g (12oz) hot smoked salmon fillets,
flaked into chunks
200g (7oz) prawns, cooked,
peeled, and deveined
salt and freshly ground black pepper
30g (1oz) butter
30g (1oz) plain flour
450ml (15fl oz) milk
2 tbsp chives, chopped
1 tbsp capers in brine,
rinsed and drained
60g (2oz) Cheddar cheese, grated
30g (1oz) fresh white breadcrumbs

1 Preheat the oven to 200°C (400°F/Gas 6). Cook the potatoes in a large saucepan of boiling salted water for 15 minutes, or until soft. Drain the potatoes, return to the pan and mash well with a potato masher until there are no lumps. Add the 2 tablespoons milk, mash again until smooth, then season to taste with salt and black pepper. Set the potatoes aside.

2 Arrange the salmon, and prawns in the ovenproof dish so that they are evenly distributed. Season with salt and black pepper, and set aside.

3 Gently melt the butter in a pan over a low heat. Remove from the heat and stir in the flour with a wooden spoon. Add a little milk and beat until smooth. Return the pan to the heat, and continue adding the milk, a little at a time, stirring constantly, until the sauce has thickened. Whisk to get rid of any lumps, then stir through the chives and capers.

4 Pour the sauce over the prawns and salmon, and stir well. Cover with the mashed potato. Combine the cheese and breadcrumbs, season well, and sprinkle evenly over the mash. Bake for 15–20 minutes until heated through and the topping is crisp and golden.

Using chopped fresh dill in the pastry of this rich tart helps to complement the dill used in the filling. Smoked salmon is considered luxurious, but salmon trimmings are cheap and work well here.

SMOKED SALMON AND DILL TART

 SERVES 4–6   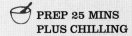 PREP 25 MINS PLUS CHILLING   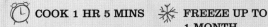 COOK 1 HR 5 MINS   ❄ FREEZE UP TO 1 MONTH

1 To make the pastry, rub the flour and butter together with your fingertips until the mixture resembles breadcrumbs. Add the egg yolk and dill to the flour mixture, then add 1–2 tablespoons cold water and bring together to form a smooth dough. Wrap in cling film and chill for 30 minutes.

2 Preheat the oven to 180°C (350°F/Gas 4). Roll out the pastry on a floured surface to a circle large enough to line the tart tin. Place the pastry in the tin, pressing it down well into the bottom and around the edges. Trim off any excess pastry, then prick the bottom with a fork. Line with baking parchment and fill with baking beans. Place the tin on a baking tray and bake for 20 minutes. Remove the beans and paper and return to the oven for a further 5 minutes to crisp.

3 For the filling, arrange the salmon in the bottom of the pastry case. Place the soured cream, milk, the 2 eggs, Grana Padano cheese, and dill in a large jug, season generously with black pepper, and beat well. Pour over the salmon and bake for 35–40 minutes or until golden and set in the middle. Serve hot or warm.

EQUIPMENT
20cm (8in) tart tin, baking beans

INGREDIENTS

FOR THE PASTRY
(For visual step by step instructions
   see shortcrust pastry p104)
150g (5½oz) plain flour
75g (2½oz) butter, chilled and diced
1 egg yolk
2 tbsp dill, finely chopped

FOR THE FILLING
140g (5oz) smoked salmon trimmings
100ml (3½fl oz) soured cream
4 tbsp milk
2 eggs
20g (¾oz) Grana Padano cheese, grated
3 tbsp dill, chopped
freshly ground black pepper

Smoked trout often has a more delicate colour and flavour than smoked salmon. Horseradish is hot, so if you don't like it fiery add a little and taste before adding any more. Serve with a green salad.

SMOKED TROUT TARTLETS

 MAKES 6    PREP 30 MINS
PLUS CHILLING   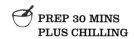 COOK 30 MINS    FREEZE UP TO
1 MONTH

EQUIPMENT
6 x 10cm (4in) tartlet tins,
baking beans

INGREDIENTS

FOR THE PASTRY
(For visual step by step instructions
see shortcrust pastry p104)
125g (4½oz) plain flour,
plus extra for dusting
75g (1½oz) butter, chilled and diced
a pinch of salt
1 small egg

FOR THE FILLING
115ml (4fl oz) crème fraîche
1 tsp creamed horseradish
½ tsp lemon juice
grated zest of ½ lemon
1 tsp capers, rinsed and chopped
salt and freshly ground black pepper
4 egg yolks, beaten
200g (7oz) smoked trout
bunch of dill, chopped

1 To make the pastry, place the flour, butter, and salt in a food processor and process until the mixture resembles breadcrumbs. Add the egg and mix until incorporated. To make by hand, rub the flour, butter, and salt together with your fingertips until the mixture resemble breadcrumbs. Add the egg and mix to form a soft dough, adding a little water if necessary.

2 Roll out the dough on a lightly floured surface and use to line the tartlet tins. Line the pastry cases with greaseproof paper and fill with baking beans. Chill in the refrigerator for 30 minutes.

3 Preheat the oven to 200°C (400°F/Gas 6). Bake the pastry cases for 10 minutes, then remove the beans and paper and bake for a further 5 minutes.

4 To make the filling, mix the crème fraîche, horseradish, lemon juice and zest, and capers in a bowl, and season to taste with salt and black pepper. Stir in the egg yolks, smoked trout, and dill.

5 Divide the filling evenly among the tartlet cases and bake for 10–15 minutes until the filling is set. Set aside to cool for 5 minutes before removing the tartlets from the tins and serving warm.

These traditional Spanish pastry parcels are often served as a tapas or starter. They can be quickly made from a few store cupboard essentials, and make a great picnic dish or canapé.

EMPANADAS

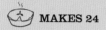 MAKES 24   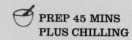 PREP 45 MINS PLUS CHILLING   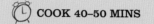 COOK 40–50 MINS   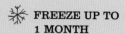 FREEZE UP TO 1 MONTH

EQUIPMENT
9cm (3½in) round pastry cutter, baking tray

INGREDIENTS

FOR THE PASTRY
(For visual step by step instructions see shortcrust pastry p104)
450g (1lb) plain flour, plus extra for dusting
½ tsp salt
85g (3oz) butter, diced
2 eggs, beaten, plus 1 egg, beaten to glaze

FOR THE FILLING
1 tbsp olive oil, plus extra for greasing
1 onion, finely chopped
120g can tomatoes, drained
2 tsp tomato purée
140g can tuna, drained
2 tbsp parsley, finely chopped
salt and freshly ground black pepper

1 To make the pastry, sift the flour into a large bowl with the salt. Add the butter and rub it in with your fingertips until it resembles fine breadcrumbs. Add the 2 beaten eggs with 4–6 tablespoons water and combine to form a dough. Cover with cling film and chill in the refrigerator for 30 minutes.

2 Meanwhile, heat the olive oil in a frying pan, add the onion, and fry over a medium heat, stirring frequently, for 5–8 minutes until translucent. Add the tomatoes, tomato purée, tuna, and parsley, and season to taste with salt and black pepper. Reduce the heat and simmer for 10–12 minutes, stirring occasionally.

3 Preheat the oven to 190°C (375°F/Gas 5). Roll out the pastry on a lightly floured surface to 3mm (⅛in) thick and cut out 24 circles with the pastry cutter. Put 1 teaspoon of the filling on each circle, then brush the edges with water, fold over, and pinch together.

4 Grease a baking tray, then place the empanadas on the tray and brush with beaten egg. Bake for 25–30 minutes until golden brown. Serve warm.

An all-time children's favourite, leave out the spring onions for fussy eaters, or add more vegetables for the more adventurous child. Use extra Cheddar for the topping, instead of the mozzarella if you like.

CHEESY POTATO-TOPPED TUNA PIE

 SERVES 4   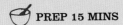 PREP 15 MINS   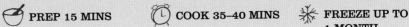 COOK 35–40 MINS   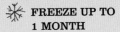 FREEZE UP TO 1 MONTH

1 Cook the potatoes in a large saucepan of salted boiling water for 15 minutes, or until tender. Drain the potatoes, return to the pan and mash. Stir in the butter and the milk and mix well to combine. Season to taste with salt and black pepper and set aside. Preheat the oven to 200°C (400°F/Gas 6).

2 For the filling, melt the butter in a medium pan. Stir in the flour and cook for 2–3 minutes over a medium heat, stirring constantly with a wooden spoon, until a smooth paste is formed. Gradually add the milk, stirring constantly, to make a white sauce.

3 Stir in the Cheddar cheese, tuna, sweetcorn, peas, spring onions, and parsley and season well. Transfer to the ovenproof dish. Top with the mash, spreading it in an even layer, and sprinkle over the grated mozzarella. Place the dish on a baking tray and bake for 15–20 minutes or until golden brown.

EQUIPMENT
2.5 litre (4¼ pints) ovenproof dish

INGREDIENTS

FOR THE TOPPING
1kg (2¼lb) floury potatoes,
 such as Maris Piper, peeled
 and chopped into small chunks
salt and freshly ground black pepper
50g (1¾oz) butter
50ml (2fl oz) whole milk

FOR THE FILLING
50g (1¾oz) butter
50g (1¾oz) plain flour
300ml (10fl oz) whole milk
115g (4oz) mature Cheddar cheese, grated
2 x 185g cans tuna in spring water, drained
195g (7oz) can sweetcorn, drained
150g (5½oz) frozen peas
4 spring onions, finely chopped
2 tbsp parsley, finely chopped
salt and freshly ground black pepper
100g (3½oz) firm mozzarella cheese, grated
 (or ready-grated mozzarella)

A mixture of smoked fish can be used as a filling for a fish pie when you want something a little different. Topped with a cheesy mashed potato, this rich dish just needs a green salad as an accompaniment.

SMOKED FISH PIE

 SERVES 4–6　　 PREP 20 MINS　　 COOK 50–55 MINS　　 FREEZE UP TO 1 MONTH

EQUIPMENT
2.5 litre (4¼ pint) ovenproof dish

INGREDIENTS

FOR THE TOPPING
800g (1¾lb) floury potatoes, such as Maris Piper, peeled and chopped into small chunks
300g (10oz) sweet potatoes, peeled and chopped into small chunks
salt and freshly ground black pepper
45g (1½oz) butter
3 tbsp whole milk
50–75g (1¾–2½oz) Red Leicester cheese, grated

FOR THE FILLING
45g (1½oz) butter, plus extra for greasing
45g (1½oz) plain flour
350–450ml (12–15fl oz) whole milk
50g (1¾oz) Gruyère cheese, grated
2 tbsp parsley, chopped
grated zest of 1 lemon
juice of ½ lemon
3 tsp capers in brine, drained and rinsed
300g (10oz) undyed smoked haddock fillet, skinned and chopped into bite-size pieces
300g (10oz) undyed smoked cod fillet, skinned and chopped into bite-size pieces
125g (4½oz) smoked salmon trimmings

1 To make the topping, cook the floury and sweet potatoes in a large saucepan of salted boiling water for 15 minutes, or until tender. Drain the potatoes, return to the pan, and mash with a potato masher. Stir in the butter and milk, and mix well to combine. Season to taste with salt and black pepper and set aside. Preheat the oven to 180°C (350°F/Gas 4).

2 For the filling, melt the butter in a small non-stick pan over a low heat. Stir in the flour and cook for 2–3 minutes over a medium heat, stirring constantly with a wooden spoon, until a smooth paste is formed. Gradually add the milk, stirring constantly, to make a white sauce. Bring to the boil stirring, then add the Gruyère, parsley, lemon zest and juice, and capers, and season well with black pepper. Stir until all the cheese has melted. Remove from the heat and set aside.

3 Grease the ovenproof dish and place all the fish in the dish. Pour the sauce over and stir well to thoroughly coat the fish. Top with the mash and the grated Red Leicester cheese. Place the dish on a baking tray and bake for 25–30 minutes or until golden brown and bubbling.

This fabled, whole fish pie heralds from Cornwall where there is even a folk tale to explain the origins of the dish. Spectacular to look at, it is not as difficult to prepare as it seems. Eat on the day it is made.

STARGAZY PIE

 SERVES 4–6   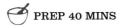 PREP 40 MINS   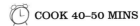 COOK 40–50 MINS

1 Preheat the oven to 200°C (400°F/ Gas 6). Boil the eggs in a saucepan for 6 minutes until they are hard-boiled. Set aside to cool, then slice into thin slices. Cook the potatoes in a large pan of boiling salted water for 5 minutes. Drain and rinse them under a cold tap.

2 Meanwhile, heat the olive oil in a pan and fry the bacon and onion for 5 minutes, or until the bacon is crisp and the onion is soft, but not brown.

3 Roll out the pastry on a floured surface and use to line the pie dish. Trim off the excess pastry, leaving a 1cm (½in) edge overhanging. Re-roll the remaining pastry into a disc big enough to cover the top.

4 Layer two-thirds of the cooked potatoes over the bottom of the dish, then cover with half the onion and bacon mixture. Scatter with half the chopped parsley and season. Arrange the sliced egg over the filling in a single layer. Lay the sardines over the filling in a single layer, cut-side down, with the tails at the centre and the heads at the edge of the pie. If the fish are too long, snip the ends off and use offcuts to fill in the spaces between the fish. Scatter over the remaining onion mix, parsley, and a final layer of potato.

5 Whisk the mustard into the cream and pour over the filling. Brush the edges of the pie with beaten egg and lay the lid on top. Where you can see the fish heads poking up snip a little slit. Ease the fish heads through the slits, moulding the pastry around them. Crimp the edges of the pie together to seal, and trim off any excess pastry. Use offcuts to make a few small pastry stars. Brush the top with egg and stick on the stars. Brush the stars with egg and bake the pie on a baking tray for 30–40 minutes until golden brown. Set aside to cool for 10–15 minutes before serving.

EQUIPMENT
23cm (9in) deep dish pie tin with sloping sides

INGREDIENTS

FOR THE FILLING
2 large eggs
400g (14oz) waxy potatoes, peeled weight, cut into 5mm (¼in) slices
salt and freshly ground black pepper
2 tbsp olive oil
100g (3½oz) unsmoked streaky bacon, chopped into 1cm (½in) strips
1 onion, finely sliced
1 heaped tbsp flat-leaf parsley, finely chopped
4 sardines, scaled and gutted with head still intact, rinsed and patted dry
1 tbsp Dijon mustard
150ml (5fl oz) single cream

FOR THE PASTRY
500g (1lb 2oz) ready-made puff pastry (or to make your own, see pp110–113)
plain flour, for dusting
1 egg, lightly beaten, to glaze

A fabulous dinner party dish, this is more of a deconstructed pie. The layers of buttery puff pastry are made crisp and flat by sandwiching them in between two baking trays halfway through cooking.

INDIVIDUAL HALIBUT AND SPINACH PIES

 SERVES 4    PREP 10 MINS   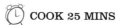 COOK 25 MINS

EQUIPMENT
2 baking trays

INGREDIENTS

FOR THE PASTRY
300g (10oz) sheet ready-rolled puff pastry
(or to make your own, see pp110–113)
plain flour, for dusting
1 tbsp butter, for brushing

FOR THE FILLING
4 x 125g (4½oz) pieces of halibut fillets,
or salmon can be used
salt and freshly ground black pepper
a large knob of unsalted butter
2 tbsp olive oil
1 garlic clove, crushed
200g (7oz) ready-washed
baby spinach leaves
1 small jar or 8 tbsp ready-made
hollandaise sauce
grated zest of ½ lemon

1 Preheat the oven to 190°C (375°F/Gas 5). Roll out the pastry on a floured surface to 5mm (¼in) thick. Using the fish fillets as a template, cut the pastry into 8 equal rectangles, about 12 x 7cm (5 x 2¾in). They should be the same size as the fish. Gently score a diagonal stripe across the rectangles, taking care not to cut right through the pastry. Melt the tablespoon of butter and use it to brush the pastry pieces well.

2 Use a fish slice to place the pastry pieces on a baking tray, and bake for 5–7 minutes until they start to colour and puff up. Place a similarly sized baking tray on top of the pastry, pushing down firmly, then bake for a further 7–10 minutes until the pastry is flat, crisp, and golden brown.

3 Season the fish fillets well on both sides. Fry them in 1 tablespoon butter and 1 tablespoon olive oil for 2–3 minutes each side, until they are just firm to the touch when gently pressed with a finger in the centre.

4 Heat the remaining butter and olive oil in a large saucepan. Add the garlic and cook for 1–2 minutes, until it is soft. Add the spinach to the pan, season well, and cook for 2–3 minutes, stirring occasionally, until it has just broken down. Heat the hollandaise sauce in a small pan over a gentle heat until warmed through. Watch over the pan, as there is a risk of it splitting. Add the lemon zest and season with black pepper.

5 Place 1 piece of pastry on each of the 4 serving plates. Cover the pastry with the spinach, then spread 1 tablespoon of hollandaise over the spinach and place a fish on top. Cover with another spoonful of hollandaise and top with the remaining pastry. Serve.

Herring and apple is a traditional British pairing, and here the strong taste of the fish is matched with a sweet, creamy filling. Best eaten on the day, but, if liked, chill overnight and eat cold the next day.

HERRING, APPLE, AND ONION PIE

 SERVES 4–6　　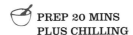 PREP 20 MINS PLUS CHILLING　　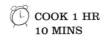 COOK 1 HR 10 MINS　　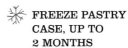 FREEZE PASTRY CASE, UP TO 2 MONTHS

1 To make the pastry, rub the flour, salt, butter, and lard together with your fingertips until it resembles loose breadcrumbs. Add 4–6 tablespoons cold water and bring the mixture together to form a dough. Wrap well in cling film and chill for 30 minutes.

2 Preheat the oven to 180°C (350°F/Gas 4). Roll out the pastry on a well-floured surface to 7mm (¼in) thick and use to line the pie tin, trimming the edges of all but 1cm (½in) overhang of pastry. Prick the bottom with a fork, line with greaseproof paper, and fill with baking beans. Place on a baking tray and bake for 15–20 minutes until the pastry is lightly cooked. Remove the beans and paper and bake for a further 5 minutes to crisp the bottom. Trim the edges.

3 Blanch the potato slices in a large saucepan of boiling, salted water for 2–3 minutes until they begin to soften. Drain well. Lay half the fish over the bottom of the pastry. Spread half the sliced apple and onion over the fish, then top with half the potato slices. Press down firmly to evenly distribute the filling in the dish. Place the last of the fish over the potatoes in a single layer, the remaining apple and onion, and top with the remaining potatoes, layered in an overlapping ring around the edge. Fill the centre with another, smaller ring of potatoes, so that the top is covered.

4 Whisk the cream, egg yolk, and mustard together and season well. Pour the cream over the filling. Place on a baking tray and bake for 40–45 minutes until golden brown and the centre yields easily when pierced with a skewer. Set aside to cool for 5 minutes.

EQUIPMENT
23cm (9in) deep-dish metal pie tin, baking beans

INGREDIENTS

FOR THE PASTRY
(For visual step by step instructions see p104)
200g (7oz) plain flour, plus extra for dusting
a pinch of salt
75g (2½oz) butter, at room temperature
25g (scant 1oz) lard or vegetable shortening

FOR THE FILLING
500g (1lb 2oz) waxy potatoes such as charlottes, peeled and very finely sliced
salt and freshly ground black pepper
4 small- or 5 medium-sized herring, scaled, gutted, and filleted, or sardines can be used
1 large dessert apple, peeled, cored, and finely sliced
1 onion, peeled, halved and finely sliced
200ml (7fl oz) single cream
1 egg yolk
1 heaped tsp Dijon mustard

The filling of this dish is based on a recipe for a "mouclade", a French dish where mussels are smothered in a mild, curry-flavoured cream. Serving it as a mini, puff pastry-topped pie gives it a modern twist

INDIVIDUAL CURRIED MUSSEL PIES

 MAKES 4   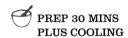 PREP 30 MINS PLUS COOLING    COOK 40–45 MINS    FREEZE UP TO 1 MONTH

EQUIPMENT
4 x 10cm (4in) round pie dishes (3cm/1¼in deep)

INGREDIENTS

FOR THE FILLING
1kg (2¼lb) mussels, scrubbed and beards removed
1 tbsp olive oil
1 onion, roughly chopped
1 bunch parsley
120ml (4fl oz) dry white wine
30g (1oz) butter
4 baby leeks, finely chopped
2 carrots, finely diced
salt and freshly ground black pepper
1–2 tsp medium curry powder
4 tbsp single cream
2 tbsp chopped coriander

FOR THE PASTRY
215g (7½oz) sheet ready-rolled puff pastry (or to make your own, see pp110–113)
1 egg, beaten, to glaze

1. Preheat the oven to 200°C (400°F/Gas 6). Discard any mussels that stay open when sharply tapped.

2. Heat the olive oil in a large saucepan and gently fry the onion for 5 minutes. Add the parsley, wine, mussels, and 120ml (4fl oz) water and bring to the boil. Cover and cook for 5 minutes. Discard any mussels that do not open. Strain the mussels through a sieve and reserve the cooking liquid.

3. Melt the butter in a medium pan over a medium heat, add the leeks and carrots, season well, then cover with a lid and fry gently for 5 minutes, stirring occasionally. Add the curry powder and cook for 5 more minutes. Stir 250ml (9fl oz) of the reserved cooking liquid into the vegetable mixture and simmer for 5 minutes to reduce. Set aside to cool for 15 minutes.

4. Remove the cooked mussels from their shells and add to the creamy vegetable mixture. Stir in the cream and coriander, and season well. Divide the mussel mixture among the pie dishes.

5. Cut the pastry into 4 lids to fit the top of the pie dishes. Moisten the rim of each dish with water and press the lids on firmly to seal. Brush with the egg and cut a hole in the centre of each lid to allow steam to escape. Place the pies on a baking tray and bake for 15–20 minutes until browned.

This light, delicate seafood pie is perfect for summer entertaining. Slice through the crunchy filo topping to reveal a rich, creamy, and luxurious filling. Serve with a green salad and baby new potatoes.

FILO-TOPPED SEAFOOD PIE

 SERVES 4–6    PREP 20 MINS   🕐 COOK 30–35 MINS

EQUIPMENT
28 x 20 x 5cm (11 x 8 x 2in) ovenproof dish

INGREDIENTS

FOR THE FILLING
65g (2oz) butter, plus extra for greasing
140g (5oz) mixture of watercress, rocket, and spinach leaves
45g (1½oz) plain flour
150ml (5fl oz) single cream
300ml (10fl oz) dry white wine
100g tub fresh brown crab meat
2 tbsp parsley, chopped
juice and zest of ½ lemon
freshly ground black pepper
180g tub fresh cooked mussels, in brine (drained weight)
200g (7oz) scallops, coral removed
150g (5½oz) king prawns, peeled and deveined

FOR THE PASTRY
175g (6oz) ready-made filo pastry
(4 x 26 x 44cm/10 x 16in sheets)

1 Preheat the oven to 200°C (400°F/Gas 6). Grease the ovenproof dish.

2 Place the watercress, rocket, and spinach in a colander and pour boiling water from the kettle over to wilt. Set aside to cool and drain. Once cool, squeeze out the excess liquid and chop finely.

3 For the filling, melt 45g (1½oz) of the butter in a medium non-stick saucepan over a low heat. Stir in the flour and cook for 2–3 minutes over a medium heat, stirring constantly, until a smooth paste is formed. Gradually add the cream and then the wine, then bring to the boil to thicken, stirring to make a creamy, smooth sauce. Stir in the chopped greens, crab, parsley, lemon juice and zest, and season well with black pepper. Set aside.

4 Drain and rinse the mussels and stir into the sauce. Add the scallops and prawns and stir well to mix.

5 Spoon the seafood mixture into the prepared dish. Roughly tear the filo pastry into strips and arrange half the strips over the seafood, folded and twisted to give texture. Drizzle or brush 10g (¼oz) melted butter over, then top with the remaining filo strips and butter.

6 Place the dish on a baking tray and bake for 20–25 minutes or until the pastry is golden brown and crisp. Serve immediately.

A dish for a special occasion, the musky fragrance of the saffron gently flavours the delicate seafood filling. You can store the cooked case, well wrapped, for up to 2 days before finishing.

CRAB AND PRAWN SAFFRON TART

 SERVES 2–4 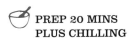 PREP 20 MINS PLUS CHILLING 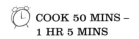 COOK 50 MINS – 1 HR 5 MINS  FREEZE UP TO 2 MONTHS

1 To make the pastry, rub the flour and butter together with your fingertips until the mixture resembles breadcrumbs. Add the egg yolk and 1 tablespoon cold water and bring the mixture together to form a soft dough. Add a little extra water if it is too dry. Wrap in cling film and chill for 30 minutes.

2 Preheat the oven to 180°C (350°F/Gas 4). Roll out the pastry on a floured surface to a large circle about 3mm (⅛in) thick, and use to line the tart tin, making sure it overlaps the sides. Trim off all but 2cm (¾in) of the overhanging pastry. Use your fingers to push the pastry down into the tin. Prick the bottom with a fork, line with baking parchment, and fill with baking beans. Place the case on a baking tray and bake for 20–25 minutes until cooked. Remove the beans and paper and bake for a further 5 minutes to crisp. Cool.

3 For the filling, splash 1 tablespoon of hot water over the saffron in a small bowl. Put the crab meat and prawns into a sieve and press down well over a sink to remove any excess water. Mix the crab and prawns together with your fingers, then scatter them over the surface of the tart.

4 Whisk together the cream and egg in a jug. Add the herbs, saffron and its soaking water, and seasoning, and mix well. Place the pastry case on the baking tray and, with the oven door open, rest it half on, half off the middle oven shelf. Hold the tray with one hand and with the other pour as much of the cream and egg mix as possible into the tart, then slide it into the oven. Bake for 30–35 minutes until golden in places and puffed up. Set aside to cool for 10 minutes, then trim off the overhanging pastry and remove the tart from the tin. Serve warm or cold.

EQUIPMENT
15cm (6in) loose-bottomed tart tin, baking beans

INGREDIENTS

FOR THE PASTRY
(For visual step by step instructions see shortcrust pastry p104)
100g (3½oz) plain flour, plus extra for dusting
50g (1¾oz) unsalted butter, chilled and diced
1 egg yolk

FOR THE FILLING
a pinch of saffron
125g (4½oz) white crab meat
100g (3½oz) small cold water prawns, peeled and deveined
200ml (7fl oz) double cream
1 egg
1 tbsp tarragon or chervil, finely chopped
sea salt and freshly ground black pepper

VEGETARIAN PIES AND TARTS

All the flavours of a high summer's day resonate in the filling of these delicious tarts. If you can't find baby plum tomatoes use any others, but make sure they are ripe to bring out their full flavour.

TOMATO AND PESTO TARTS

 MAKES 4   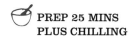 PREP 25 MINS
PLUS CHILLING   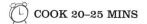 COOK 20–25 MINS    FREEZE UP TO
1 MONTH

EQUIPMENT
4 x 12cm (5in) loose-bottomed
fluted tart tins

INGREDIENTS

FOR THE PASTRY
**(For visual step by step instructions
see shortcrust pastry p104)**
200g (7oz) plain flour,
plus extra for dusting
100g (3½oz) butter, diced,
plus extra for greasing
½ tsp salt

FOR THE FILLING
4 tbsp red pesto
handful of basil leaves,
plus extra to garnish
6 sun-dried tomatoes in oil,
drained and finely chopped
12–16 baby plum tomatoes,
halved lengthways
salt and freshly ground black pepper
1 egg
100ml (3½fl oz) single cream
75g (2½oz) mozzarella cheese, grated

1 To make the pastry, rub the flour and butter together in a bowl with your fingertips until the mixture resembles fine breadcrumbs. Stir in the salt and add 3–4 tablespoons cold water to bring together to form a smooth dough. Wrap in cling film and chill for 30 minutes. Lightly grease the tart tins.

2 Divide the pastry equally into 4 portions. Roll out one-quarter of the pastry on a well-floured surface to a circle large enough to line one of the tins. Place the pastry in the tin and trim the edges. Prick the bottom with a fork and place on a baking tray. Repeat using the remaining pastry. Chill for 30 minutes.

3 Preheat the oven to 200°C (400°F/Gas 6). Line each tartlet case with foil, pressing it down well. Bake for 5 minutes then remove the foil. Spread 1 tablespoon pesto over the bottom of each tart. Cover the pesto with one-quarter of the basil leaves and spoon one-quarter of the chopped sun-dried tomatoes into the centre of each tart. Arrange 3 or 4 halved plum tomatoes around the edge of each tart and season to taste with black pepper.

4 Beat the egg and cream together in a small jug, season well, and pour carefully over the tomatoes. Sprinkle the mozzarella over and bake for 15–20 minutes. Serve garnished with fresh basil leaves.

Nothing could be easier to make than this simple tomatoey tart, which takes only minutes to prepare. Serve with a mixed salad for an after-work dinner or an informal starter at a dinner party.

TOMATO AND HARISSA TART

 SERVES 6    PREP 30 MINS    COOK 15 MINS

1 Preheat the oven to 200°C (400°F/Gas 6). Roll out the pastry on a floured surface to a large rectangle or square. Lay on a baking tray, then use a sharp knife to score a border about 5cm (2in) in from the edges all the way around, being careful not to cut all the way through the pastry. Using the back of the knife, score the pastry around the outer edges.

2 Working inside the border, smother the pastry with the tapenade. Arrange the plum and cherry tomatoes on top in an even pattern, cut-side up. Mix the harissa with the olive oil, and drizzle over the tomatoes. Scatter over the thyme leaves.

3 Bake for about 15 minutes until the pastry is cooked and golden. Serve hot.

EQUIPMENT
baking tray

INGREDIENTS

FOR THE PASTRY
400g (14oz) ready-made puff pastry
  (or to make your own, see pp110–113)
plain flour, for dusting

FOR THE FILLING
2 tbsp vegetarian tapenade or
  regular tapenade
3 plum tomatoes, halved
12 cherry tomatoes, halved
2–3 tbsp harissa paste
1 tbsp olive oil
4 sprigs of thyme, leaves only

This simple tart is ideal when tomatoes are in season and they are dark red, ripe, and plentiful. Here a normal shortcrust pastry is given a lift with the addition of fresh Parmesan and basil.

TOMATO AND DIJON TART WITH A PARMESAN AND BASIL CRUST

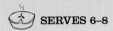 **SERVES 6–8**   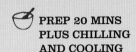 **PREP 20 MINS PLUS CHILLING AND COOLING**   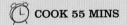 **COOK 55 MINS**   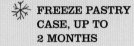 **FREEZE PASTRY CASE, UP TO 2 MONTHS**

1 To make the pastry, process the flour, Parmesan, butter, basil leaves, and salt together in a food processor until the mixture resembles fine green breadcrumbs. Add the egg and 1 tablespoon cold water, and bring the mixture together to form a soft dough. Add a little extra water if needed. Wrap and chill for 30 minutes. Preheat the oven to 200°C (400°F/Gas 6).

2 Roll out the pastry on a well-floured surface to a large circle about 3mm (⅛in) thick and use to line the tart tin, making sure it overlaps the sides. Trim all but 1cm (½in) of the overhanging pastry. Prick the bottom with a fork, line with greaseproof paper, and fill with baking beans. Place it on a baking tray and bake for 15 minutes until the pastry is lightly cooked. Remove the beans and paper, and bake for a further 5 minutes to crisp. Trim off any ragged edges while still warm. Reduce the heat to 180°C (350°F/Gas 4).

3 For the filling, place the tomatoes in an overlapping circle around the edge of the tart. Fill the centre with a smaller circle of tomato slices. Scatter the chopped parsley over the tomatoes. Whisk together the cream, crème fraîche, eggs, mustard, salt, and black pepper in a large bowl. Place the tart back on a baking tray and carefully pour the cream mixture over the tomatoes. Scatter the grated Parmesan over the top.

4 Bake for 35 minutes, or until golden on top and the filling has just set. Set the tart aside to cool for at least 30 minutes before eating warm or cold. This is best eaten the day it is made.

EQUIPMENT
22cm (9in) loose-bottomed tart tin, baking beans

INGREDIENTS

FOR THE PASTRY
(For visual step by step instructions
see shortcrust pastry p104)
160g (5¾oz) plain flour,
  plus extra for dusting
20g (¾oz) grated vegetarian-style
  Parmesan or regular Parmesan
90g (3oz) unsalted butter, softened
10 basil leaves
½ tsp salt
1 egg

FOR THE FILLING
3–4 ripe, medium tomatoes, all of
  similar size and shape, thinly sliced
1 tbsp flat-leaf parsley, finely chopped
150ml (5fl oz) single cream
150ml (5fl oz) crème fraîche
2 eggs
1 heaped tbsp Dijon mustard
salt and freshly ground black pepper
20g (¾oz) grated vegetarian-style
  Parmesan or regular Parmesan

These delicious individual slices make a light, tasty vegetarian alternative to pork pies. Good served warm or cold, they transport well and make a perfect picnic pie or lunchbox treat.

MEDITERRANEAN JALOUSIE

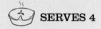 SERVES 4   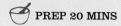 PREP 20 MINS   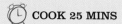 COOK 25 MINS

EQUIPMENT
baking tray

INGREDIENTS

FOR THE PASTRY
500g (1lb 2oz) ready-made puff pastry (or to make your own, see pp110–113)
plain flour, for dusting
beaten egg or milk, to glaze

FOR THE FILLING
3 tbsp green pesto
200g (7oz) mozzarella cheese, cut into 1cm (½in) cubes, or grated
140g (5oz) artichokes in oil, drained
140g (5oz) sun-dried tomatoes in oil, drained
30g (1oz) pitted green olives
freshly ground black pepper

1 Preheat the oven to 220°C (425°F/Gas 7). Roll out just less than half the pastry on a lightly floured surface to a 30 x 15cm (12 x 6in) rectangle, then place the pastry on a large dampened baking tray. Roll out the remaining pastry to a 30 x 18cm (12 x 7in) rectangle, lightly dust with flour, then fold in half lengthways. Make cuts 1cm (½in) apart along the folded edge to within 2.5cm (1in) of the outer edge.

2 Spread the pesto over the pastry on the baking tray to within 2.5cm (1in) of the edges, and top with half the cheese. Pat the artichokes and tomatoes with kitchen paper to remove any excess oil, and arrange on top of the cheese with the olives. Scatter with the remaining cheese and season to taste with black pepper.

3 Dampen the edges of the pastry with water. Carefully place the second piece of pastry on top and press the edges together to seal; trim away the excess. Brush the top with beaten egg and bake for 25 minutes, or until golden brown and crisp. Set aside to cool for a few minutes before slicing and serving. This is good served with a green salad.

This Italian-inspired tart is the perfect thing to serve on a hot summer's day. To make this easy tart even quicker, use some ready-roasted red peppers from a jar or the deli counter.

ROASTED RED PEPPER TART

 SERVES 6–8   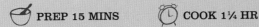 PREP 15 MINS   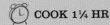 COOK 1¼ HR

1 Preheat the oven to 200°C (400°F/Gas 6). Put the peppers in a roasting tin. Using your hands, smear each one with the olive oil. Roast in the oven for about 20 minutes until lightly charred. Transfer to a plastic bag and set aside until cool enough to handle before skinning and deseeding.

2 Meanwhile, roll out the pastry on a floured surface, and use to line the tart tin. Trim away the excess pastry. Line the pastry case with greaseproof paper and fill with baking beans. Bake for 15–20 minutes until the edges are golden. Remove the beans and paper, brush the bottom of the case with beaten egg, and bake for a further 2–3 minutes to crisp. Remove from the oven and set aside. Reduce the heat to 180°C (350°F/Gas 4).

3 Whiz the roasted peppers, eggs, mascarpone, and basil in a food processor until combined. Season with salt and black pepper. Spread the pesto over the bottom of the pastry case, then pour in the pepper mixture. Bake for 25–35 minutes until set. Set aside to cool for 10 minutes before garnishing with basil, and serving with a wild rocket and fennel salad.

EQUIPMENT
23cm (9in) square loose-bottomed fluted tart tin, baking beans

INGREDIENTS

FOR THE FILLING
4 large red peppers
1 tbsp olive oil
2 eggs
1 tbsp mascarpone
handful of basil leaves,
    plus extra to garnish
salt and freshly ground black pepper
1 tsp red pesto

FOR THE PASTRY
300g (10oz) ready-made shortcrust pastry
    (or to make your own, see p104)
plain flour, for dusting
1 egg, lightly beaten, to glaze

A jar of tapenade is a wonderful thing to keep in the cupboard, here adding depth of flavour to a few basic ingredients. This tart is delicious served with a rocket salad dressed with a nutty vinaigrette.

OLIVE, ROSEMARY, AND RED ONION TART

 SERVES 4–6   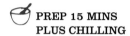 PREP 15 MINS PLUS CHILLING   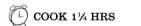 COOK 1¼ HRS    FREEZE UP TO 1 MONTH

EQUIPMENT
22cm (9in) loose-bottomed fluted tart tin, baking beans

INGREDIENTS

FOR THE PASTRY
115g (4oz) unsalted butter
3 tbsp milk
150g (5½oz) self-raising flour

FOR THE FILLING
3 tbsp olive oil
3 red onions, finely sliced
1 tsp caster sugar
2 tbsp rosemary leaves, finely chopped
1 tsp salt
240ml (8fl oz) double cream
3 eggs, beaten
freshly ground black pepper
30g (1oz) Parmesan cheese, finely grated
2 tbsp vegetarian black olive tapenade or regular tapenade
5–10 pitted green olives
5–10 pitted black olives

1 To make the pastry, heat the butter and milk together in a saucepan until the butter is melted. Stir in the flour and mix until a ball forms. Set aside to cool. When cool enough to handle, press the pastry into the tart tin and chill for 30 minutes.

2 Preheat the oven to 200°C (400°F/Gas 6). Line the pastry case with baking paper, fill with baking beans, and bake for 15 minutes. Remove the paper and beans and return to the oven for a further 5 minutes or until firm to the touch and golden brown.

3 For the filling, heat the olive oil in a heavy-based frying pan. Add the onions, and fry, stirring, over a high heat for 5 minutes. Add the sugar, rosemary leaves, and salt. Reduce the heat and cook slowly, stirring occasionally, for 20 minutes, or until the onions are very soft and slightly caramelized. Meanwhile, whisk the cream, eggs, black pepper, and Parmesan cheese together in a bowl.

4 Reduce the heat to 190°C (375°F/Gas 5). Place the tart tin on a baking tray and spread the tapenade over the bottom of the pastry. Spread the onions on top, carefully pour over the cream filling, and arrange the olives on top. Bake for 25 minutes, or until just set and turning golden on top. Serve warm or cold.

This crispy filo pie is dense, yet incredibly moreish. No cream or eggs are used to bring together the filling, as the potatoes and cheese seem to work well on their own. Serve the pie hot or cold.

POTATO AND BLUE CHEESE FILO PIE

 SERVES 6    PREP 35–40 MINS   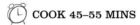 COOK 45–55 MINS

1 Preheat the oven to 180°C (350°F/Gas 4). Melt the butter in a saucepan, then brush the tin with a little of the butter. Lay a damp tea towel on a work surface, and unroll the filo pastry sheets onto the towel.

2 Using the tin as a guide, cut through the pastry to leave a 7.5cm (3in) border around the tin. Cover with a second damp towel.

3 Put 1 filo sheet on a third damp towel and brush with butter, then press into the tin. Repeat with another sheet, putting it in the tin at a right angle to the first. Continue until half the filo is used.

4 Arrange half the potatoes in the tin. Sprinkle with half the cheese, shallots, herbs, salt, and black pepper. Repeat with the remaining filling ingredients. Cover the pie with the remaining filo, buttering and layering, then cut a 7.5cm (3in) hole from the centre with a knife, so the filling shows.

5 Bake for 45–55 minutes until golden brown. While still hot, spoon the soured cream into the centre of the pie and serve in wedges. The pie can be prepared ahead up to the point of baking, wrapped in cling film, and chilled in the refrigerator for 2 days.

EQUIPMENT
28cm (11in) springform cake tin

INGREDIENTS

FOR THE PASTRY
190g (6½oz) unsalted butter
500g (1lb 2oz) ready-made filo pastry

FOR THE FILLING
1kg (2¼lb) potatoes, very thinly sliced
125g (4½oz) blue cheese, crumbled
4 shallots, finely chopped
4–5 sprigs each parsley, tarragon, and chervil, leaves finely chopped
salt and freshly ground black pepper
3–4 tbsp soured cream

A good vegetarian alternative to chicken or tuna empanadas, for a party serve a selection of all three of these fillings. Make these in advance and store in a container for up to two days.

CHEESE AND POTATO EMPANADAS

 **MAKES 24**　　 **PREP 40 MINS**　　 **COOK 55 MINS**　　 **FREEZE UP TO 3 MONTHS**

EQUIPMENT
7.5cm (3in) round cutter, baking tray

INGREDIENTS

FOR THE PASTRY
juice of 1 lemon
100g (3½oz) butter, diced
225g (8oz) plain flour, sifted, plus extra for dredging and dusting
a pinch of salt

FOR THE FILLING
400g (14oz) potatoes, par-boiled, peeled, and diced into 1cm (½in) cubes
salt and freshly ground black pepper
1 tbsp olive oil
1 medium onion, finely chopped
1 tsp dried dill
1 tsp dried mint
150ml (5fl oz) dry white wine
125g (4oz) mature Cheddar cheese, coarsely grated
oil, for greasing

1 To make the pastry, place the lemon juice, butter, and 100ml (3½fl oz) of water in a medium saucepan and heat gently for 2–3 minutes until the butter melts. Put the mixture into a large bowl and cool for 2–3 minutes. Add the flour and salt, and mix well. On a floured surface, knead the dough, dredging 2–3 tablespoons more flour into the dough until it is smooth and no longer sticky. Wrap and chill for 30 minutes.

2 For the filling, place the potatoes in a medium-sized pan of salted boiling water, bring to the boil, then reduce the heat and simmer for about 5 minutes. Drain the potatoes and set aside.

3 Heat the olive oil in a large frying pan and fry the onion and a little salt gently for 15 minutes until soft. Stir in the herbs, and add the wine. Increase the heat to high and cook for 2–3 minutes until the wine has evaporated. Stir in the potatoes, reduce the heat to low and cook for 5–10 minutes until the potatoes start to break up and are cooked. Transfer the mixture to a large bowl and set aside to cool for 10 minutes.

4 Roll out the pastry on a well-floured surface to 5mm (¼in) thick. Cut out 16 circles with the pastry cutter and set aside. Re-roll the remaining pastry and repeat until you have 24 circles. Set aside.

5 Add the cheese to the filling and season. Preheat the oven to 180°C (350°F/Gas 4). Oil the baking tray. Divide the filling into 24 portions. Spoon a portion into the centre of one of the pastry circles, compressing it with the spoon. Brush water on the pastry in a circle right around the filling. Fold the pastry across the filling and crimp the edges. Bake for 20–25 minutes. Cool for 5 minutes, then cool completely on a wire rack.

A wonderful dish to take on a picnic, this crisp filo pie is good served cold or at room temperature when the rich, ripe flavours of the vegetable filling really seem to come into their own.

MEDITERRANEAN FILO PIE

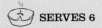 SERVES 6   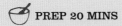 PREP 20 MINS    COOK 50–55 MINS

1 Heat the olive oil in a large non-stick frying pan. Add the onions and cook over a medium heat for 5 minutes. Add the garlic, peppers, courgette, and aubergine and stir well. Cook over a medium-high heat for 15 minutes, or until all the vegetables are tender, stirring occasionally to stop them sticking. Set aside.

2 Preheat the oven to 200°C (400°F/Gas 6). Place a sheet of filo pastry in the bottom of the cake tin, so the edges are hanging over the sides. Brush it generously with melted butter and place another sheet of pastry across the first, so they form a cross shape in the bottom. Brush with more butter. Repeat the pastry layers until all the pastry is used up and the bottom of the tin is completely covered.

3 Spoon half the vegetables into the pastry case, top with half the pesto, then half the basil leaves, and half the crumbled feta. Season well with black pepper. Repeat the layers once. Carefully pull the overhanging layers of pastry into the centre, to cover the filling. Brush the finished pie with the remaining melted butter. Place the tin on a baking tray and bake for 35–40 minutes or until the pastry is golden brown and crisp. Remove the outer ring of the tin and leave the pie to rest for 15 minutes before slicing.

EQUIPMENT
20cm (8in) loose-bottomed cake tin

INGREDIENTS

FOR THE FILLING
1 tbsp olive oil
2 red onions, finely sliced
2 garlic cloves, finely chopped
1 red pepper, finely sliced
1 yellow pepper, finely sliced
1 courgette, sliced
1 small aubergine, sliced
4 tbsp sun-dried tomato pesto
leaves from 1 bunch of basil
200g (7oz) feta cheese,
   roughly crumbled
freshly ground black pepper

FOR THE PASTRY
270g (9½oz) ready-made filo pastry
   (6 x 26 x 44cm/10½ x 17¼in sheets)
30g (1oz) butter, melted

The more usual meat-based filling of a Shepherd's Pie is substituted with a tasty mix of mushrooms and pulses to produce a delicious vegetarian dish. Use brown lentils instead of aduki beans, if preferred.

SHEPHERDLESS PIE

 SERVES 4 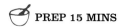 PREP 15 MINS 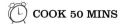 COOK 50 MINS

EQUIPMENT
ovenproof dish

INGREDIENTS

FOR THE TOPPING
675g (1½lb) floury potatoes, peeled and quartered
2 knobs of butter

FOR THE FILLING
1 tbsp olive oil
1 onion, finely chopped
1 bay leaf
salt and freshly ground black pepper
3 celery sticks, finely chopped
3 carrots, finely chopped
200g (7oz) chestnut mushrooms, roughly chopped
handful of thyme sprigs, leaves picked
splash of dark soy sauce
400g tin aduki beans, drained and rinsed
150ml (5fl oz) hot vegetable stock

1 Preheat the oven to 200°C (400°F/Gas 6). To make the topping, cook the potatoes in a large saucepan of salted boiling water for 15–20 minutes until soft. Drain, then return the potatoes to the pan and mash. Add a knob of butter and mash again, then set aside.

2 Heat the olive oil in a large frying pan over a low heat. Add the onion, bay leaf, and a pinch of salt, and sweat for about 5 minutes until the onion is soft. Next, add the celery and carrots, and continue to sweat gently for a further 5 minutes.

3 Pulse the mushrooms in a food processor until broken down, you want them shredded but not mushy. Add these to the pan, along with the thyme leaves and soy sauce, and cook for a further 5–10 minutes until the mushrooms begin to release their juices. Add the aduki beans, and season well with salt and black pepper. Pour over the stock, bring to the boil, reduce the heat slightly, and simmer gently for 5 minutes.

4 Tip the filling into the dish, and top with the set-aside mashed potato. Dot with the remaining butter and bake until the top starts to become crisp and golden. Serve hot.

These exotic little hand pies can be served hot or cold. Try swapping the potatoes in the filling for sweet potatoes and playing with the spicing until you get the balance of flavours you prefer.

VEGETABLE SAMOSAS

 MAKES 16   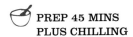 PREP 45 MINS
PLUS CHILLING    COOK 35–40 MINS    FREEZE
UNCOOKED, UP TO
1 MONTH

1 To make the pastry, sift the flour into a bowl with the salt. Stir in the vegetable oil and gradually add 120ml (4fl oz) warm water, mixing to form a dough. On a floured surface, knead the dough until smooth, then wrap in cling film and chill for at least 30 minutes.

2 For the filling, cook the potatoes in a large saucepan of boiling water for 15–20 minutes or until tender. Drain and, when the potatoes are cool enough to handle, peel and chop into small pieces.

3 Blanch the cauliflower florets and fresh peas, if using, in another pan of boiling water for 2–3 minutes or until just tender, then drain.

4 Heat the oil in a large frying pan and fry the shallots for 3–4 minutes, stirring frequently, until soft. Add the potatoes, cauliflower, peas, curry powder, coriander, and lemon juice and cook over a low heat for 2–3 minutes, stirring occasionally. Set aside to cool.

5 Divide the dough into 8 equal pieces and roll them out on a floured surface so each forms an 18cm (7in) circle. Cut each circle in half and shape into a cone, dampening the edges to seal. Spoon a little of the filling into each cone, dampen the top edge of the dough, and press down over the filling to enclose it. Repeat with the rest of the dough and filling.

6 Half-fill the deep-fat fryer or saucepan with oil and heat to 180°C (350°F/Gas 4). Fry the samosas in batches for 3–4 minutes or until golden brown on both sides. Drain on kitchen paper and serve hot or cold. Arrange on a serving plate with ribbons of cucumber and some raita or chutney. The samosas can be prepared 1 day ahead, chilled, and fried just before serving.

EQUIPMENT
deep-fat fryer or large saucepan

INGREDIENTS

FOR THE PASTRY
350g (12oz) plain flour,
   plus extra for dusting
½ tsp salt
6 tbsp vegetable oil or ghee,
   plus extra for frying

FOR THE FILLING
450g (1lb) potatoes, unpeeled
225g (8oz) cauliflower, chopped into
   small pieces
175g (6oz) peas, thawed if frozen
3 tbsp vegetable oil or ghee
2 shallots, sliced
2 tbsp curry powder or paste
2 tbsp chopped coriander leaves
1 tbsp lemon juice

Late summer is a perfect time to make this delicious Mediterranean-inspired tart. The sweet, rich flavours of the vegetables are offset nicely with the sharp tang of the goat's cheese.

ROASTED VEGETABLE AND GOAT'S CHEESE TART

 SERVES 6 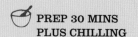 PREP 30 MINS PLUS CHILLING  COOK 1¼–1½ HRS 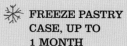 FREEZE PASTRY CASE, UP TO 1 MONTH

EQUIPMENT
20cm (8in) round tart tin, baking beans

INGREDIENTS

FOR THE PASTRY
(For visual step by step instructions see shortcrust pastry p104)
150g (5½oz) plain flour, plus extra for dusting
75g (2½oz) butter, chilled and diced
30g (1oz) mature Cheddar cheese, finely grated
1 egg yolk

FOR THE FILLING
½ red pepper, finely chopped
½ red onion, finely chopped
2 garlic cloves, finely chopped
2 baby courgettes, finely sliced
2 baby aubergines, finely sliced
4 baby plum tomatoes, halved
1 tbsp olive oil
½ tsp dried basil
salt and freshly ground black pepper
120ml (4fl oz) single cream
2 eggs
100g (3½oz) log of goat's cheese, thinly sliced

1 To make the pastry, rub the flour and butter together with your fingertips until the mixture resembles fine breadcrumbs. Stir the cheese and egg yolk into the flour mixture. Add 1–2 teaspoons of cold water, and bring the ingredients together to form a smooth dough. Wrap and chill for 30 minutes.

2 Preheat the oven to 200°C (400°F/Gas 6). Place the pepper, onion, garlic, courgette, aubergine, and tomatoes in a roasting tin. Add the olive oil and basil, season, and toss well to coat the vegetables. Roast for 20 minutes, or until the vegetables are tender. Reduce the oven temperature to 180°C (350°F/Gas 4).

3 Roll out the pastry on a floured surface to a circle large enough to line the tart tin. Place the pastry in the tin, pressing down well into the bottom and around the edges. Trim off any excess pastry, prick the bottom of the tart with a fork, and line with baking parchment. Place the tin on a baking tray and fill with baking beans. Bake for 15 minutes, then remove the beans and paper, and bake for a further 10 minutes.

4 Place the cream and eggs in a jug, season well, and whisk to combine. Arrange the roasted vegetables over the pastry case, and place the sliced goat's cheese on top. Carefully pour the cream and egg mixture over the vegetables and cheese, then bake for 30–35 minutes until golden.

A cross between an Indian samosa and a Cornish Pasty, here a gently spiced vegetable filling is encased in shortcrust pastry and baked. You can vary the vegetables used according to the season.

CURRIED VEGETABLE PIES

 MAKES 4   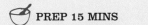 PREP 15 MINS    COOK 45 MINS   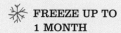 FREEZE UP TO 1 MONTH

1 Preheat the oven to 200°C (400°F/Gas 6). Cook the carrots and potatoes in a large saucepan of boiling, salted water for 15 minutes until soft, then drain well.

2 Roll out the pastry on a floured surface and cut out 4 rounds using the cutter. Place the pastry rounds on a baking tray and brush the edges with a little of the beaten egg.

3 Place the carrots and potatoes in a bowl, and gently mix with the curry paste and yogurt. Add the garlic, ginger, spring onions, coriander, and lemon juice, and season well with salt and black pepper. Stir through gently until well mixed.

4 Divide the vegetable mixture evenly among the pastry circles, spooning it into the centre of each one. Fold over the pastry to make a half-moon shape and pinch the edges together to seal. Using a sharp knife, cut 2 slashes in the top of each pie, then brush all over with the remaining beaten egg. Bake for 20–30 minutes until golden. Serve hot or cold.

EQUIPMENT
15cm (6in) round cutter, baking tray

INGREDIENTS

FOR THE FILLING
2 carrots, diced
2 potatoes, peeled and finely diced
salt and freshly ground black pepper
1 tbsp curry paste
2 tbsp Greek-style yogurt
1 garlic clove, grated or finely chopped
2cm (1in) piece of root ginger,
  finely chopped
2 spring onions, finely sliced
handful of coriander, finely chopped
juice of ½ lemon

FOR THE PASTRY
450g (1lb) ready-made shortcrust pastry
  (or to make your own, see p104)
plain flour, for dusting
1 egg, lightly beaten, to glaze

Some people have been put off beetroot by only trying the pickled variety. Try roasting fresh beetroot and you will soon be won over by its sweet, earthy flavour. Tangy goat's cheese is a perfect pairing here.

BEETROOT TARTE TATIN

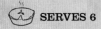 SERVES 6   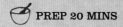 PREP 20 MINS    COOK 35–45 MINS

EQUIPMENT
23cm (9in) cast-iron frying pan, or a similar pan with an ovenproof handle

INGREDIENTS

FOR THE FILLING
25g (scant 1oz) butter
2 tbsp balsamic vinegar
1 tbsp caster sugar
1 tbsp sage, finely chopped
salt and freshly ground black pepper
450g (1lb) cooked beetroot, not preserved in vinegar, drained and chopped
100g (3½oz) firm or semi-firm goat's cheese, finely sliced

FOR THE PASTRY
200g (7oz) ready-made puff pastry (or to make your own, see pp110–113)
plain flour, for dusting

1 Preheat the oven to 200°C (400°F/Gas 6). Melt the butter in the frying pan. Add the balsamic vinegar and caster sugar, and cook briefly, until the sugar dissolves and the mixture turns syrupy. Scatter the chopped sage over the bottom of the frying pan and season well with salt and black pepper.

2 Fry the beetroot in the balsamic glaze for 5–10 minutes over a medium heat, or until they start to darken and the juices reduce, until they just cover the bottom of the pan. Spread the beetroot out evenly in the frying pan, packing them in tightly, then use the sliced goat's cheese to cover the beetroot.

3 Roll out the pastry on a lightly floured surface to a circle a little larger than the pan and about 5–7mm (¼–¾ in) thick, and drape it over the frying pan. Trim the excess pastry around the edges with a small, sharp knife. Now take any excess pastry and tuck it under the edges of the beetroot, to make an edge to the tart when you turn it over and to contain the juices.

4 Bake for 25–30 minutes until the pastry is puffed up and golden brown. Remove from the oven, and place a large, flat serving plate over the top. Holding the bottom of the frying pan with a tea towel, flip the tart over onto the plate in a quick movement. Leave the tart with the frying pan on top for 1–2 minutes, to allow all the beetroot to dislodge before taking it off.

5 Serve the tart warm, or at room temperature, as it is, or with extra goat's cheese crumbled over to make a more substantial dish. Best eaten the same day.

Use either home-made or shop-bought shortcrust pastry to make this double-crusted pie. Suitable for vegetarians, its rich, cheesy filling is offset by the sharpness of the onions.

CHEESE AND ONION PIE

 **SERVES 4**

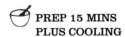 **PREP 15 MINS PLUS COOLING**

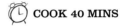 **COOK 40 MINS**

 **FREEZE UP TO 6 MONTHS**

EQUIPMENT
18cm (7in) round pie tin

INGREDIENTS

FOR THE FILLING
1 tbsp olive oil
1 large onion, finely chopped
salt and freshly ground black pepper
2 eggs
200g (7oz) mature Cheddar cheese, grated

FOR THE PASTRY
350g (12oz) ready-made shortcrust pastry
(or to make your own, see p104)
plain flour, for dusting

1 Preheat the oven to 200°C (400°F/Gas 6). Heat the olive oil in a small pan over a low heat. Add the onion and a pinch of salt, and sweat for 2 minutes until transparent and just starting to soften. Tip into a bowl and set aside to cool completely.

2 Lightly beat 1 of the eggs in a small bowl and stir into the cooled onion with the cheese. Season with salt and black pepper.

3 Halve the pastry, then roll out each piece on a floured surface. Use one of the pastry circles to line the pie tin, allowing the pastry to hang over the edge, and fill with the cheese and onion mixture. Dampen the edge of the pastry with water, then top with the other circle of pastry. Trim away the excess pastry. Using your thumb and finger, pinch the edges of the pastry together to seal. Cut 2 slits in the top to allow the steam to escape.

4 Lightly beat the remaining egg and brush all over the top of the pie. Bake for 25–35 minutes until cooked and golden. Serve with a mixed salad and boiled or steamed new potatoes.

A well-cooked onion tart is one of the most delightful dishes imaginable. Take care to cook the onions long and slow, so that they become soft and sweet, and use a rich, buttery pastry for the best result.

ONION TART

 SERVES 8   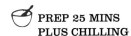 PREP 25 MINS PLUS CHILLING   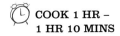 COOK 1 HR – 1 HR 10 MINS    FREEZE UP TO 2 MONTHS

1 Heat the olive oil and butter in a saucepan. Add the onions and season well with salt and black pepper. When sizzling, reduce the heat to low, cover, and cook for 20 minutes, stirring occasionally, until the onions are soft, but not brown. Uncover the pan, increase the heat, and cook the onions for a further 5–10 minutes to allow any water to evaporate.

2 Put the onions in the pastry case and spread them out. Whisk together the cream, egg, egg yolk, and salt and black pepper. Place the tart on a baking tray and pour the cream mixture over the onions. Use a fork to help distribute the cream evenly, by pushing the onions from side to side a little.

3 Bake for 30 minutes until just set, lightly golden, and puffy on top. Remove from the oven, trim the edges of the pastry, and set aside to cool for 10 minutes before eating warm or cold. This tart is best eaten the day it is made, but it can be chilled overnight and gently reheated in a medium oven. The pastry case can be prepared up to 2 days in advance, wrapped in cling film, and chilled in the refrigerator until needed.

EQUIPMENT
22cm (9in) loose-bottomed tart tin

INGREDIENTS

FOR THE FILLING
2 tbsp olive oil
25g (scant 1oz) butter
500g (1lb 2oz) finely sliced onions
sea salt and freshly ground black pepper
200ml (7fl oz) double cream
1 large egg, plus 1 egg yolk

FOR THE PASTRY CASE
ready-made shortcrust pastry case
  (or to make your own, see p104
  and pp122–123)

Tarte Tatin is usually a sweet tart, but try making a savoury version for an interesting twist on a classic, such as shallot or beetroot. Contrast the sweet and sour flavours with a simple green salad.

CARAMELIZED SHALLOT TARTE TATIN

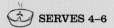 SERVES 4–6   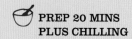 PREP 20 MINS PLUS CHILLING   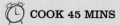 COOK 45 MINS

EQUIPMENT
large ovenproof frying pan

INGREDIENTS

FOR THE PASTRY
(For visual step by step instructions
see shortcrust pastry p104)
150g (5½oz) plain flour,
plus extra for dusting
a pinch of sea salt
75g (2½oz) butter
or 250g (9oz) ready-made
shortcrust pastry

FOR THE FILLING
25g (scant 1oz) butter
2 tbsp extra virgin olive oil
400g (14oz) shallots, peeled and
split in half lengthways
2 tbsp balsamic vinegar
a few sprigs of thyme

1 To make the pastry, combine the flour, salt, and butter in a food processor, and mix to form fine breadcrumbs, or to make by hand, rub with your fingertips. With the motor running, add enough cold water, a tablespoon at a time, until the pastry starts to stick together. If making by hand, add the water in the same way, but bring the dough together between each addition. Form the pastry into a ball, wrap in cling film, and chill in the refrigerator for 30 minutes.

2 Preheat the oven to 200°C (400°F/Gas 6). Melt the butter with the olive oil in the frying pan. Put the shallots in, cut-side down, and cook very gently for 10 minutes until browned. Turn them over and cook for a further 5 minutes. Add the vinegar and 2 tablespoons water, then remove from the heat. Tuck the thyme sprigs between the shallots.

3 Roll out the pastry on a lightly floured surface to a circle a little larger than the frying pan. Lay the pastry over the shallots, trim, and tuck it in. Transfer the pan to the oven and cook for 30 minutes, or until the pastry is golden brown.

4 Remove the pan from the oven and bang gently to loosen the shallots. Run a knife around the edges of the pastry, then put a large plate over the pan and quickly turn it over. Serve warm with a green salad.

The slow-cooked onions melt down to a soft sweetness, and combined with the tangy saltiness of the blue cheese make this a wonderful vegetarian quiche, which is perfect to serve on any occasion.

ONION AND ROQUEFORT QUICHE

 SERVES 6–8   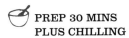 PREP 30 MINS PLUS CHILLING   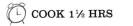 COOK 1½ HRS    FREEZE UP TO 1 MONTH

1 To make the pastry, sift the flour on to a surface and make a well in the centre. Add the egg yolk, salt, 3 tablespoons water, and butter to the well. Mix the ingredients with your fingertips, then work the flour into the ingredients until breadcrumbs form. Press the dough into a ball.

2 On a lightly floured surface, knead the dough by pushing it away from you with the heel of your hand for 1–2 minutes until it is smooth and peels away from the surface in one piece. Form into a ball, wrap in cling film, and chill for 30 minutes until firm.

3 Grease the tin. Roll out the pastry on a floured surface to a 30cm (12in) circle and use to line the tin, allowing the sides to overhang. Trim off the excess pastry. Press the dough evenly up the side, then prick the bottom with a fork. Chill for 15 minutes until firm.

4 Preheat the oven to 220°C (425°F/Gas 7). Line the pastry case with greaseproof paper. Fill with baking beans and bake for 15 minutes. Remove the paper and beans and reduce the oven temperature to 190°C (375°F/Gas 5). Bake for 5–8 minutes until browned. Set aside.

5 Melt the butter. Add the onions, thyme, and seasoning. Put greased foil on top and cover with the lid. Cook, stirring occasionally, for 20–30 minutes, until soft but not brown. Whisk the egg, yolk, milk, salt, black pepper, nutmeg, and cream. Crumble the cheese into the onions; stir until melted. Cool slightly. Spread it evenly into the pastry case. Put the tin on a baking tray. Pour the custard over the onions, and mix in with a fork. Bake for 30–35 minutes until a skewer inserted into the centre comes out clean and the custard has a slight wobble. Serve warm or at room temperature.

EQUIPMENT
25cm (10in) tart tin, baking beans

INGREDIENTS

FOR THE PASTRY
(For visual step by step instructions see shortcrust pastry p104)
200g (7oz) plain flour,
  plus extra for dusting
1 egg yolk
½ tsp salt
100g (3½oz) unsalted butter, softened,
  plus extra for greasing

FOR THE FILLING
30g (1oz) unsalted butter
500g (1lb 2oz) onions, sliced
2–3 thyme sprigs, leaves picked
salt and freshly ground black pepper
1 egg, plus 1 egg yolk
125ml (4fl oz) milk
a pinch of ground nutmeg
4 tbsp double cream
175g (6oz) vegetarian Roquefort-style
  blue cheese, or regular Roquefort

A mixture of Gruyère and feta cheese is used to flavour this classic spinach tart. Picking up a bag of baby spinach and some ready-made pastry from the supermarket makes this a great last-minute dish.

SPINACH, CHEESE, AND THYME TART

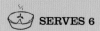 SERVES 6   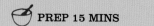 PREP 15 MINS   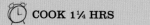 COOK 1¼ HRS   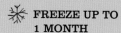 FREEZE UP TO 1 MONTH

EQUIPMENT
23cm (9in) loose-bottomed fluted tart tin, baking beans

INGREDIENTS

FOR THE PASTRY
300g (10oz) ready-made shortcrust pastry (or to make your own, see p104)

FOR THE FILLING
1 tbsp olive oil
1 onion, finely chopped
salt and freshly ground black pepper
2 garlic cloves, grated or finely chopped
leaves from 1 bunch fresh thyme
250g (9oz) baby spinach
125g (4½oz) each Gruyère and feta cheese
200ml (7fl oz) double cream
2 eggs

1 Preheat the oven to 200°C (400°F/Gas 6). Roll out the pastry on a floured surface and use to line the tart tin. Trim off the excess pastry, line the pastry case with greaseproof paper, and fill with baking beans. Bake for 15–20 minutes. Remove the beans and paper. Bake for a further 1–2 minutes to crisp. Set aside. Reduce the heat to 180°C (350°F/Gas 4).

2 Heat the olive oil in a saucepan over a low heat. Add the onion and a pinch of salt, and sweat gently for 5 minutes until soft. Add the garlic and thyme, and cook for a few seconds, then add the spinach and stir for 5 minutes until the spinach wilts.

3 Assemble the tart (see below). Bake for 30–40 minutes until set and golden. Set aside to cool for 10 minutes. Serve warm or at room temperature.

For the tart filling

1 Spoon the onion and spinach mixture into the pastry case and make sure it covers the bottom.

2 Sprinkle over grated Gruyère, and scatter evenly with feta cubes. Season with salt and black pepper.

3 Mix the cream and 2 eggs in a jug, until well combined, and carefully pour over the tart filling.

A traditional Greek recipe, this crispy filo pie will become a firm family favourite. For variety, add a pinch of grated nutmeg to the filling. This pie is best served either warm or at room temperature.

FILO PIE WITH SPINACH, RICOTTA, PINE NUTS, AND RAISINS

 SERVES 4   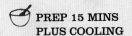 PREP 15 MINS PLUS COOLING   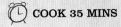 COOK 35 MINS

1 Preheat the oven to 180°C (350°F/Gas 4). Heat the olive oil in a frying pan over a low heat. Add the onion and a pinch of salt, and sweat gently for about 5 minutes until soft. Add the garlic, and cook for a few more seconds until the garlic turns white.

2 Tip in the spinach, and cook, stirring, for about 3 minutes until it wilts. Season well with salt and black pepper. Remove from the heat, stir through the raisins and pine nuts, and set aside to cool. Add the ricotta and beaten egg, and stir well.

3 Lay 2 sheets of filo pastry one on top of the other in the cake tin, letting them hang over the edge on 2 sides. Next, lay 2 more sheets of filo at right angles to the first layer. Continue in this way until you have used 8 sheets for the bottom of the pie.

4 Spoon the spinach and ricotta mixture into the pie. Fold in the edges of the pastry, and top the pie with the remaining 4 sheets of filo pastry, tucking them in neatly. Brush all over with the melted butter, and bake for 20–30 minutes until golden and crisp.

EQUIPMENT
20cm (8in) round or square loose-bottomed cake tin

INGREDIENTS

FOR THE FILLING
1 tbsp olive oil
1 onion, finely chopped
salt and freshly ground black pepper
2 garlic cloves, grated or finely chopped
550g (1¼lb) fresh
  spinach leaves
handful of raisins
75g (2½oz) pine nuts, toasted
200g (7oz) ricotta cheese
1 egg, lightly beaten

FOR THE PASTRY
12 sheets ready-made
  filo pastry
30g (1oz)
  butter, melted

I love the vibrant colour of this tart, which will become a perennial favourite with both friends and family. Be sure to wash the spinach and watercress to remove any dirt and drain well before using.

CREAMY SPINACH TART

 **SERVES 4–6** 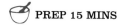 **PREP 15 MINS**   **COOK 1 HR**

EQUIPMENT
20cm (8in) round loose-bottomed fluted tart tin, baking beans

INGREDIENTS

FOR THE PASTRY
300g (10oz) ready-made shortcrust pastry
(or to make your own, see p104)
plain flour, for dusting
1 egg, lightly beaten, to glaze

FOR THE FILLING
1 tbsp olive oil
1 onion, finely chopped
salt and freshly ground black pepper
2 garlic cloves, grated or finely chopped
450g (1lb) fresh spinach
200g (7oz) watercress
200ml (7fl oz) double cream
2 eggs
a pinch of freshly grated nutmeg

1 Preheat the oven to 200°C (400°F/Gas 6). Roll out the pastry on a lightly floured surface and use to line the tart tin. Trim off the excess, then line the pastry case with greaseproof paper, and fill with baking beans. Bake for 15–20 minutes until the edges are golden. Remove the beans and paper, brush the bottom of the case with a little of the beaten egg, and bake for a further 2–3 minutes to crisp. Set aside. Reduce the oven temperature to 180°C (350°F/Gas 4).

2 For the filling, heat the olive oil in a large frying pan over a low heat. Add the onion and a pinch of salt and sweat gently for about 5 minutes until soft. Add the garlic and cook for a few more seconds until the garlic turns white, then spoon into the pastry case.

3 Put the spinach and watercress in a food processor, and pulse a couple of times until broken up but not mushy. Pour in the cream and the 2 eggs, and pulse again until everything is combined. Season well with salt and black pepper and pulse once more. Carefully pour into the pastry case and sprinkle over the nutmeg. Bake for 20–30 minutes until set. Set aside to cool for 10 minutes before releasing from the tin. Serve with boiled or steamed new potatoes and a fresh tomato salad.

Spinach and goat's cheese are the classic combination for a tasty quiche. Serve warm or cold for a summer lunch or picnic with salad. It is best eaten on the day it is made, but can be chilled overnight.

SPINACH AND GOAT'S CHEESE QUICHE

 SERVES 4–6

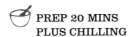 PREP 20 MINS PLUS CHILLING

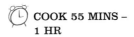 COOK 55 MINS – 1 HR

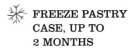 FREEZE PASTRY CASE, UP TO 2 MONTHS

1 To make the pastry, rub the flour, butter, and salt together with your fingertips until the mixture resembles fine breadcrumbs. Add 3–4 tablespoons cold water a little at a time and bring the mixture together to form a soft dough. Add a little more water if it is too dry. Wrap in cling film and chill for 30 minutes. Preheat the oven to 180°C (350°F/Gas 4).

2 Roll out the pastry on a floured surface to a large circle about 3mm (⅛in) thick, and use to line the tart tin, making sure it overlaps the sides. Trim all but 1cm (½in) of the overhanging pastry. Prick the bottom with a fork, line with greaseproof paper, and fill with baking beans. Place on a baking tray and bake for 20–25 minutes until the pastry is lightly cooked. Remove the beans and paper and bake for a further 5 minutes to crisp. Trim any ragged edges from the pastry case while it is still warm.

3 For the filling, cook the spinach in a large saucepan with the olive oil and garlic for 2–3 minutes until it softens. Place the spinach in a sieve and press out any excess water. Set aside to cool.

4 Once the spinach is cool whiz it in a blender with the goat's cheese, cream, and eggs until the mixture is smooth. Season well with salt and black pepper.

5 Place the tart on a baking tray and carefully pour in the spinach and goat's cheese mixture. Bake for 30 minutes until the mixture has just set. Set aside to cool for at least 15 minutes before serving.

EQUIPMENT
22cm (9in) loose-bottomed fluted tart tin, baking beans

INGREDIENTS

FOR THE PASTRY
(For visual step by step instructions see shortcrust pastry p104)
150g (5½oz) plain flour, plus extra for dusting
75g (2½oz) unsalted butter, at room temperature, cut into small pieces
½ tsp salt

FOR THE FILLING
200g (7oz) baby spinach
1 tbsp olive oil
1 garlic clove, crushed
200g (7oz) soft goat's cheese
100ml (3½fl oz) single cream
2 eggs
salt and freshly ground black pepper

Make sure you chill these pasties in the refrigerator before baking; this helps firm up the pastry and hold them together during cooking. These much-loved, wholesome pies are delicious hot or cold.

WHOLEMEAL SPINACH AND POTATO PASTIES

 MAKES 4   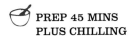 PREP 45 MINS PLUS CHILLING   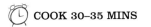 COOK 30–35 MINS    FREEZE UP TO 1 MONTH

1 To make the pastry, rub the two kinds of flour and butter together with your fingertips until the mixture resembles breadcrumbs. Add the salt and about 4 tablespoons cold water, to bring the mixture together to form a soft dough. Wrap and chill for 30 minutes.

2 For the filling, cook the potato chunks in a small saucepan of boiling water for 10 minutes. Drain and set aside to cool. Place the spinach in a colander and pour boiling water over it, from a kettle, to wilt it. Squeeze out all the liquid and chop finely. Place the spinach in a large bowl with the garlic, cheeses, nutmeg, salt, and black pepper, and stir well. Set aside.

3 Preheat the oven to 190°C (375°F/Gas 5). Line the baking trays with baking parchment. Stir the cooled potato into the spinach and cheese mixture.

4 On a well-floured surface, cut the dough into 4 equal pieces. Roll each piece into a circle about 20cm (8in) across and a thickness of 5mm (¼in). Using a small plate (about 20cm/8in in diameter) cut out a circle from each rolled circle of dough. Arrange one-quarter of the filling on half of each circle, leaving a 1cm (½in) border around the edge. Brush the edges with the beaten egg, bring them together to seal, and crimp for a decorative finish. Chill the pies for 10 minutes.

5 Place the pies on the prepared baking trays and brush with the remaining beaten egg. Cut a slit in the top of each pasty and bake for 20–25 minutes. Serve the pasties either hot or cold.

EQUIPMENT
2 baking trays

INGREDIENTS

FOR THE PASTRY
(For visual step by step instructions see shortcrust pastry p104)
150g (5½oz) plain wholemeal flour
150g (5½oz) plain flour, plus extra for dusting
150g (5½oz) butter, chilled and diced
½ tsp salt
1 egg, beaten, to glaze

FOR THE FILLING
300g (10oz) unpeeled waxy potatoes, such as charlotte, cut into small chunks
225g (8oz) spinach
1 garlic clove, finely chopped
250g (9oz) ricotta cheese
75g (2½oz) vegetarian-style Grana Padano cheese, or regular Grana Padano, grated
freshly grated nutmeg
salt and freshly ground black pepper

Long, slow cooking of the fennel ensures a soft, sweet filling for this tart. It is best served on the day it is made, but if making it in advance it can be stored in the refrigerator overnight.

ROASTED FENNEL AND PARMESAN TART

 SERVES 6–8

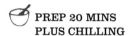 PREP 20 MINS
PLUS CHILLING

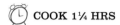 COOK 1¼ HRS

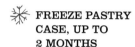 FREEZE PASTRY
CASE, UP TO
2 MONTHS

EQUIPMENT
22cm (9in) loose-bottomed
fluted tart tin, baking beans

INGREDIENTS

FOR THE PASTRY
(For visual step by step instructions
see shortcrust pastry p104)
150g (5½oz) plain flour,
plus extra for dusting
75g (2½oz) unsalted butter, softened
½ tsp salt

FOR THE FILLING
2 large fennel bulbs, 10oz (300g)
trimmed weight, finely sliced
(green fronds reserved)
1 onion, finely sliced
2 tbsp olive oil
1 tbsp butter, softened
juice and zest of 2 lemons
300ml (10fl oz) double cream
2 large eggs
50g (1¾oz) vegetarian Parmesan-style
cheese, or regular Parmesan grated
salt and freshly ground black pepper

1 To make the pastry, rub the flour, butter, and salt together with your fingertips until the mixture resembles fine breadcrumbs. Add 3–4 tablespoons of water, a little at a time, and bring together to form a soft dough. Wrap in cling film and chill for 30 minutes.

2 Preheat the oven to 180°C (350°F/Gas 4). Roll out the pastry on a floured surface to a large circle about 3mm (⅛in) thick and use to line the tart tin, making sure it overlaps the sides. Trim all but 1cm (½in) of the overhanging pastry. Prick the bottom of the pastry with a fork, line with greaseproof paper, fill with baking beans, and put on a baking tray. Bake for 20–25 minutes until the pastry is lightly cooked. Remove the beans and paper and bake for a further 5 minutes to crisp. Trim off any ragged edges from the pastry case.

3 Meanwhile, cook the fennel and onion in the olive oil, butter, and lemon juice for 20 minutes until soft. Stir occasionally to prevent it from sticking. If it looks like it's starting to burn, cover the pan with a lid, but remove it for the last 5 minutes of cooking time, to evaporate any excess water. Set aside to cool.

4 Whisk the cream, eggs, Parmesan, and lemon zest together and season well. Add a tablespoon or two of the reserved fennel fronds, finely chopped.

5 Pile the cooked fennel mixture into the tart case and spread it around evenly without packing it too tightly. Carefully pour the cream mixture over the fennel and bake for 30 minutes until just set. Set aside to cool for 30 minutes before eating warm or cold.

These delicious strudels make a fantastic vegetarian alternative at any party. Preparing them a few hours in advance means that there is no last-minute panic when serving lots of dishes at the same time.

BUTTERNUT SQUASH AND GOAT'S CHEESE STRUDELS

 MAKES 4    PREP 15 MINS    COOK 30–35 MINS    FREEZE UP TO 1 MONTH

1 Preheat the oven to 200°C (400°F/Gas 6). Heat the olive oil in a frying pan over a medium heat. Add the onions and cook for about 5 minutes until soft. Add the vinegar, sugar, season well with salt and black pepper, and cook over a low heat for 5 minutes.

2 If using filo, lay out 4 sheets of pastry, one for each strudel on a well-floured surface. Brush the sheets with melted butter, cover with a second layer, and brush again. Repeat with the remaining pastry sheets. Brush the top layer with butter, being careful to brush around the edges first (this will help to seal the strudels later).

3 Now scatter the grated butternut squash evenly over the strudel bases, leaving a clean border of at least 2cm (¾in) around all the edges except those nearest to you. Scatter the cooked onions on top, then the chopped sage. Finally, add the goat's cheese, and season with black pepper and a little salt.

4 Fold in the 2 sides of each strudel that are free of filling, then carefully roll up, starting with the side nearest you. Take care to tuck the sides in as you roll, and finish with the joins tucked underneath. Transfer the strudels to the baking tray and brush the tops with any remaining melted butter.

5 Bake at the top of the oven for 20–25 minutes until golden brown and crisp. If serving hot, set the strudels aside to cool for at least 10 minutes; they are also good cold. The uncooked strudels can be stored in the refrigerator, covered, a few hours before baking. The cooked strudels can be warmed 1 day later.

EQUIPMENT
baking tray

INGREDIENTS

FOR THE FILLING
2 tbsp olive oil
3 red onions, finely sliced
2 tbsp balsamic vinegar
a pinch of sugar
salt and freshly ground black pepper
500g (1lb 2oz) butternut squash, peeled, deseeded, and coarsely grated
2 tbsp finely chopped sage leaves
250g (9oz) soft goat's cheese, roughly diced

FOR THE PASTRY
1 quantity strudel pastry (or to make your own, see pp114–115), or 12 sheets filo pastry, about 25 x 25cm (10 x 10in)
plain flour, for dusting
50g (1¾oz) unsalted butter, melted

Squash is a wonderfully versatile vegetable. Roasting it gives it a depth of flavour, and contrasting it with a salty cheese, such as Dolcelatte complements its sweet, earthy tones.

THYME-ROASTED SQUASH AND DOLCELATTE TART

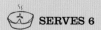 **SERVES 6**   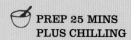 **PREP 25 MINS PLUS CHILLING**    **COOK 1½ HRS**    **FREEZE UP TO 1 MONTH**

EQUIPMENT
20cm (8in) loose-bottomed tart tin, baking beans

INGREDIENTS

FOR THE PASTRY
(For visual step by step instructions see shortcrust pastry p104)
225g (8oz) plain flour
115g (4oz) butter, chilled

FOR THE FILLING
450g (1lb) squash, peeled and deseeded
1–2 tbsp olive oil
leaves from 1 bunch fresh thyme or 1 tsp dried thyme
400g (14oz) rocket
2 large eggs, plus 1 egg yolk
300ml (10fl oz) double cream
50g (1¾oz) vegetarian Parmesan-style cheese or regular Parmesan, grated
grated nutmeg
salt and freshly ground black pepper
115g (4oz) Dolcelatte cheese

1 To make the pastry, put the flour and butter into a food processor and pulse until it resembles breadcrumbs. Add just enough water to bring it together into a dough. Roll it out on a floured surface, and use to line the tart tin. Chill for 30 minutes.

2 Preheat the oven to 180°C (350°F/Gas 4). Prick the bottom of the tart case, line it with greaseproof paper, and fill with baking beans. Bake for 10 minutes, then remove the paper and beans, and bake for a further 10 minutes to crisp up.

3 Slice the squash into thick slices, put on a roasting tray, brush lightly with olive oil and sprinkle the thyme over. Bake for 30 minutes, or until tender. Meanwhile, place the rocket and a little olive oil in a saucepan and wilt over a medium heat for 1–2 minutes. Drain and set aside to cool. Whisk the eggs, egg yolk, cream, Parmesan, and nutmeg together and season to taste with salt and black pepper.

4 Squeeze the rocket dry and spread it across the bottom of the tart case, then add slices of squash and crumble over the Dolcelatte. Pour in the egg mixture and bake for 30–40 minutes, or until the filling is set. Remove from the oven and set it aside for 10 minutes before serving.

These crisp little filo parcels are a version of a popular Middle Eastern snack. Variations of these savoury snacks are available all over the Middle East and North Africa.

SPICY BUTTERNUT SQUASH AND FETA PARCELS

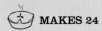 MAKES 24   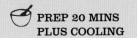 PREP 20 MINS PLUS COOLING    COOK 30 MINS   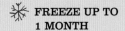 FREEZE UP TO 1 MONTH

1 Place the squash in a small saucepan and pour in enough water to just cover it. Bring to the boil, cover, then reduce the heat, and simmer gently for 5 minutes, or until tender. Drain and set aside to cool.

2 Preheat the oven to 180°C (350°F/Gas 4) and grease the baking tray. Mix the squash with the pine nuts and feta. Season with black pepper and add the spices and chilli flakes. Set aside.

3 Lay the filo sheets on top of each other and cut into 4 long strips, about 7.5cm (3in) wide. Stack the strips on top of each other and cover with dampened kitchen paper.

4 Taking one strip of pastry at a time, brush with melted butter and fill one end with a heaped teaspoon of the squash mixture 2.5cm (1in). Fold over the end of the strip of pastry to cover the filling.

5 Fold a corner of the pastry over diagonally to form a triangular pocket of filled pastry. Working upwards, keep folding diagonally, from one side to the other, to retain the triangular shape, until all the pastry is folded. Make sure any gaps in the pastry are pressed closed. Keep the triangles in a pile on a lightly floured surface, covered with a damp cloth to stop them drying out, while preparing the other pastries. Transfer the triangles to the baking tray.

6 Brush with the remaining butter and bake for 20–25 minutes until crisp and golden. Serve while still warm. The pastries can be prepared up to 24 hours before baking, and chilled.

EQUIPMENT
baking tray

INGREDIENTS

FOR THE FILLING
100g (3½oz) butternut squash, peeled, deseeded, and finely diced
25g (scant 1oz) toasted pine nuts
100g (3oz) feta cheese, finely crumbled
freshly ground black pepper
½ tsp ground coriander
½ tsp ground cumin
½ tsp dried chilli flakes

FOR THE PASTRY
6 sheets filo pastry, 40 x 30cm (16 x 12in)
50g (1¾oz) butter, melted, plus extra for greasing
plain flour, for dusting

If you don't have much time use shop-bought puff pastry, rather than making your own. Buy a butter-based one, and it will be all but indistinguishable from the home-made variety.

SWEET POTATO, RED ONION, AND THYME GALETTES WITH CHILLI

 MAKES 4    PREP 20 MINS   COOK 50 MINS

EQUIPMENT
1 or 2 baking trays

INGREDIENTS

FOR THE FILLING
2 medium-sized sweet potatoes,
300g (10oz) peeled weight
2 red onions, cut into 1cm (½in) cubes
1 tbsp olive oil
salt and freshly ground black pepper
½ red chilli, deseeded and finely chopped
1 tsp finely thyme, chopped

FOR THE PASTRY
375g (12oz) ready-made puff pastry
(or to make your own, see pp110–113)
plain flour, for dusting
1 egg yolk, beaten

1 Preheat the oven to 200ºC (400ºF/Gas 6). Dice the sweet potatoes into 1cm (½in) cubes. Toss the sweet potato and red onions in the olive oil in a large bowl and season well with salt and black pepper. Turn the vegetables out onto a baking tray and bake for 30 minutes until softened and golden at the edges.

2 Roll out the puff pastry on a lightly floured surface into a square about 30 x 40cm (12 x 16in) and cut it into quarters. Lay the pastry rectangles on one or two baking trays, and brush them with beaten egg yolk.

3 Toss the cooked vegetables with the chopped chilli and thyme, and divide the mixture equally between the 4 pastry rectangles. Spread the vegetables out, leaving a 1cm (½in) clear edge to the pastry.

4 Bake the galettes for 20 minutes, or until the pastry is puffed up and golden brown at the edges, and the bottom is firm to the touch and golden. Best eaten hot, but set aside to cool for 5 minutes before serving with a leafy green salad. The cooked galettes can be stored in the refrigerator for up to 2 days and warmed through again before serving.

Any combination of mushrooms can be used in this rich, nutty tart. For an added depth of flavour, reconstitute a handful of dried porcini in stock or boiling water, then chop and add them to the filling.

MIXED MUSHROOM AND WALNUT TART

 SERVES 6    **PREP 15 MINS**    **COOK 1 HR**   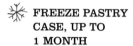 **FREEZE PASTRY CASE, UP TO 1 MONTH**

EQUIPMENT
12 x 35cm (5 x 14in) rectangular loose-bottomed fluted tart tin, baking beans

INGREDIENTS

FOR THE PASTRY
250g (9oz) ready-made shortcrust pastry (or to make your own, see p104)
plain flour, for dusting
1 egg, lightly beaten, to glaze

FOR THE FILLING
3–4 tbsp olive oil
140g (5oz) exotic mushrooms (such as porcini or shiitake), roughly chopped
200g (7oz) chestnut mushrooms, roughly chopped
3 garlic cloves, grated or finely chopped
50g (1¾oz) walnut halves, roughly chopped
salt and freshly ground black pepper
2 handfuls of fresh spinach leaves, roughly chopped
200ml (7fl oz) double cream
2 eggs

1 Preheat the oven to 200°C (400°F/Gas 6). Roll out the pastry on a floured surface and use to line the tart tin. Trim away the excess pastry. Line the pastry case with greaseproof paper and fill with baking beans. Bake for 15–20 minutes until the edges are golden, then remove the beans and paper, brush the bottom of the case with a little of the beaten egg, and bake for a further 2–3 minutes to crisp. Remove from the oven and set aside. Reduce the heat to 180°C (350°F/Gas 4).

2 Heat the olive oil in a large, deep-sided frying pan over a low heat. Add the mushrooms, garlic, and walnuts, and season well with salt and black pepper. Cook, stirring occasionally, for about 10 minutes until the mushrooms release their juices. Tip in the spinach, and cook, stirring, for a further 5 minutes until just wilted. Spoon the mixture into the pastry case.

3 Mix together the cream and the eggs. Season well with salt and black pepper and pour the cream mixture over the mushroom filling. Sprinkle with a pinch of black pepper and bake for 15–20 minutes until set. Set aside to cool for 10 minutes before releasing from the tin. Serve hot or cold.

These tempting little tarts make a great starter, being both meat-free and easy to finish at the last minute. For an even faster version, use a jar of good-quality hollandaise sauce.

CREAMY MUSHROOM HOLLANDAISE TARTLETS

 MAKES 6 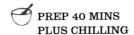 PREP 40 MINS PLUS CHILLING 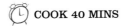 COOK 40 MINS

1 To make the pastry, pulse the flours and butter in a food processor until the mixture resembles breadcrumbs. Add the egg and process until the pastry comes together into a ball, adding 1–2 drops of water if necessary. Put the pastry on a floured surface, divide into 6 pieces, roll out, and use to line the tins. Prick the bottom of the pastry, then chill for 30 minutes.

2 Preheat the oven to 200°C (400°F/Gas 6). Line the pastry cases with greaseproof paper and fill with baking beans. Bake for 10 minutes, then remove the paper and beans and bake for a further 5 minutes, or until crisp. Set aside. Don't turn off the oven.

3 Pour boiling water over the dried mushrooms and leave for 10 minutes to soften. Melt the butter in a frying pan and cook the onion and mushrooms over a medium heat. Drain the dried mushrooms, chop, and add to the onion mix. Once all the mushrooms have wilted, increase the heat and boil until the liquid has evaporated. Add the lemon juice and seasoning. Cool.

4 Whiz the mushroom mixture with the cream cheese in a food processor until fairly smooth. Season. For the hollandaise, melt the butter in a small saucepan. Whiz the yolks, black pepper, and vinegar in a food processor for 1 minute, then gradually add the melted butter while the processor is running, until the sauce is thickened. Adjust the seasoning and set aside.

5 Turn the oven to 190°C (375°F/Gas 5). Spoon the filling into the tartlets, pour over the sauce, and bake for 10 minutes. Serve hot, topped with chopped chives.

EQUIPMENT
6 loose-bottomed tartlet tins, baking beans

INGREDIENTS

FOR THE PASTRY
(For visual step by step instructions see shortcrust pastry p104)
85g (3oz) plain flour, plus extra for dusting
85g (3oz) wholemeal plain flour
85g (3oz) butter, chilled and diced
1 small egg

FOR THE FILLING
15g (½oz) dried wild mushrooms
30g (1oz) unsalted butter
1 red onion, chopped
400g (14oz) mixed mushrooms, such as portabellini, oyster, shiitake, chestnut, or button, sliced
juice of ½ lemon
175g (6oz) cream cheese
salt and freshly ground black pepper

FOR THE HOLLANDAISE SAUCE
225g (8oz) unsalted butter
4 egg yolks
freshly ground black pepper
1 tbsp white wine vinegar
small bunch of chives, chopped

The addition of rolled oats to a classic shortcrust pastry gives this tart a nutty flavour. Unusually, yogurt is used in the filling instead of cream, which lends a tanginess to the finished dish.

GOAT'S CHEESE TARTLETS

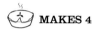 **MAKES 4**

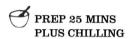 **PREP 25 MINS PLUS CHILLING**

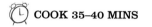 **COOK 35–40 MINS**

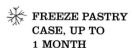 **FREEZE PASTRY CASE, UP TO 1 MONTH**

EQUIPMENT
4 x loose-bottomed tartlet tins, 12.5cm (5in) in diameter and 2.5cm (1in) deep, baking beans

INGREDIENTS

FOR THE PASTRY
(For visual step by step instructions see shortcrust pastry p104)
85g (3oz) plain flour, plus extra for dusting
a pinch of salt
25g (scant 1oz) rolled oats
60g (2oz) butter chilled and diced

FOR THE FILLING
2 large eggs
90ml (3fl oz) Greek yogurt
150ml (5fl oz) milk
2 tbsp chives, chopped
salt and freshly ground black pepper
85g (3oz) goat's cheese, crumbled

1 To make the pastry, sift the flour and salt into a large bowl and stir in the oats. Rub in the butter with your fingertips until the mixture resembles breadcrumbs. Sprinkle over 2 tablespoons of chilled water and mix in with a round-bladed knife. Gather the dough together and, on a floured surface, knead lightly for a few seconds, or until smooth. Wrap the dough in cling film and chill for 30 minutes.

2 Preheat the oven to 200°C (400°F/Gas 6) and place a baking tray inside to heat. Divide the dough into 4 pieces. Roll out each one thinly on a lightly floured surface and use to line the tartlet tins. Prick the bottom of the pastry several times with a fork, then line each tin with foil and fill with baking beans. Bake for 10 minutes, then remove the foil and beans and return to the oven for 5 minutes. Remove from the oven and set aside. Reduce the heat to 180°C (350°F/Gas 4).

3 Whisk the eggs, yogurt, milk, chives, and salt and black pepper in a jug. Divide the cheese between the pastry cases, then carefully pour over the egg mixture. Bake for 20–25 minutes until the filling is lightly set and beginning to brown.

4 Set aside to cool slightly, then remove from the tins and serve warm, or at room temperature. Make the pastry and line the tartlet tins up to 1 day in advance. If serving cold, the tartlets can be refrigerated, and covered with cling film, for up to 48 hours.

A classic Swedish recipe, all the flavour comes from the buttery, crisp pastry and the strong cheese. Serve with a leafy, green salad and a sharp dressing to complement the richness of the tart.

SWEDISH CHEESE TART

 SERVES 6–8   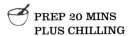 PREP 20 MINS PLUS CHILLING   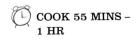 COOK 55 MINS – 1 HR   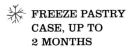 FREEZE PASTRY CASE, UP TO 2 MONTHS

1 To make the pastry, rub the flour, butter, and salt together with your fingertips until the mixture resembles fine breadcrumbs. Add 3–4 tablespoons cold water a little at a time and bring the mixture together to form a soft dough. Wrap in cling film and chill for 30 minutes. Preheat the oven to 180°C (350°F/Gas 4).

2 Roll out the pastry on a well-floured surface to a large circle about 3mm (⅛in) thick and use to line the tart tin, making sure it overlaps the sides. Trim all but 1cm (½in) of the overhanging pastry, then use your fingers to push the pastry down into the corners of the tin, making sure it clings to the sides well. Prick the bottom of the pastry with a fork, line with greaseproof paper, and fill with baking beans. Place the tart case on a baking tray and bake for 20–25 minutes until the pastry is lightly cooked. Remove the beans and paper and bake for a further 5 minutes to crisp. Trim off any ragged edges from the pastry case while warm.

3 Whisk together the cream, milk, and eggs and season well with black pepper, and a little salt – not too much as the cheese is quite salty.

4 Scatter the cheese over the bottom of the cooked tart case, spreading it out evenly. Put the tart case on a baking tray and carefully pour the cream mixture over the cheese. Bake for 30 minutes until just set, slightly puffy and golden brown.

5 Set the tart aside to rest for at least 15 minutes before serving warm or at room temperature. Best eaten on the day it is made, but can be stored in the refrigerator overnight.

EQUIPMENT
22cm (9in) loose-bottomed fluted tart tin, baking beans

INGREDIENTS

FOR THE PASTRY
(For visual step by step instructions
   see shortcrust pastry p104)
150g (5½oz) plain flour,
   plus extra for dusting
75g (2½oz) unsalted butter, softened
½ tsp salt

FOR THE FILLING
175ml (6fl oz) single cream
75ml (2½oz) full-fat milk
2 large eggs
salt and freshly ground black pepper
250g (9oz) Västerbotten cheese, or other
   sharp cheese such as aged Cheddar, grated

Spinach seems to work well with strong, sharp cheeses, such as Stilton, goat's cheese, or feta. Here, the classic filling is given a makeover, encased in a filo pie with herbs, and baked until crisp.

HERBY FETA FILO PIE

 SERVES 6   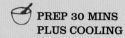 PREP 30 MINS PLUS COOLING   COOK 1 HR

EQUIPMENT
20cm (8in) round springform tin

INGREDIENTS

FOR THE FILLING
900g (2lb) spinach, rinsed
100g (3½oz) butter,
plus extra for greasing
2 onions and garlic cloves, finely chopped
120g (4oz) roasted peppers in oil,
drained and chopped
a handful of basil leaves
3 tbsp mint leaves, chopped
3 tbsp parsley, chopped
salt and freshly ground black pepper
300g (10oz) feta cheese, crumbled

FOR THE PASTRY
6 sheets ready-made filo pastry,
40 x 30cm (16 x 12in)

1 Pack the spinach leaves into a large saucepan, cover, and cook for 8–10 minutes until just wilted. Drain well. Set aside, still draining, to cool.

2 Melt 25g (scant 1oz) butter until bubbling and gently fry the onions, stirring occasionally, for 3 minutes. Add the garlic and fry for a further 2 minutes. Stir in the peppers and herbs, and set aside. Preheat the oven to 200°C (400°F/Gas 6). Grease and line the tin.

3 Blot the spinach with kitchen paper, then chop finely. Stir into the onion mixture, and season to taste. Melt the remaining butter. Brush the tin with a little melted butter and assemble the pie (see below).

4 Brush the top of the pastry with any remaining butter and place the tin on a baking tray. Bake for 35–40 minutes until crisp and golden. Be sure to leave the pie to stand for 10 minutes before carefully releasing from the tin. Serve hot or warm, cut into wedges. Good with a crisp salad or seasonal vegetables.

Layering filo sheets

1 Cover the bottom with a sheet of pastry, leaving the edges to overhang, and brush with butter.

2 Continue with 5 more sheets, brushing each with butter. Leave the edges overhanging.

3 Add half the filling, then feta, then filling. Put the overhanging pastry over the top, brushing with butter.

A simple yet sophisticated tart, the flavours of this dish belie the simple list of ingredients. Try to use really fresh ricotta, and the young tips of the rosemary. Best eaten on the day it is made.

RICOTTA, ROSEMARY, AND PINE NUT TART

 SERVES 6

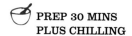 **PREP 30 MINS PLUS CHILLING**

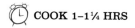 **COOK 1–1¼ HRS**

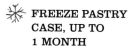 **FREEZE PASTRY CASE, UP TO 1 MONTH**

EQUIPMENT
20cm (8in) round tart tin

INGREDIENTS

FOR THE PASTRY
(For visual step by step instructions see shortcrust pastry p104)
150g (5½oz) plain flour,
plus extra for dusting
75g (2½oz) butter, chilled and diced
1 tsp dried rosemary
1 egg yolk

FOR THE FILLING
1 tbsp olive oil
2 red onions, finely sliced
2 garlic cloves, finely chopped
salt and freshly ground black pepper
250g (9oz) ricotta cheese
2 eggs
85g (3oz) toasted pine nuts
1 tbsp fresh rosemary leaves, finely chopped

1 To make the pastry, rub the flour and butter together with your fingertips until the mixture resembles fine breadcrumbs. Add the rosemary and egg yolk to the flour mixture, then add 1–2 teaspoons cold water and bring together to form a smooth dough. Wrap in cling film and chill for 30 minutes.

2 Meanwhile, heat the olive oil in a non-stick frying pan over a medium heat. Add the onions and cook for 10 minutes. Add the garlic and cook for a further 2 minutes. Season well and transfer to a large bowl. Add the ricotta and stir well. Add the eggs and beat the mixture until it is well combined. Stir in the pine nuts and fresh rosemary. Set aside.

3 Preheat the oven to 180°C (350°F/Gas 4). Roll out the pastry on a floured surface to a circle large enough to line the tart tin. Place the pastry in the tin, pressing down well into the bottom and around the edges. Trim off any excess pastry, prick the bottom with a fork, and line with baking parchment. Place the tin on a baking tray and fill with baking beans. Bake for 20 minutes. Remove the beans and paper and bake for a further 5 minutes.

4 Pour the ricotta and onion mixture into the pastry case and bake for 25–30 minutes until golden.

The classic ingredients of a Waldorf salad can be turned into a delicious tangy tart. Adding chopped walnuts to the pastry gives the crust added texture and taste. Serve with salad for a summer lunch.

STILTON, APPLE, AND CELERY TART

 SERVES 6–8 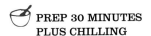 PREP 30 MINUTES PLUS CHILLING 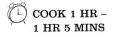 COOK 1 HR – 1 HR 5 MINS 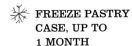 FREEZE PASTRY CASE, UP TO 1 MONTH

1 To make the pastry, rub the flour and butter together with your fingertips until the mixture forms fine breadcrumbs. Add the egg yolk and chopped walnuts to the flour mixture, then add 2–3 tablespoons cold water and bring together to form a smooth dough. Wrap in cling film and chill for 30 minutes.

2 For the filling, melt the butter in a medium non-stick frying pan and gently fry the celery for 5 minutes. Remove from the pan with a slotted spoon. Add the apple slices to the pan and gently fry for a further 5 minutes, or until just browning.

3 Whiz the Stilton, milk, eggs, and plenty of black pepper in a food processor until well combined.

4 Preheat the oven to 180°C (350°F/Gas 4). Roll out the pastry on a floured surface to a circle large enough to line the tart tin. Place the pastry in the tin, pressing down well into the bottom and around the edges. Trim off any excess pastry, prick the bottom with a fork, and line with baking parchment. Place the tin on a baking tray and fill with baking beans. Bake for 20 minutes. Remove the beans and paper and bake for a further 5 minutes to crisp up the bottom.

5 Sprinkle the celery and walnuts over the pastry base and arrange the apples in 3 rows, over the top. Carefully pour the Stilton mixture over the apple slices and bake for 25–30 minutes until golden.

EQUIPMENT
20cm (8in) loose-bottomed square tart tin

INGREDIENTS

FOR THE PASTRY
(For visual step by step instructions see shortcrust pastry p104)
225g (8oz) plain flour, plus extra for dusting
115g (4oz) butter, chilled and diced
1 egg yolk
2 tbsp walnuts, very finely chopped

FOR THE FILLING
25g (scant 1oz) butter
4 stalks celery (115g/4oz), finely chopped
2 red eating apples eg Gala, quartered, cored and each sliced into 16 pieces
140g (5oz) Stilton cheese, roughly crumbled
150ml (5fl oz) whole milk
2 eggs
freshly ground black pepper
25g (scant 1oz) walnuts, roughly chopped

These little cigar-shaped filo pastries are stuffed with flavoured feta and quickly baked to a crisp, golden finish. A handful of toasted pine nuts or some chopped dill make a good addition to this basic recipe.

BOREKS

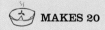 MAKES 20   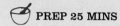 PREP 25 MINS   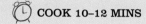 COOK 10–12 MINS   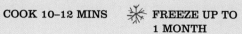 FREEZE UP TO 1 MONTH

EQUIPMENT
baking tray

INGREDIENTS

FOR THE FILLING
175g (6oz) feta cheese, finely crumbled
a pinch of ground nutmeg
1 tsp dried mint
freshly ground black pepper

FOR THE PASTRY
8 sheets of ready-made filo pastry,
40 x 30cm (16 x 12in)
60g (2oz) butter, melted,
plus extra for greasing
plain flour, for dusting

1 Preheat the oven to 180°C (350°F/Gas 4). Place the feta cheese in a bowl, add the nutmeg and mint, then season to taste with black pepper.

2 Lay the filo sheets on top of each other and cut into 3 long strips, 10cm (4in) wide.

3 Taking one strip of pastry at a time, brush with melted butter and place 1 heaped teaspoon of the cheese mixture at one end. Roll up the pastry, like a cigar, folding the ends in about one-third of the way down to encase the filling completely, then continue to roll. Make sure the ends are tightly sealed.

4 On a lightly floured surface, keep the rolled pastries in a pile, covered with a damp cloth, while preparing the remainder.

5 Place the pastries in a single layer on a large greased baking tray. Brush with the remaining butter and bake for 10–12 minutes or until crisp and golden. Best served hot or slightly warm. The pastries can be prepared 24 hours ahead of baking.

This quiche is an all-time spring favourite. A hidden layer of cream cheese and Cheddar under the asparagus adds flavour to the finished dish. Serve warm or cold with a crisp green salad.

ASPARAGUS CREAM CHEESE QUICHE

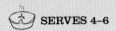 SERVES 4–6   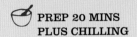 PREP 20 MINS
                                         PLUS CHILLING   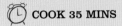 COOK 35 MINS

1 Sift the flour and salt into a bowl. Add the fat and rub in with your fingertips until the mixture resembles fine breadcrumbs. Mix with 2 tablespoons of cold water to form a firm dough. Knead gently on a lightly floured surface. Roll out and use to line the flan ring set on a baking tray. Chill for 30 minutes.

2 Preheat the oven to to 180°C (350°F/Gas 4). Toss the asparagus in a little olive oil and cook on a hot griddle pan for 2 minutes each side, until bright green and just tender.

3 Spread the cream cheese over the bottom of the prepared pastry case. Sprinkle with the thyme, some black pepper, and the Cheddar. Trim the asparagus spears to fit the flan, as necessary. Scatter the asparagus trimmings over the cheese and lay the whole spears attractively on top.

4 Beat the eggs and cream together with a little salt and black pepper, and pour into the flan. Bake for 30 minutes or until golden and set. Serve warm or cold.

EQUIPMENT
20cm (8in) flan ring,
baking beans

INGREDIENTS

FOR THE PASTRY
**(For visual step by step instructions
   see shortcrust pastry p104)**
175g (6oz) plain flour
a pinch of salt
45g (1½oz) lard, chilled and diced
45g (1½oz) butter, chilled and diced

FOR THE FILLING
175g (6oz) green asparagus spears
a little olive oil
115g (4oz) cream cheese
2 tsp chopped thyme
salt and freshly ground black pepper
85g (3oz) mature Cheddar cheese, grated
2 eggs
150ml (5fl oz) single cream

A perfect dish to cook in early summer, this tart looks as good as it tastes. Puréeing the peas gives them a wonderfully vibrant green colour and adds a sweet, fresh flavour to the creamy filling.

ASPARAGUS, PEA, AND MINT TART

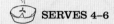 **SERVES 4–6**

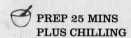 **PREP 25 MINS PLUS CHILLING**

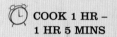 **COOK 1 HR – 1 HR 5 MINS**

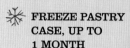 **FREEZE PASTRY CASE, UP TO 1 MONTH**

EQUIPMENT
20cm (8in) tart tin, baking beans

INGREDIENTS

FOR THE PASTRY
(For visual step by step instructions see shortcrust pastry p104)
150g (5½oz) plain flour, plus extra for dusting
75g (2½oz) butter, chilled and diced
20g (¾oz) vegetarian-style Parmesan cheese or regular Parmesan, finely grated
1 egg yolk

FOR THE FILLING
115g (4oz) frozen peas
125g (4½oz) fine asparagus stems, cut into 6cm (2½in) lengths
100ml (3½fl oz) whole milk
2 eggs
2 garlic cloves, roughly chopped
salt and freshly ground black pepper
3 tbsp mint leaves, chopped
50g (1¾oz) Cheddar cheese, grated

1 To make the pastry, rub the flour and butter together with your fingertips until the mixture resembles fine breadcrumbs. Stir the Parmesan cheese and egg yolk into the flour mixture. Add 1–2 tablespoons cold water and bring together to form a smooth dough. Wrap and chill for 30 minutes.

2 For the filling, cook the peas in a small saucepan of boiling water for 2 minutes, or until tender. Drain. Steam the asparagus for 5 minutes, or until just tender. Drain and place on kitchen paper to absorb any excess moisture. Whiz the peas, milk, eggs, garlic, and plenty of seasoning in a food processor until well combined.

3 Preheat the oven to 180°C (350°F/Gas 4). Roll out the pastry on a floured surface to a circle large enough to line the tart tin. Place the pastry in the tin, pressing down well into the bottom and around the edges. Trim off any excess pastry, prick the bottom with a fork, and line with baking parchment. Place the tin on a baking tray and fill with baking beans. Bake for 20 minutes, then remove the beans and paper and bake for a further 5 minutes.

4 Sprinkle the chopped mint over the pastry case and arrange the asparagus spears, like the spokes of a wheel, on top. Carefully pour the creamy pea mixture over the asparagus and sprinkle the Cheddar cheese over. Bake for 25–30 minutes until golden.

For a meat-free feast, try cooking up the best your garden has
to offer in this delicious potato-topped pie. The types of vegetables
used can be varied according to the season. Serve hot.

KITCHEN GARDEN PIE

 SERVES 4   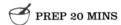 PREP 20 MINS    COOK 1¼–1½ HRS

1 Preheat the oven to 200°C (400°F/Gas 6). Place
the leeks, parsnips, squash, carrots, onion, and
garlic in a large roasting tin. Add the olive oil, chilli
flakes, and rosemary, season well, and toss to coat
the vegetables. Roast for 35–45 minutes, or until the
vegetables are tender.

2 To make the topping, cook the potatoes in a
saucepan of boiling, salted water for 15 minutes,
or until tender. Drain and mash, stir in the butter,
whole milk, and Cheddar cheese. Mix well to combine,
season to taste, and set aside.

3 Place the parsley, bread, and Parmesan in a food
processor, and pulse to form fine crumbs. Season,
and stir in the lemon zest.

4 Melt the butter in a medium pan. Stir in the
flour and cook for 2–3 minutes over a medium
heat, stirring constantly with a wooden spoon, until
a smooth paste is formed. Gradually add the milk,
stirring constantly, to make a white sauce. Stir in
the mustard powder, Cheddar cheese, and roasted
vegetables, and season well.

5 Transfer to the ovenproof dish. Top with the mash,
spreading it in an even layer, and sprinkle over the
breadcrumb mixture. Place the dish on a baking tray
and bake for 20 minutes.

EQUIPMENT
2.5 litre (4¼ pint) ovenproof dish

INGREDIENTS

FOR THE FILLING
100g (3½oz) baby leeks, sliced
200g (7oz) parsnips, chopped
  into bite-sized pieces
300g (10oz) butternut squash,
  chopped into bite-sized pieces
200g (7oz) baby carrots,
  chopped into bite-sized pieces
1 red onion, finely chopped
2 garlic cloves, finely chopped
2 tbsp olive oil
½ tsp dried red chilli flakes
2 tbsp fresh rosemary, chopped
  or 1 tsp dried rosemary
salt and freshly ground black pepper
small bunch of curly parsley,
  stalks removed
50g (1¾oz) white bread
30g (1oz) Parmesan cheese, grated
zest of 1 lemon
50g (1¾oz) butter
50g (1¾oz) plain flour
450ml (15fl oz) whole milk
½ tsp English mustard powder
60g (2oz) mature Cheddar cheese, grated

FOR THE TOPPING
1kg (2¼lb) floury potatoes, such as
  Maris Piper, peeled and chopped
  into small chunks
50g (1¾oz) butter
50ml (1½fl oz) whole milk
60g (2oz) mature Cheddar cheese, grated

Sometimes a few staple ingredients can be combined to produce a simple yet sumptuous dish. Baked in minutes, these are great served fresh from the oven with new potatoes and a tomato salad.

BROCCOLI, TOMATO, AND MOZZARELLA GALETTES

 MAKES 4    PREP 20 MINS   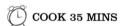 COOK 35 MINS

EQUIPMENT
baking tray

INGREDIENTS

FOR THE FILLING
175g (6oz) broccoli, cut into tiny florets
salt and freshly ground black pepper
100g (3½oz) mozzarella cheese, grated
6 sun-dried tomatoes in oil, drained and finely chopped
6 tbsp crème fraîche, plus extra for brushing

FOR THE PASTRY
375g (13oz) sheet ready-rolled puff pastry (about 23 x 40cm/9 x 16in), (or to make your own, see pp110–113)

1 Cook the broccoli in a saucepan of boiling, lightly salted water for 2 minutes until almost tender. Drain, rinse with cold water, and drain again. Preheat the oven to 220°C (425°F/Gas 7). Sprinkle a little water over the baking tray to dampen.

2 Place the broccoli florets in a large bowl, add the mozzarella, tomatoes, and crème fraîche. Season with salt and black pepper and stir well to combine.

3 Cut the pastry into quarters. Pile one-quarter of the filling at one end of each oblong, leaving a border, then brush the pastry edges with water. Fold over the uncovered halves of pastry, press the edges together to seal, and transfer to the dampened baking tray. Make a few slashes in the tops and brush some crème fraîche over the top to glaze. Bake for 30 minutes until puffy, crisp, and golden.

If you don't have a food processor, try making a traditional shortcrust pastry the old-fashioned way. It only takes minutes to prepare and is surprisingly satisfying, when you have the time.

BROCCOLI AND MUSHROOM QUICHE

 SERVES 6–8 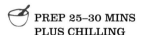 PREP 25–30 MINS PLUS CHILLING 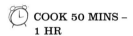 COOK 50 MINS – 1 HR  FREEZE UP TO 1 MONTH

1 To make the pastry, sift the flour on to a work surface and make a well in the centre. Put the egg yolk, salt, butter, and 3 tablespoons water in the well. Work the flour into the other ingredients with your fingertips until coarse breadcrumbs form. Press the dough lightly into a ball. If it is too dry, sprinkle with a little more water. On a lightly floured surface, knead the dough for 1–2 minutes until it is smooth. Shape into a ball, wrap in cling film, and chill for 30 minutes.

2 Preheat the oven to 220°C (425°F/Gas 7). Grease the tart tin. Roll out the pastry on a floured surface to a 30cm (12in) circle, and use to line the tin. With your thumb and forefingers, press the dough evenly up the side, from the bottom, to increase the height of the dough rim. Prick the bottom with a fork and chill for at least 15 minutes until firm.

3 Line the pastry with foil, fill with baking beans, and bake for 12–15 minutes until starting to turn golden. Remove the foil and beans, reduce the heat to 190°C (375°F/Gas 5) and bake for a further 5 minutes.

4 Cook the broccoli in a saucepan of salted boiling water for 3–5 minutes, then drain. Melt the butter in a frying pan, add the mushrooms and garlic and sauté until all the liquid has evaporated. Whisk together the eggs, yolks, milk, cream, seasoning, and nutmeg. Spread the mushrooms in the case. Lay the broccoli on top and sprinkle the cheese over. Ladle the egg mix over to fill almost to the rim. Bake for 30–35 minutes until browned and the filling has a slight wobble in the centre. Serve at room temperature.

EQUIPMENT
25cm (10in) fluted tart tin, baking beans

INGREDIENTS

FOR THE PASTRY
(For visual step by step instructions see shortcrust pastry p104)
200g (7oz) plain flour, plus extra for dusting
1 egg yolk
½ tsp salt
100g (3½ oz) unsalted butter, softened, plus extra for greasing

FOR THE FILLING
1–2 heads of broccoli, total weight about 500g (1lb 2oz), cut into florets
salt and freshly ground black pepper
30g (1oz) butter
85g (3oz) chestnut mushrooms, sliced
85g (3oz) button mushrooms, halved
2 garlic cloves, finely chopped
3 eggs, plus 2 egg yolks
375ml (12fl oz) milk
250ml (9fl oz) double cream
a pinch of ground nutmeg
115g (4 oz) mature Cheddar cheese, grated

This classic leek pie originates from the Picardy region of northern France. Although not traditional, the inclusion of blue cheese adds piquancy to the gentle sweetness of the leeks. Serve warm or cold.

FLAMICHE

 SERVES 4–6    PREP 20 MINS   🕐 COOK 40–45 MINS

EQUIPMENT
18cm (7in) loose-bottomed
cake tin

INGREDIENTS

FOR THE FILLING
50g (1¾oz) unsalted butter
2 tbsp olive oil
500g (1lb 2oz) leeks, washed, trimmed,
and finely shredded
sea salt and freshly ground black pepper
grated nutmeg
2 tbsp plain flour
250ml (9fl oz) milk
100g (3½oz) vegetarian blue cheese,
or regular blue cheese, such
as Stilton (optional)

FOR THE PASTRY
500g (1lb 2oz) ready-made puff pastry
(or to make your own, see pp110–113)
flour, for dusting
oil, for greasing
1 egg, beaten, to glaze

1 Preheat the oven to 200°C (400°F/Gas 6). Melt the butter and olive oil in a large saucepan. Add the leeks and cook over a low heat for 10 minutes, stirring occasionally, until well softened but not browned. Season well with salt, black pepper, and a little nutmeg. Scatter the flour over the surface of the leeks and stir it in well.

2 Pour the milk onto the leeks, a little at a time, stirring constantly. The mixture will thicken to begin with, then gradually loosen as all the milk is added. Bring to the boil, reduce the heat, and cook for 3–5 minutes until well thickened. Remove from the heat and stir in the cheese (if using).

3 Roll out the pastry on a well-floured surface into a 20 x 40cm (8 x 16in) rectangle, about 3–5mm (⅛–¼in) thick. Place the tin onto one short edge of the pastry and cut a circle around it to make the lid; the remaining pastry should be large enough to line the bottom of the tin. Oil the tin, trim the remaining pastry and use it to line the tin, allowing the sides to overhang slightly. Brush the inside with a little beaten egg and set aside for 5 minutes.

4 Fill the pastry case with the leek mixture and brush a little beaten egg around the edges of the pastry. Top with the disc of pastry and press around the edges to seal. Brush the top with beaten egg, then cut 2 small slits in the top to allow steam to escape.

5 Bake for 25–30 minutes until puffed up and golden brown. Remove from the oven, trim the excess pastry, and set aside to cool for at least 10 minutes before serving. Chill the flamiche overnight. Gently reheat, or bring back to room temperature to serve.

The humble leek is a vastly underrated vegetable. Commonly used to complement other vegetables, leeks and onions both flourish alone when cooked long and slow to bring out their natural sweetness.

LEEK QUICHE

 **SERVES 6–8**   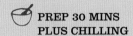 **PREP 30 MINS PLUS CHILLING**    **COOK 1–1½ HRS**   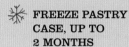 **FREEZE PASTRY CASE, UP TO 2 MONTHS**

1 To make the pastry, rub the flour, butter, and salt together with your fingertips until the mixture resembles fine breadcrumbs. Add 4–6 tablespoons cold water a little at a time and bring the mixture together to form a soft dough. Add a little extra water if it is too dry. Wrap in cling film and chill for 30 minutes. Preheat the oven to 180°C (350°F/Gas 4).

2 Roll out the pastry on a floured surface to a large circle about 5mm (¼in) thick, and use to line the tin, making sure the pastry overlaps the sides. Trim all but 1cm (½in) of the overhanging pastry. Prick the bottom of the pastry with a fork, line with greaseproof paper, and fill with baking beans. Place the case on a baking tray and bake for 20–25 minutes until the pastry is lightly cooked. Remove the beans and paper and bake for a further 5 minutes to crisp. Trim off any ragged edges from the pastry case while still warm.

3 To make the the filling, melt the butter in a large saucepan, add the leeks and cook over a medium heat for 15 minutes, stirring occasionally until soft, but not brown. Place the leeks in the pastry case and spread them out evenly to cover the bottom.

4 Whisk the cream, crème fraîche, eggs, thyme, and seasoning together in a bowl. Place the pastry case on a baking tray and carefully pour the cream mixture over the leeks. Bake for 45 minutes until the mixture has just set, and is lightly golden.

5 Remove the tart from the oven and set aside to cool for at least 15 minutes before eating warm or cold. This is best eaten the day it is made, but it can be stored in the refrigerator overnight.

EQUIPMENT
22cm (9in) loose-bottomed fluted tart tin with deep sides (3cm/1¼in)

INGREDIENTS

FOR THE PASTRY
(For visual step by step instructions see shortcrust pastry p104)
200g (7oz) plain flour, plus extra for dusting
100g (3½oz) unsalted butter, at room temperature, cut into small pieces
½ tsp salt

FOR THE FILLING
50g (1¾oz) butter
500g (1lb 2oz) leeks, prepared weight, sliced into 1cm (½in) discs
200ml (7fl oz) single cream
100g (3½oz) crème fraîche
2 eggs
½ tbsp thyme, finely chopped
salt and freshly ground black pepper

This pie is full of woody forest flavours and would make an ideal supper dish served with creamy mashed potato and a green vegetable. It is also perfect as a vegetarian Christmas alternative.

CHESTNUT AND MUSHROOM PIE

 **SERVES 4–6**　　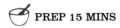 **PREP 15 MINS**　　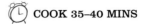 **COOK 35–40 MINS**

EQUIPMENT
23cm (9in) pie dish

INGREDIENTS

FOR THE FILLING
1 tbsp olive oil
1 red onion, finely chopped
2 garlic cloves, finely chopped
500g (1lb 2oz) mixed mushrooms, such as portabellini, oyster, shiitake, chestnut, button, sliced if large or left whole
200ml (7fl oz) red wine
leaves from 4 sprigs of fresh thyme or 1 tsp dried thyme
salt and freshly ground black pepper
150g (5½oz) cooked and peeled ready-to-eat chestnuts, cooked, peeled and halved

FOR THE PASTRY
215g (7½oz) sheet ready-rolled puff pastry (or to make your own, see pp110–113)
1 egg, beaten, to glaze

1 Heat the olive oil in a large, heavy-based, non-stick frying pan and gently fry the onion for 3 minutes. Add the garlic and cook for a further 1–2 minutes.

2 Add the mushrooms, red wine, and thyme. Season well, bring to a simmer, and cook over a medium heat for 5 minutes. Stir the chestnuts into the mushroom mixture and cook for a further 5 minutes, stirring occasionally. Spoon the mushroom mixture into the pie dish. Preheat the oven to 200°C (400°F/Gas 6).

3 Cut enough 2cm (¾in) wide strips from the edge of the pastry to fit round the rim of the pie dish. Brush the edge of the dish with water and place the strips on the rim. Cover the pie with the remaining pastry, trim, and press firmly to seal. Brush with the beaten egg and cut a hole in the centre of the lid to allow steam to escape. Place on a baking tray and bake for 15–20 minutes or until browned.

Salting the grated courgettes is an important stage of this recipe.
It helps to draw out as much moisture as possible from them, which
stops the delicate filo pastry going soggy after cooking.

COURGETTE AND FETA PIE

 SERVES 4–6    PREP 1 HR    COOK 50–55 MINS

1 Toss the grated courgettes in the salt and drain in
a colander over a bowl for 30 minutes. To help the
liquid drain, cover them with a clean saucer and put
a heavy weight on top. After 30 minutes, push the
courgettes down firmly with your hand to make sure
that as much liquid as possible is extracted.

2 Heat the olive oil in a frying pan, add the onion
and garlic and fry for 5 minutes until soft. Add the
courgettes and cook for 10–15 minutes over a low heat,
stirring occasionally, so that all the liquid evaporates.
Set the courgette mixture aside to cool.

3 Preheat the oven to 180°C (350°F/ Gas 4). Mix the
the eggs, yogurt, and mint into the courgette mix,
and season well with black pepper. Mix in the feta.

4 Brush the bottom of the tin with a little olive oil.
Layer the first sheet of filo into the tin lengthways,
and brush with a little olive oil. Lay the next one at
right angles to the first, making sure it touches one
of the short edges of the tin, and brush with more oil.
Place a third in the same direction touching the other
edge and again brush with oil. Repeat until you have
used 6 pieces of filo. Spread the filling evenly over the
bottom of the pie. Lay 1 piece of filo lengthways over
the filling. Fold half the overhanging edges over the
top piece of filo. Brush with oil and add a further piece
lengthways, folding the remaining edges over and
brushing with oil. Put a third sheet of filo on top and
place the last piece over the pie, tucking any edges in.

5 Brush the top with a little olive oil and bake
for 35–40 minutes. Set aside to cool for at least
10 minutes before serving hot or warm. This pie can
be refrigerated, covered, for up to 2 days. It can be
eaten cold, or reheat before use.

EQUIPMENT
20 x 30cm (8 x 12in) brownie tin

INGREDIENTS

FOR THE FILLING
600g (1lb 5oz) courgettes,
   trimmed and coarsely grated
1 tsp fine salt
6 tbsp olive oil
1 red onion, finely chopped
1 garlic clove, crushed
2 eggs, beaten
1 tbsp Greek yogurt
3–4 tbsp mint, chopped
freshly ground black pepper
200g (7oz) feta cheese, crumbled

FOR THE PASTRY
10 sheets ready-made filo pastry
olive oil, for brushing

These light, delicate mini quiches are filled with the produce of an early summer harvest. Using cheese in the crust adds a sharpness, which contrasts well with the sweetness of the vegetables.

COURGETTE, BROAD BEAN, AND PEA MINI QUICHES

 MAKES 6   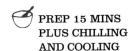 **PREP 15 MINS PLUS CHILLING AND COOLING**   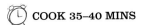 **COOK 35–40 MINS**    **FREEZE UP TO 1 MONTH**

1 Preheat the oven to 170°C (350°F/Gas 4). In a food processor, spin the flour for a minute, then drop the butter down the chute in small knobs. To make by hand, rub the butter into the flour until it resembles breadcrumbs. Once incorporated, add the egg yolk, Parmesan, and some salt and black pepper. Tip out onto a work surface and bring the dough together with a little milk. Wrap in cling film and chill for 30 minutes.

2 Bring a saucepan of salted water to the boil and drop in the broad beans. Blanch them for 3 minutes, then drain under cold running water, and shell them.

3 Grease the tart tins with butter, then dust with flour. Roll the pastry out on a lightly floured surface and use to line the tart tins. Chill in the refrigerator for 10 minutes, then line the pastry case with greaseproof paper and bake for 8 minutes. Set aside to cool, then fill with the vegetables.

4 Mix together the egg yolks and cream, add the chopped mint, season with some salt and black pepper, and pour over the tarts, right up to the top. Bake for 25 minutes until the custard has just set. Let them stand for 5 minutes before serving with a few dressed mixed leaves.

EQUIPMENT
6 x 10 x 4cm (4 x 2in) fluted tart tins, baking beans

INGREDIENTS

FOR THE PASTRY
(For visual step by step instructions
   see shortcrust pastry p104)
200g (7oz) plain flour,
   plus extra for dusting
100g (3½oz) unsalted butter,
   plus extra for greasing
1 egg yolk
40g (1½oz) vegetarian Parmesan-style
   cheese or regular Parmesan, grated
salt and freshly ground black pepper
a little milk

FOR THE FILLING
650g (1½lb) broad beans in the pod
   (or 220g/8oz frozen)
200g (7oz) courgettes,
   cut into 1cm (½in) dice
400g (14oz) fresh peas
   (120g/4–4½oz podded weight)
6 egg yolks
150ml (5fl oz) double cream
1 tbsp chopped mint

These savoury tartlets are good served either as an individual portion or as small as you like for a quick and easy canapé. If you are making bite-sized ones, reduce the cooking time accordingly.

APPLE AND CAMEMBERT TARTLETS

 MAKES 4    PREP 10 MINS   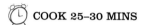 COOK 25–30 MINS

EQUIPMENT
baking tray

INGREDIENTS

FOR THE PASTRY
200g (7oz) ready-made puff pastry
(or to make your own, see pp110–113)
plain flour, for dusting
1 egg yolk, beaten with a little water
1 tsp Dijon mustard

FOR THE FILLING
250g (9oz) Camembert cheese (underripe, if possible), sliced very thinly
4 small dessert apples, such as Cox or Gala, sliced very thinly
salt and freshly ground black pepper

1 Preheat the oven to 200°C (400°F/Gas 6). Roll out the pastry on a lightly floured surface to about 5mm (¼in) thick. Cut out four 15cm (6in) rounds with a saucer or a small plate. Brush the rounds with the egg yolk, and then with the mustard.

2 Lay 2 slivers of the sliced cheese over the pastry bases. If the cheese is too ripe to slice, pinch pieces off between your fingers and dot them over the surface of the pastry, leaving a 2cm (¾in) edge free. Lay the apple slices on top of the cheese in a circular pattern, overlapping them slightly. Season the apple with salt and black pepper and finish the tarts by dotting the remaining cheese over the surface of the apple.

3 Bake for 25–30 minutes until golden brown and puffed up. Cool for 5 minutes before serving.

These rustic pies are practically a national dish in Finland. They are made with rye flour and shaped into rough, hand-finished oval shapes, before being baked and topped with a traditional egg butter.

KARELIAN PIES

 MAKES 8   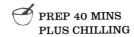 PREP 40 MINS
PLUS CHILLING    COOK 40 MINS

1 Place the flours and salt in a large bowl and add 5–6 tablespoons cold water and mix well, to form a soft dough. Wrap in cling film and chill for 30 minutes.

2 Cook the potatoes in a saucepan of salted, boiling water for 15 minutes, or until tender. Drain, transfer to a food processor, and blend until smooth.

3 Heat the milk in a small pan until warm and add it to the food processor with the egg yolk, season and process until well combined.

4 Place the eggs in a small pan of cold water, bring to the boil and simmer gently for 8 minutes. Remove from the pan, rinse under cold water, and set aside. Preheat the oven to 230°C (450°F/Gas 8) and line the baking trays with baking parchment.

5 On a well-floured surface, divide the dough into 8 equal pieces. Form each piece of dough into a ball and roll it thinly into an oval shape about 10 x 15cm (4 x 6in). Sprinkle each oval with rye flour and cover with a tea towel, to prevent it drying out. Place a mound of the potato purée down the centre of each oval (about 2 dessertspoons), leaving a 2cm (¾in) border all around the edge. Fold the edges of the dough over and pinch them tightly to form an open oval pie.

6 Place the pies on baking trays and brush the pastry and potato with the melted butter. Bake for 10–15 minutes until just starting to turn golden brown. Meanwhile, shell and finely chop the hard-boiled eggs. In a small bowl, cream the butter and stir in the chopped egg. Remove the pies from the oven and cover with a tea towel, so the crust does not harden. Serve the pies warm, topped with the egg butter.

EQUIPMENT
2 baking trays

INGREDIENTS

FOR THE PASTRY
115g (4oz) rye flour,
   plus extra for dusting
25g (scant 1oz) plain flour,
   plus extra for dusting
½ tsp salt

FOR THE FILLING
500g (1lb 2oz) floury potatoes,
   such as Maris Piper, peeled and
   chopped into small chunks
90ml (3fl oz) whole milk
1 egg yolk
40g (1¼oz) butter, melted

FOR THE EGG BUTTER
2 eggs
115g (4oz) butter, softened
salt and freshly ground black pepper

FRUIT PIES AND TARTS

A classic comfort food, for many people apple pie is the taste of home. Lard or white vegetable fat is used here to make the shortcrust pastry, but butter can be easily substituted if desired.

APPLE PIE

 SERVES 6–8   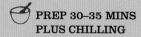 PREP 30–35 MINS PLUS CHILLING   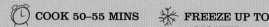 COOK 50–55 MINS   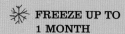 FREEZE UP TO 1 MONTH

EQUIPMENT
23cm (9in) shallow pie dish

INGREDIENTS

FOR THE PASTRY
(For visual step by step instructions
see sweet shortcrust pastry p105)
330g (11oz) plain flour,
plus extra for dusting
½ tsp salt
150g (5½oz) lard or white vegetable fat,
plus extra for greasing
2 tbsp caster sugar,
plus extra for sprinkling
1 tbsp milk, to glaze

FOR THE FILLING
1kg (2¼lb) tart apples
juice of 1 lemon
2 tbsp plain flour
½ tsp ground cinnamon,
or to taste
¼ tsp grated nutmeg,
or to taste
100g (3½oz) caster sugar,
or to taste

1 To make the pastry, sift the flour and salt into a bowl. Add the fat, cutting it in with 2 round-bladed knives, then rub the fat into the flour with your fingertips until the mixture resembles breadcrumbs. Add the sugar. Sprinkle with 6–7 tablespoons cold water. Mix with a fork. Press the crumbs into a ball, wrap and chill for 30 minutes. Grease the dish.

2 Roll out two-thirds of the dough on a floured surface to a circle, 5cm (2in) larger than the dish. Using the rolling pin, drape the pastry over the dish, then gently push it into the contours. Trim any excess pastry, then chill for 15 minutes until firm.

3 Peel, quarter, and core the apples. Set each quarter, cut-side down, on a chopping board and cut into slices, then put them in a bowl and pour on the lemon juice. Toss to coat. Sprinkle over the flour, cinnamon, nutmeg, and sugar and toss to coat. Arrange the apples in the dish so that it is slightly mounded in the centre. Brush the edge of the pastry with water. Roll the rest of the dough to a 28cm (11in) circle. Drape it over the filling and trim the top crust. Press the edges together to seal, crimping with the back of a knife as you go.

4 Cut an "x" in the top crust. Gently pull back the point of each triangle to reveal the filling. Roll out the trimmings, cut into strips, and moisten. Lay on the pie in a criss-cross pattern. Brush the top with the milk, sprinkle over the sugar, and chill for 30 minutes. Preheat the oven to 220°C (425°F/Gas 7).

5 Bake for 20 minutes. Reduce to 180°C (350°F/Gas 4) and bake for 30–35 minutes. Insert a skewer to check the apples are tender. Serve warm.

One of the best known of all desserts, this famous Austrian dish originated in Vienna. It traditionally uses a home-made strudel pastry, but here, filo pastry works just as well and saves time.

APPLE STRUDEL

 SERVES 10–12　　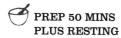 PREP 50 MINS PLUS RESTING　　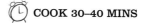 COOK 30–40 MINS

EQUIPMENT
baking tray

INGREDIENTS

FOR THE FILLING
butter, for greasing
1kg (2¼lb) dessert apples,
such as Cox or Braeburn
grated zest of ½ lemon
3 tbsp rum
60g (2oz) raisins
100g (3½ oz) caster sugar
a few drops of pure vanilla extract
60g (2oz) blanched almonds, chopped

FOR THE PASTRY
4 x 25 x 45cm (10 x 18in) sheets filo pastry
(or to make your own strudel pastry,
see pp114–115)
60g (2oz) butter, melted
60–85g (2–3oz) fresh breadcrumbs
icing sugar, for dusting

1 Preheat the oven to 180°C (350°F/Gas 4). Grease a large baking tray. To prepare the apples, peel, core, and cut the apples into small pieces. Choose crisp apples that are not too ripe, to ensure that the strudel does not turn soggy. Don't cut the fruit too small, as they will soften while baking.

2 Place the apple pieces into a bowl and mix together with the lemon zest, rum, raisins, caster sugar, vanilla extract, and chopped almonds.

3 Place a sheet of filo on a clean work surface and brush with a little of the melted butter. Lay another filo sheet on top and brush with more melted butter. Repeat with the remaining pastry sheets.

4 Sprinkle the breadcrumbs over the pastry, leaving a 2cm (¾in) border. Spoon the filling over the breadcrumbs and fold the edges of the short sides that have been left uncovered over the filling. Roll the pastry, starting from one of the longer sides, and press the ends together tightly. Transfer the strudel onto the baking tray and brush with more butter.

5 Bake for 30–40 minutes, brushing the strudel with the remaining melted butter after the first 20 minutes.

6 Remove the strudel from the oven and set aside to cool on the baking tray. Sprinkle liberally with icing sugar and serve warm or cold. This strudel is good served with a spoonful of whipped cream.

Named after the French word for a "louvred shutter", this parcel is slashed to resemble a shutter, revealing the sweet, glistening apple filling inside. For variety, use pears instead of the apples.

APPLE JALOUSIE

 **SERVES 6–8**   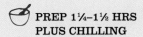 **PREP 1¼–1½ HRS PLUS CHILLING**    **COOK 30–40 MINS**   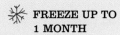 **FREEZE UP TO 1 MONTH**

1 To make the pastry, coarsely grate the butter into a bowl. Sift over the flour and salt and rub together with your fingertips until the mixture resembles coarse breadcrumbs. Pour in 90–100ml (3–3½fl oz) water and the lemon juice, and form a rough dough. Turn the dough out onto a floured surface, work into a ball, then flatten it slightly. Place the dough in a plastic bag and chill for 20 minutes.

2 Thinly roll out the dough on a floured surface to form a long rectangle, with short sides of 25cm (10in). Take one-third of the pastry and fold into the middle. Fold over the remaining third. Turn it over so the joins are easily sealed when it is re-rolled. Give it a quarter turn. Roll out again to a similar size as the original rectangle. Keep the short sides even in size.

3 Repeat the folding, turning, and rolling. Return it to the bag and chill for 20 minutes. Roll, fold, and turn the pastry twice more, then chill for 20 minutes.

4 Melt the butter in a saucepan. Add the apples, ginger, and all but 2 tablespoons of the sugar and sauté and stir for 15–20 minutes until the apples are tender and caramelized. Set aside to cool.

5 Roll out the pastry on a floured surface to 28 x 32cm (11 x 13in), then cut lengthways in half. Fold one half lengthways and cut across the fold at 5mm (¼in) gaps, leaving a border. Place the uncut dough on the baking tray and spoon the apple filling along the centre. Top with the cut dough and chill for 15 minutes. Preheat the oven to 220°C (425°F/Gas 7). Bake for 20–25 minutes. Brush with the egg white to glaze and sprinkle over the remaining sugar. Bake for 10–15 minutes. Serve the slices warm or at room temperature.

EQUIPMENT
baking tray

INGREDIENTS

FOR THE PASTRY
(For visual step by step instructions see quick puff pastry pp112–113)
250g (9oz) unsalted butter, frozen for 30 minutes
250g (9oz) plain flour, sifted, plus extra for dusting
1 tsp salt
1 tsp lemon juice

FOR THE FILLING
15g (½oz) unsalted butter
1kg (2¼lb) tart eating apples, peeled, cored, and diced
2.5cm (1in) fresh root ginger, finely chopped
100g (3½oz) caster sugar
1 egg white, beaten, to glaze

An all-time classic tart, this French dish uses a combination of puréed apple as a filling and finely sliced apple as a topping. Serve with vanilla ice cream for a delicious finale to a Sunday lunch.

TARTE AUX POMMES

 SERVES 8   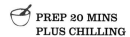 PREP 20 MINS PLUS CHILLING    COOK 1¼ HRS    FREEZE UP TO 1 MONTH

EQUIPMENT
23cm (9in) fluted tart tin, baking beans

INGREDIENTS

FOR THE PASTRY
375g (13oz) ready-made sweet shortcrust pastry (or to make your own, see p105)
plain flour, for dusting
2 tbsp apricot jam, sieved

FOR THE FILLING
50g (1¾oz) butter
750g (1lb 10oz) cooking apples, peeled, cored, and chopped
125g (4½oz) caster sugar
finely grated zest and juice of ½ lemon
2 tbsp Calvados or brandy
2 dessert apples

1 Roll the pastry out on a lightly floured surface and use to line the tart tin. Trim around the top of the tin and prick the bottom of the pastry with a fork. Chill the pastry case for 30 minutes.

2 Preheat the oven to 200°C (400°F/Gas 6). Line the pastry case with greaseproof paper and fill with baking beans. Bake for 15 minutes. Remove the paper and beans, then return to the oven for a further 5 minutes, or until the pastry is a light golden colour.

3 Melt the butter in a saucepan and add the cooking apples. Cover and cook over a low heat, stirring occasionally, for 15 minutes, or until soft and mushy.

4 Push the cooked apple through a sieve to produce a smooth purée, then return it to the pan. Reserve 1 tablespoon caster sugar and add the rest to the apple purée, then stir in the lemon zest and Calvados. Return the pan to the heat and simmer, stirring constantly until it thickens.

5 Spoon the purée into the pastry case. Peel, core, and thinly slice the dessert apples and arrange on top of the purée. Brush with the lemon juice and sprinkle with the reserved caster sugar. Bake for 30–35 minutes until the apple slices have softened and are starting to turn pale golden. Warm the apricot jam and brush it over the top. Cut into slices and serve.

These light, delicate individual tartlets couldn't be easier to make and can be ready in a matter of minutes. Make sure to coat the apple slices with the lemon juice to prevent them discolouring.

APPLE AND ALMOND GALETTES

 MAKES 8   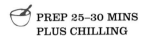 PREP 25–30 MINS PLUS CHILLING   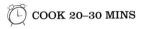 COOK 20–30 MINS

1 Roll out half the pastry on a lightly floured surface to a 35cm (14in) square, about 3mm (⅛in) thick. Using a 15cm (6in) plate as a guide, cut out 4 circles.

2 Sprinkle the baking trays with water. Set the circles on a baking tray, and prick each with a fork, avoiding the edge. Repeat with the remaining dough. Chill for 15 minutes. Divide the marzipan into 8 portions and roll each into a ball.

3 Spread a sheet of baking parchment on the work surface. Set a ball of marzipan on the parchment, and cover with another sheet of parchment. Roll out the marzipan to a 12.5cm (5in) circle between the sheets and set on top of a pastry circle, leaving a border of 1cm (½in). Repeat with the remaining marzipan and pastry circles. Chill until ready to bake.

4 Cut the lemon in half, and squeeze the juice from one half into a small bowl. Peel, halve, and core the apples; then cut into thin slices. Drop the slices into the lemon juice and toss until they are coated.

5 Preheat the oven to 220°C (425°F/Gas 7). Arrange the apple slices, overlapping them slightly, in an attractive spiral over the marzipan circles. Leave a thin border of pastry dough around the edge. Bake for 15–20 minutes until the pastry edges have risen around the marzipan and are light golden. Sprinkle the apples evenly with the granulated sugar.

6 Return to the oven and bake for 5–10 minutes until the apples are golden brown, caramelized around the edges, and tender when tested with the tip of a small knife. Transfer to warmed serving plates, dust with a little icing sugar, and serve at once.

EQUIPMENT
2 baking trays

INGREDIENTS

FOR THE PASTRY
600g (1lb 5oz) ready-made puff pastry (or to make your own, see pp110–113)
plain flour, for dusting
icing sugar, for dusting

FOR THE FILLING
215g (7½oz) marzipan
1 lemon
8 small, tart dessert apples
50g (1¾oz) granulated sugar

This upside-down tart is a true French classic. The caramelized apples give a sweet, tangy flavour to the dish, and the rich sweet pastry helps soak up any of the escaping juices.

APPLE TARTE TATIN

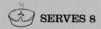 **SERVES 8**   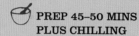 **PREP 45–50 MINS PLUS CHILLING**   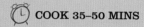 **COOK 35–50 MINS**

EQUIPMENT
23–25cm (9–10in) ovenproof frying pan or tatin dish

INGREDIENTS

FOR THE PASTRY
175g (6oz) plain flour, plus extra for dusting
2 egg yolks
1½ tbsp caster sugar
a pinch of salt
75g (2½oz) unsalted butter, softened

FOR THE FILLING
14–16 apples, total weight about 2.4kg (5¼lb)
1 lemon
125g (4½oz) unsalted butter
200g (7oz) caster sugar

1 To make the pastry, sift the flour into a bowl and make a well in the centre. Add the egg yolks, sugar, salt, butter and 1 tablespoon of water, and using your fingertips, work until mixed. Work in the flour until coarse breadcrumbs form. Press the dough into a ball. On a floured surface, knead the dough for 2 minutes until smooth. Wrap in cling film, and chill in the refrigerator for 30 minutes until firm.

2 For the filling, peel the apples, then halve and core them. Cut the lemon in half, and rub the apples all over with it. Melt the butter in the pan. Add the sugar and stir it together. Cook over a medium heat, stirring occasionally until caramelized. Set aside to cool to tepid.

3 Put the apple in concentric circles to fill the pan and cook over a high heat for 15–25 minutes until caramelized. Turn once. Set aside to cool for 15 minutes. Preheat the oven to 190°C (375°F/Gas 5). Make the tatin (see below). Spoon some caramel over the apples. Serve with crème fraîche.

Constructing the tarte

1 Roll out the pastry to a circle, 2.5cm (1in) larger than the pan. Drape it over the pan.

2 Tuck the edges of the pastry down around the apples and bake for 20–25 minutes until golden.

3 Set aside to cool to tepid, then set a plate on top, hold firmly together, and invert.

A traditional apple and blackberry crumble is given a wholesome twist with the addition of oats to the topping. These help to give the crumble a lovely, chewy texture.

OATY BLACKBERRY AND APPLE CRUMBLE

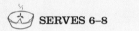 SERVES 6–8   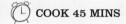 PREP 15–20 MINS    COOK 45 MINS   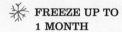 FREEZE UP TO 1 MONTH

1 Preheat the oven to 180°C (350°F/Gas 4). To make the filling, put the apples in the wide, shallow ovenproof dish and add the blackberries. Sprinkle the sugar over the fruit, then cover with foil and bake for 15 minutes just to get the fruit to start to soften.

2 To make the crumble, work the butter and flour together with your fingertips until it resembles breadcrumbs. Add the sugar, then the oats (you could do this in a blender, but add the oats last so they don't get chopped too finely).

3 Remove the fruit from the oven, give it a quick stir, and spread the crumble all over the top. Bake for a further 30 minutes, or until the fruit is oozing out from beneath the golden crumble. Serve immediately with double cream or custard.

EQUIPMENT
2¼ litre (4 pint) ovenproof dish

INGREDIENTS

FOR THE FILLING
1 kg (2¼lb) apples, peeled, cored
  and thickly sliced
350g (12oz) blackberries
60g (2oz) dark muscovado sugar

FOR THE CRUMBLE TOPPING
(For visual step by step instructions
  see crumble topping p121)
125g (4½oz) butter, diced
125g (4½oz) plain flour
140g (5oz) dark muscovado sugar
125g (4½oz) coarse oatmeal
  or porridge oats

Not strictly a pie, but a popular French "pie-like" classic, this recipe is great when eaten as a dessert, warm from the oven with thick cream, but will keep for several days to serve cold.

APPLE TOURTE WITH NUTS AND RAISINS

 SERVES 8    PREP 20 MINS   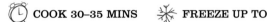 COOK 30–35 MINS    FREEZE UP TO 2 MONTHS

EQUIPMENT
20cm (8in) round springform cake tin

INGREDIENTS

100g (3½oz) unsalted butter, plus extra for greasing
100g (3½oz) caster sugar
1 tsp vanilla extract
2 eggs
150g (5½oz) self-raising flour
1 tsp ground cinnamon
2 dessert apples, peeled, cored, and finely sliced
30g (1oz) raisins
30g (1oz) walnuts, roughly chopped

1 Preheat the oven to 180°C (350°F/Gas 4). Grease and line the bottom of the cake tin. Melt the butter and set aside to cool.

2 Whisk the sugar, vanilla extract, and eggs together in a large bowl. Whisk in the cooled, melted butter until all the ingredients are thoroughly mixed. Sift in the flour and cinnamon, and fold it together well. Finally, fold in the apples, raisins, and walnuts.

3 Pour the mixture into the prepared cake tin and smooth the top. Bake for 30–35 minutes until it is well risen and golden brown, and a skewer inserted into the centre comes out clean.

4 Set the tourte aside to rest for at least 15 minutes before serving warm with whipped cream, or cold as a cake. Best eaten the same day, but can be stored, well wrapped, for up to 2 days.

Depending on whether you bought blackberries or gathered them from the hedgerows, blackberries can vary in taste from very sweet to super-sharp, so taste the filling as you go adding sugar as required.

BLACKBERRY AND APPLE PIE

 SERVES 4–6   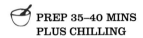 PREP 35–40 MINS PLUS CHILLING   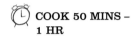 COOK 50 MINS – 1 HR    FREEZE UP TO 1 MONTH

EQUIPMENT
1 litre (1¾ pint) pie dish, pie funnel

INGREDIENTS

FOR THE PASTRY
(For visual step by step instructions see sweet shortcrust pastry p105)
215g (7½oz) plain flour, plus extra for dusting
1½ tbsp caster sugar
¼ tsp salt
45g (1½oz) lard or white vegetable fat, chilled and diced
60g (2oz) unsalted butter, chilled and diced

FOR THE FILLING
875g (1lb 15oz) Granny Smith apples, peeled, cored, and diced
juice of 1 lemon
150g (5½oz) caster sugar, or to taste
500g (1lb 2oz) blackberries

1 To make the pastry, sift the flour, sugar, and salt into a bowl. Add the lard and butter, and rub together with your fingertips until the mixture resembles breadcrumbs. Sprinkle water over the mix, 1 tablespoon at a time, stopping as soon as clumps form; too much water toughens the pastry. Press the dough lightly into a ball, wrap in cling film, and chill for 30 minutes.

2 For the filling, put the apples in a bowl, add the lemon juice and all but 2 tablespoons of sugar and toss until coated. Add the blackberries and toss again.

3 Roll out the dough on a lightly floured surface to a shape 7.5cm (3in) larger than the top of the pie dish. Invert the dish onto the pastry. Cut a 2cm (¾in) strip off the dough, leaving a shape 4cm (1½in) larger than the dish. Turn the pie dish the right way up, place a pie funnel in the centre and spoon the fruit around.

4 Dampen the edge of the dish with water and transfer the strip of pastry, pressing firmly. Brush the strip with cold water and transfer the pastry top, pressing down to seal. Cut a hole over the pie funnel and trim the edges. Chill for 15 minutes.

5 Preheat the oven to 190°C (375°F/Gas 5). Bake for 50–60 minutes until lightly browned and crisp. Sprinkle with the remaining sugar and serve hot or warm. The pastry can be made 2 days ahead and stored in the refrigerator, wrapped in cling film.

The classic autumnal pairing of sweet, soft apples and tart blackberries is given a twist here with a cobbler topping. Add a hint of ground cinnamon or mixed spice for an additional layer of flavour.

APPLE AND BLACKBERRY COBBLER WITH CINNAMON

 SERVES 6–8    PREP 20 MINS   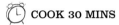 COOK 30 MINS

1 Preheat the oven to 190°C (375°F/Gas 5). For the filling, toss the apples and blackberries in the lemon juice, then mix them together with the 2 types of sugar. Put them in the dish and dot with the butter.

2 To make the cobbler topping, sift the flour, baking powder, caster sugar, salt, and cinnamon into a bowl. Rub in the butter with your fingertips until the mixture resembles fine breadcrumbs. Whisk the egg and buttermilk together in another bowl, then add the liquid to the dry ingredients, and bring it together to form a soft, sticky dough.

3 Drop heaped tablespoonfuls of the dough over the surface of the fruit, leaving a little space between them. Sprinkle with the soft light brown sugar.

4 Bake for 30 minutes, or until golden and bubbling. The cobbler is ready when a skewer inserted into the centre of the topping comes out clean. Set aside to cool for at least 5 minutes before serving with ice cream, custard, or cream.

EQUIPMENT
shallow ovenproof dish

INGREDIENTS

FOR THE FILLING
1kg (2¼lb) apples, peeled, cored
   and roughly chopped
250g (9oz) blackberries
juice of ½ lemon
2 tbsp caster sugar
2 tbsp soft light brown sugar
25g (scant 1oz) unsalted butter,
   chilled and diced

FOR THE COBBLER TOPPING
(For visual step by step instructions
   see cobbler dough pp118–119)
225g (8oz) self-raising flour
2 tsp baking powder
75g (2½oz) caster sugar
a pinch of salt
½–¾ tsp ground cinnamon, to taste
75g (2½oz) unsalted butter
1 egg
100ml (3fl oz) buttermilk
1 tbsp soft light brown sugar

For a warm and satisfying pudding, a simple filling of apples, brown sugar, and spices is topped with a crunchy mix of buttery breadcrumbs and baked until golden. Serve with whipped cream.

APPLE BROWN BETTY

 SERVES 4   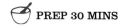 PREP 30 MINS   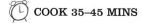 COOK 35–45 MINS

EQUIPMENT
1.2 litre (2 pint) baking dish

INGREDIENTS

FOR THE TOPPING
85g (3oz) butter
175g (6oz) fresh breadcrumbs

FOR THE FILLING
900g (2lb) apples, such as Bramley, Granny Smith, or Golden Delicious
85g (3oz) soft brown sugar
1 tsp ground cinnamon
½ tsp mixed spice
zest of 1 lemon
2 tbsp lemon juice
1 tsp pure vanilla extract

1 Preheat the oven to 180°C (350°F/Gas 4). For the topping, melt the butter in a saucepan, add the breadcrumbs, and mix well.

2 For the filling, peel, quarter, and core the apples. Cut each quarter into slices and place in a bowl. Add the sugar, cinnamon, mixed spice, lemon zest and juice, and vanilla extract, and mix well.

3 Put half the apple mixture into the baking dish. Cover with half the breadcrumbs, then put in the rest of the apples and top with the remaining breadcrumbs.

4 Bake for 35–45 minutes, checking after 35 minutes. If it is getting too brown, reduce the oven temperature to 160°C (325°F/Gas 3) and cover with greaseproof paper. It is cooked when the crumbs are golden brown and the apples are soft. Serve warm.

Here the mellow flavours of pears contrast with the nuttiness of the pastry. Adding ground nuts such as walnuts, hazelnuts, or almonds to a sweet pastry can make an elegant alternative to a simple dessert.

PEAR PIE WITH WALNUT PASTRY

 **SERVES 6–8**   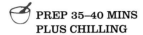 **PREP 35–40 MINS PLUS CHILLING**   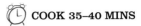 **COOK 35–40 MINS**

1 To make the pastry, finely grind the walnuts with half the sugar in a food processor. Sift the flour onto a surface, add the ground nuts, and make a large well in the centre. Put the egg, remaining sugar, butter, salt, and cinnamon into the well, and using your fingertips, work the ingredients until mixed, then work in the flour until coarse breadcrumbs form. Press the dough into a ball. On a lightly floured surface, knead the dough for 1–2 minutes until very smooth. Form into a ball, wrap, and chill for 30 minutes until firm.

2 Brush the tin with melted butter, then roll out two-thirds of the pastry on a floured surface to a 28cm (11in) circle. Re-wrap and chill the unrolled dough. Line the tin with the rolled-out pastry. Trim off the excess pastry and add the trimmings to the chilled pastry. Press the dough up the side of the tin, then chill in the refrigerator for 1 hour.

3 Peel the pears. Using the tip of a knife, cut out the stalk and flower ends from each pear. Cut each pear into quarters, then scoop out the central stalks and cores, being sure to remove all the hard fibres and working gently to keep the pear quarters intact. Put the pear wedges into a bowl. Add the black pepper and lemon juice, and toss until the pears are coated.

4 Shaking off the excess lemon juice, arrange the pears in a cartwheel pattern on the bottom of the pastry shell. Roll out the dough to a 25cm (10in) circle; stamp out a circle from the centre, using a cutter and drape it over the pears. Trim the excess pastry. Press the dough edges together to seal. Brush with water and sprinkle with sugar. Chill for 15 minutes. Preheat the oven to 190°C (375°F/Gas 5). Heat a baking tray. Bake the pie on the tray for 35–40 minutes until browned.

EQUIPMENT
23cm (9in) loose-bottomed tart tin, 5cm (2in) circle cutter

INGREDIENTS

FOR THE PASTRY
60g (2oz) walnut pieces
135g (4¾oz) caster sugar
250g (9oz) plain flour, plus extra for dusting
1 egg
150g (5½oz) unsalted butter, slightly softened, plus extra for brushing
½ tsp salt
1 tsp ground cinnamon
1 tbsp caster sugar, for sprinkling

FOR THE FILLING
875g (1lb 15oz) pears
½ tsp freshly ground black pepper
juice of 1 lemon

A classic frangipane-filled tart, this recipe hails from Normandy in northern France where they grow the most wonderful pears. Best eaten warm or at room temperature the day it is made.

NORMANDY PEAR TART

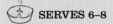 SERVES 6–8   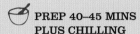 PREP 40–45 MINS PLUS CHILLING    COOK 35–45 MINS    FREEZE UP TO 1 MONTH

1 For the pastry, sift 175g (6oz) flour onto a work surface, make a well in the centre, add 3 egg yolks, 60g (2oz) sugar, salt, 75g (2½oz) butter, and vanilla and mix with your fingertips. Work the flour into the ingredients until the mixture resembles breadcrumbs. If dry, add a little water. On a floured surface, knead for 1–2 minutes. Wrap and chill for 30 minutes. Grease the tin. Roll out the dough on a floured surface to a circle, 5cm (2in) larger than the tin, and use to line the tin. Prick the bottom with a fork. Chill for 15 minutes.

2 Preheat the oven to 200°C (400°F/Gas 6). Grind the almonds to a "flour" in a food processor; prepare the frangipane (see below). Toss the pears with the lemon juice. Spread the frangipane over the pastry; place the pears in a spiral pattern. Set the tin on a baking tray. Bake for 12–15 minutes. Reduce the heat to 180°C (350°F/Gas 4). Bake for 25–30 minutes until set. Melt the jam with the Kirsch, and work it through a sieve. Cool, unmould, then brush with the glaze. Serve warm.

EQUIPMENT
23–25cm (9–10in) loose-bottomed, fluted tart tin

INGREDIENTS

FOR THE PASTRY
175g (6oz) plain flour, plus 2 tbsp extra
3 egg yolks
160g (5½oz) caster sugar
a pinch of salt
200g (7oz) unsalted butter, softened, plus extra for greasing
½ tsp vanilla extract

FOR THE FILLING
125g (4½oz) whole blanched almonds
1 egg, plus 1 egg yolk
3–4 pears, peeled, cored, and cut in wedges
juice of 1 lemon
150g (5½oz) apricot jam
2–4 tbsp Kirsch

For the frangipane

1 With an electric whisk, beat 125g (4½oz) butter and 100g (3½oz) sugar for 2–3 minutes until fluffy.

2 Gradually add 1 egg and the remaining egg yolks, beating well after each addition.

3 Add 1 tablespoon Kirsch, then gently stir in the almonds and remaining flour until well blended.

This may seem like a complicated recipe, but really it's just a few different stages, most of which are prepared ahead. The caramel sauce here is fabulous, and should become a staple recipe of any cook.

FLAKY PEAR TARTLETS

 MAKES 8   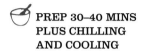 PREP 30–40 MINS PLUS CHILLING AND COOLING    COOK 30–40 MINS

EQUIPMENT
2 baking trays

INGREDIENTS

FOR THE TARTLET BASES
450g (1lb) all-butter puff pastry
(or to make your own, see pp110–113)
plain flour, for dusting
1 egg beaten with ½ tsp salt, to glaze
butter or oil, for greasing
4 pears
juice of 1 lemon
50g (1¾oz) sugar

FOR THE CARAMEL SAUCE
150g (5½oz) caster sugar
125ml (4½fl oz) double cream

FOR THE CHANTILLY CREAM
125ml (4½fl oz) double cream
1–2 tsp icing sugar
½ tsp vanilla extract

1 Sprinkle the baking trays with cold water. Roll out the puff pastry on a lightly floured surface, then cut in half lengthways, then cut diagonally at 10cm (4in) intervals along the length of each piece, to make 8 diamond shapes. Transfer to the prepared baking trays and brush with the glaze. With the tip of a knife, score a border around each. Chill for 15 minutes.

2 Preheat the oven to 220°C (425°F/Gas 7). Bake the cases for 15 minutes until they start to brown, then reduce the temperature to 190°C (375°F/Gas 5) and bake for a further 20–25 minutes until golden and crisp. Transfer to wire racks to cool, then cut out the lid from each case, and scoop out any undercooked pastry from inside.

3 For the caramel sauce, put 125ml (4fl oz) water in a saucepan, and dissolve the sugar. Boil, without stirring, until golden. Reduce the heat. Remove from the heat and add the cream. Heat gently until the caramel dissolves. Set aside to cool.

4 Pour the cream for the Chantilly cream into a bowl and whip until soft peaks form. Add the icing sugar and vanilla extract, and continue whipping until stiff peaks form. Chill in the refrigerator.

5 Grease a baking tray. Preheat the grill. Peel and core the pears. Thinly slice, keeping attached at the stalk end. With your fingers, flatten, transfer to the tray, brush with lemon, and sprinkle with sugar. Grill until caramelized.

6 Place some Chantilly cream and a pear fan in each pastry case. Pour a little cold caramel sauce over each fan, and partially cover with the pastry lids.

Canned pears are one of the few tinned fruits that bake well. Fresh pears can be unpredictable – hard one day, overripe the next. Using a good-quality canned pear means you will have a soft, yielding filling.

PEAR AND ALMOND TART

 SERVES 8   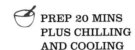 PREP 20 MINS PLUS CHILLING AND COOLING   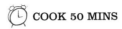 COOK 50 MINS

1 To make the pastry, place the flour, sugar, and orange zest in a food processor. Add the butter and pulse until the mixture resembles breadcrumbs. Add the egg and pulse until the dough gathers in a ball. Roll out the dough on a lightly floured surface and use to line the tart tin. Chill for 30 minutes.

2 Preheat the oven to 190°C (375°F/Gas 5). Place the tart tin on a baking tray, cover the pastry with greaseproof paper, and fill with baking beans. Bake for 10 minutes, then remove the paper and beans, and bake for a further 10 minutes. Cool on a wire rack.

3 Reduce the oven temperature to 160°C (325°F/Gas 3). Mix the mascarpone, sugar, egg, egg yolk, almond extract, and orange juice together until smooth and pour into the tart case. Arrange the pears on top, scatter with the almonds, sprinkle with sugar, and bake for 30 minutes, or until just set.

4 Warm the marmalade through by stirring in a little hot water, sieve it, and gently brush it over the tart. Serve cold. Good with whipped cream or ice cream.

EQUIPMENT
23cm (9in) loose-bottomed tart tin, baking beans

INGREDIENTS

FOR THE PASTRY
(For visual step by step instructions see sweet shortcrust pastry p105)
150g (5½oz) plain flour, plus extra for dusting
60g (2oz) caster sugar
1 tbsp grated orange zest
60g (2oz) butter, chilled and diced
1 egg

FOR THE FILLING
125g (4½oz) mascarpone
100g (3½oz) caster sugar, plus extra for sprinkling
1 egg, plus 1 egg yolk
1 tsp almond extract
2 tbsp fresh orange juice
4 canned pears, drained and sliced
45g (1½oz) almonds, toasted and sliced
2 tbsp marmalade

Although apples are the fruit traditionally used for a Tarte Tatin, pears also work well in this recipe for an upside-down tart topped with sumptuous caramelized fruit. Serve with crème fraîche.

PEAR TARTE TATIN

 **SERVES 8**

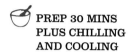 **PREP 30 MINS
PLUS CHILLING
AND COOLING**

 **COOK 45–55 MINS**

EQUIPMENT
23–25cm (9–10in) ovenproof pan
or tarte tatin dish

INGREDIENTS

FOR THE PASTRY
**(For visual step by step instructions
see sweet shortcrust pastry p105)**
**175g (6oz) plain flour,
plus extra for dusting**
2 egg yolks
1½ tbsp caster sugar
a pinch of salt
75g (2½oz) unsalted butter, softened

FOR THE FILLING
125g (4½oz) unsalted butter
200g (7oz) caster sugar
**12–14 pears, total weight
2.4kg (5¼lb), peeled, halved, cored,
and rubbed with lemon halves**

1 To make the pastry, sift the flour into a large bowl and make a well in the centre. Put the egg yolks, sugar, and salt in the well. Add the butter and 1 tablespoon water. Work the ingredients in the well with your fingertips until mixed. Work the flour into the ingredients until the mixture resembles coarse breadcrumbs. Press the dough into a ball. On a floured surface, knead the dough for 2 minutes until smooth. Wrap in cling film and chill for 30 minutes.

2 For the filling, melt the butter in the ovenproof frying pan. Add the sugar and stir together. Cook over a medium heat for 3–5 minutes, stirring, until caramelized to a deep golden brown. Remove the pan from the heat, and set aside to cool.

3 Arrange the pears on their sides in the pan, with the tapered ends towards the centre of the pan. Cook the pears over a high heat for 20–30 minutes until caramelized. Turn once to caramelize on both sides. The pears should be tender but still retain their shape, and very little juice should remain.

4 Remove the pan from the heat and set aside to cool for 10–15 minutes. Preheat the oven to 190°C (375°F/Gas 5). Roll out the pastry on a lightly floured surface to a circle 2.5cm (1in) larger than the pan. Drape it over the pan and tuck the edges around the pears. Bake for 20–25 minutes.

5 Set the tart aside to cool to tepid. Once cooled, set a plate on top, hold together, and invert. Spoon some caramel over the pears. The tart can be baked 6–8 hours ahead and warmed briefly on the hob before unmoulding.

If you have any mincemeat left over after Christmas, try making this easy dessert. Using little more than a good-quality, shop-bought puff pastry, a pear, and a jar of mincemeat, you'll have dessert in minutes.

BOOZY FRUIT AND NUT TURNOVER

 **SERVES 8**   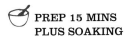 **PREP 15 MINS PLUS SOAKING**   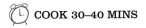 **COOK 30–40 MINS**    **FREEZE UP TO 1 MONTH**

1 Mix the mincemeat with the cherries, apricots, brandy, and orange and lemon zest together in a bowl. Set aside for 30 minutes to soak.

2 Preheat the oven to 200°C (400°F/Gas 6). Lightly grease the baking tray.

3 Lay 1 sheet of pastry on the prepared baking tray, then spoon the mincemeat mixture over, leaving a 2cm (¾in) border around the edges. Top with the pear slices and walnuts, then brush the border with beaten egg. Carefully place the second sheet of pastry on top of the first. Press the edges together, pinching the sides with your finger and thumb to decorate them.

4 Make a few slashes on the top with a knife for the steam to escape. Brush the pastry with the remaining beaten egg and bake for 30–40 minutes until the pastry is golden brown and cooked through.

EQUIPMENT
baking tray

INGREDIENTS

FOR THE FILLING
300g (10oz) mincemeat
50g (1¾oz) glacé cherries, finely chopped
50g (1¾oz) dried apricots, finely chopped
2 tbsp brandy
zest of 1 orange
zest of 1 lemon
oil, for greasing
1 ripe pear, quartered, cored, peeled, and thinly sliced
50g (1¾oz) walnuts, roughly chopped

FOR THE PASTRY
425g (14oz) puff pastry, rolled out into 2 x 28 x 20cm (11 x 8in) sheets (or to make your own, see pp110–113)
1 egg, beaten, to glaze

This recipe is so handy, because it really does make use of whatever fruit you have available. Try mixing a few of the orchard fruits and the soft fruits together to find your favourite combination.

AUTUMN FRUIT TART

 SERVES 6   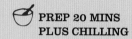 PREP 20 MINS
PLUS CHILLING    COOK 1 HR

EQUIPMENT
20cm (8in) fluted loose-bottomed tart tin, baking beans

INGREDIENTS

FOR THE PASTRY
(For visual step by step instructions see sweet shortcrust pastry p105)
175g (6oz) plain flour, plus extra for dusting
1 tbsp caster sugar
85g (3oz) butter, chilled and diced
1 egg

FOR THE FILLING
4 dessert apples or pears
3 large egg yolks
4 tbsp soft light brown sugar
200ml (7fl oz) double cream
1 tsp vanilla extract
handful of blackberries, stoned plums, or blueberries
1 tsp ground cinnamon
2 tbsp caster sugar

1 To make the pastry, place the flour, sugar, and butter in a food processor and process until the mixture resembles breadcrumbs. To make by hand, rub the butter into the flour with your fingertips until the mixture resembles breadcrumbs. Add the egg and process or bring together with your hands, until it forms a ball. Roll out the pastry on a lightly floured surface and use to line the tin. Using a fork, prick the bottom of the pastry, and chill for 30 minutes.

2 Preheat the oven to 190°C (375°F/Gas 5). Line the pastry case with greaseproof paper, fill with baking beans, and bake for 10 minutes. Remove the paper and beans and return to the oven for a further 10 minutes, then take out and set aside to cool.

3 Meanwhile, for the filling, peel, core, and thinly slice the apples. Whisk together the egg yolks, brown sugar, cream, and vanilla extract. Arrange the apples and other fruits in the pastry case and pour over the cream mixture. Sprinkle the cinnamon and caster sugar over the top and bake for 40–45 minutes, or until set. Set aside to cool in the tin and serve cold.

Using a mixture of vegetable shortening and butter gives this pastry a light, flaky quality. Traditionally, lard or shortening was often the only fat used for shortcrust pastry, but use all butter if you prefer.

VICTORIAN PLUM PIE

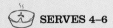 SERVES 4–6   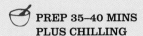 PREP 35–40 MINS PLUS CHILLING   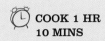 COOK 1 HR 10 MINS   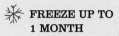 FREEZE UP TO 1 MONTH

1 To make the pastry, sift the flour, sugar, if using, and salt into a bowl. Add the fat and cut into the mixture with 2 round-bladed table knives. Rub in the fat with your fingertips until the mixture resembles breadcrumbs. Sprinkle 3–4 tablespoons water over the mixture, 1 tablespoon at a time, and mix with a fork until the crumbs are moist enough to stick together. Press into a ball, wrap, and chill for 30 minutes.

2 Preheat the oven to 180°C (350°F/Gas 4). Spread the walnut pieces evenly on a baking tray and toast for 8–10 minutes until lightly browned, stirring occasionally so that they colour evenly. Increase the oven temperature to 190°C (375°F/Gas 5).

3 Combine the plums, toasted walnuts, and caster sugar; taste, and add more sugar, if liked. Roll out the dough on a floured surface and trim to an oval 7.5cm (3in) larger than the top of the pie dish. Reserve the trimmings. Invert the pie dish onto the dough and cut a 2cm (¾in) strip from the edge of the dough, leaving an oval 4cm (1½in) larger than the dish. Set the dish, right side up, on the surface. Place the pie funnel in the centre and spoon the filling around it. With a pastry brush, moisten the edge of the dish with water. Lift the strip from around the oval of dough and transfer it to the edge of the dish, pressing it down firmly. Trim and brush the strip with water.

4 Roll up the pastry oval round a rolling pin and unroll it over the filling. Press down to seal. Cut a hole in the pastry over the pie funnel to allow steam to escape. Trim, then re-roll the trimmings and cut out leaves to decorate. Chill for 15 minutes. Meanwhile, preheat the oven to 190°C (375°F/Gas 5). Bake for 50 minutes–1 hour until crisp. Sprinkle with sugar while warm.

EQUIPMENT
1 litre (1¾ pint) oval pie dish,
pie funnel

INGREDIENTS

FOR THE PASTRY
215g (7½oz) plain flour,
   plus extra for dusting
1½ tbsp caster sugar
¼ tsp salt
45g (1½oz) white vegetable shortening,
   chilled and cut into pieces
60g (2oz) unsalted butter, chilled
   and cut into pieces
2 tbsp sugar, for sprinkling

FOR THE FILLING
125g (4½oz) walnut pieces
1.15kg (2½lb) plums,
   cut in half and stoned
100g (3½oz) caster sugar,
   plus more to taste

Brown sugar and cinnamon add a sweet, dark, and spicy flavour to the plum filling. A cobbler topping can be used to cover any fruit suitable for cooking, making it a year-round favourite.

PLUM AND CINNAMON COBBLER

 SERVES 6–8    PREP 20 MINS   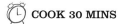 COOK 30 MINS

EQUIPMENT
shallow ovenproof dish

INGREDIENTS

FOR THE FILLING
1kg (2¼lb) plums, stoned and halved
50g (1¾oz) soft light brown sugar
1 tsp ground cinnamon
25g (scant 1oz) unsalted butter, chilled and diced

FOR THE COBBLER TOPPING
(For visual step by step instructions see cobbler dough pp118–119)
225g (8oz) self-raising flour
2 tsp baking powder
75g (2½oz) caster sugar
a pinch of salt
½–¾ tsp ground cinnamon, to taste
75g (2½oz) unsalted butter
1 egg
100ml (3fl oz) buttermilk
1 tbsp soft light brown sugar

1 Preheat the oven to 190°C (375°F/Gas 5). For the filling, toss the plums with the soft light brown sugar and ground cinnamon. Put them in the dish and dot with the diced butter.

2 To make the cobbler topping, sift the flour, baking powder, caster sugar, salt, and cinnamon into a bowl. Rub in the butter until the mixture resembles fine breadcrumbs. Whisk together the egg and buttermilk, then add the liquid to the dry ingredients, and bring it together to form a soft, sticky dough.

3 Drop heaped tablespoons of the dough over the surface of the fruit, leaving a little space between them. Sprinkle with the soft light brown sugar.

4 Bake for 30 minutes, or until golden and bubbling. The cobbler is ready when a skewer inserted into the centre of the topping comes out clean. Set aside to cool, for at least 5 minutes, before serving with ice cream, custard, or cream.

Using a quick brioche base rather than the more usual pastry, this delicious Bavarian speciality rises spectacularly on cooking, so that the soft doughy base encompasses the sweet, ripe plums.

BAVARIAN PLUM TART

 SERVES 8–10   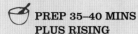 PREP 35–40 MINS
PLUS RISING   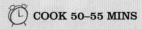 COOK 50–55 MINS

1 Sprinkle or crumble the yeast over 60ml (2fl oz) lukewarm water in a bowl. Let stand for 5 minutes until dissolved. Lightly grease a medium bowl. Sift the flour onto a surface, make a well in the centre, and add the sugar, salt, yeast, and eggs. Using your fingertips, work the ingredients until mixed. Work in the flour to form a soft dough; add more flour if it is too sticky. On a floured surface, knead for 10 minutes until elastic. Work in more flour so that the dough is slightly sticky.

2 Add the butter to the dough; pinch and squeeze to mix it in, then knead until smooth. Shape into a ball and put it into the greased bowl. Cover and chill for 1½–2 hours until doubled in size.

3 Brush the dish with melted butter. Knead the dough to knock out the air, then roll out on a floured surface to a 32cm (13in) circle and use to line the tin. Trim the excess dough. Sprinkle the breadcrumbs over the bottom of the shell. Preheat the oven to 220°C (425°F/Gas 7). Heat a baking tray.

4 Arrange the plums, cut-side up, in concentric circles on the brioche shell. Set aside at room temperature for 30–45 minutes until the edge of the dough is puffed. Whisk the yolks, two-thirds of the sugar, and the cream together. Sprinkle the plums with the remaining sugar and bake the tart on the baking tray for 5 minutes. Reduce the heat to 180°C (350°F/Gas 4). Ladle the custard over the fruit and bake for a further 45–50 minutes until the dough is browned, the fruit is tender, and the custard is set. Serve warm or at room temperature.

EQUIPMENT
28cm (11in) quiche dish

INGREDIENTS

FOR THE TART BASE
1½ tsp dried yeast, or 9g (⅓oz)
  fresh yeast
oil, for greasing
375g (13oz) plain flour,
  plus extra for dusting
2 tbsp caster sugar
1 tsp salt
3 eggs
125g (4½oz) unsalted butter, softened,
  plus extra for brushing

FOR THE FILLING
2 tbsp dried breadcrumbs
875g (1lb 15oz) purple plums,
  stoned and cut in half
2 egg yolks
100g (3½oz) caster sugar
60ml (2fl oz) double cream

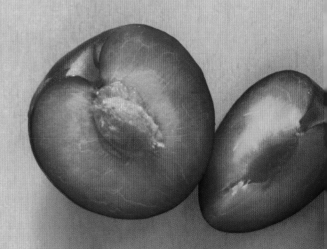

This perennial favourite never fails to delight family and friends. Make double or triple quantity of the crumble topping and store it in a plastic food bag in the freezer for last-minute puddings.

PLUM CRUMBLE

 SERVES 4   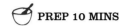 PREP 10 MINS   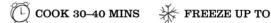 COOK 30–40 MINS    FREEZE UP TO 2 MONTHS

EQUIPMENT
medium ovenproof dish

INGREDIENTS

FOR THE CRUMBLE TOPPING
(For visual step by step instructions
see crumble topping p121)
150g (5½oz) plain flour
100g (3½oz) butter, chilled and diced
75g (2½oz) light soft brown sugar
60g (2oz) rolled oats

FOR THE FILLING
600g (1lb 5oz) plums, stoned and halved
maple syrup or honey, to drizzle

1 Preheat the oven to 200°C (400°F/Gas 6). To make the crumble topping, place the flour in a large bowl and rub in the butter with your fingertips until the mixture resembles breadcrumbs. Do not make the breadcrumbs too fine or your crumble will have a stodgy top. Stir in the sugar and oats.

2 Place the plums in the ovenproof dish, drizzle the maple syrup over, and top with the crumble mixture. Bake for 30–40 minutes until the top is golden brown and the plum juices are bubbling. Serve hot. The crumble mixture can be made 1 month in advance and stored in the freezer until ready to use.

In France, all types of fruits are used to offset this rich, buttery pastry and frangipane filling. Early summer could bring peaches, while autumn heralds pear or prune variations.

NORMANDY PEACH TART

 SERVES 6–8   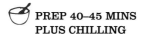 PREP 40–45 MINS PLUS CHILLING    COOK 35–45 MINS

1 Roll the pastry out on a lightly floured surface and use to line the tart tin. Trim around the top of the tin and prick the bottom of the pastry with a fork. Chill the pastry case for 30 minutes.

2 Preheat the oven to 200°C (400°F/Gas 6). Line the pastry case with greaseproof paper and fill with baking beans. Bake for 15 minutes. Remove the paper and beans, then return to the oven for a further 5 minutes, or until the pastry is a light golden colour.

3 Put a baking tray inside the oven to heat up. For the frangipane, grind the almonds to a "flour" in a food processor. Put the butter and sugar in a large bowl and whisk until fluffy. Add the egg and egg yolk and beat well. Add the Kirsch, then stir in the almonds and flour. Spoon the mixture into the prepared pastry case.

4 Immerse the peaches in a saucepan of boiling water, leave for 10 seconds, then transfer to a bowl of cold water. Cut each peach in half, remove the stone, and peel off the skin. Cut each half into thin slices and arrange on the frangipane.

5 Set the tin on the preheated baking tray and bake for 12–15 minutes. Reduce the oven temperature to 180°C (350°F/Gas 4) and bake for a further 25–30 minutes until the frangipane is puffed up and set. Set aside to cool.

6 Make a glaze by melting the jam with the extra Kirsch in a small saucepan, then push the mixture through a sieve. Unmould the tart, then brush with the glaze. The tart is best eaten the same day but can be kept for 2 days in an airtight container.

EQUIPMENT
23–25cm (9–10in) loose-bottomed tart tin, baking beans

INGREDIENTS

FOR THE FILLING
125g (4½oz) whole blanched almonds
125g (4½oz) unsalted butter, at room temperature
100g (3½oz) caster sugar
1 egg, plus 1 egg yolk
1 tbsp Kirsch
2 tbsp plain flour, sifted
1kg (2¼lb) ripe peaches

FOR THE PASTRY
375g (13oz) ready-made sweet shortcrust pastry (or to make your own, see p105)
plain flour, for dusting
150g (5½oz) apricot jam
2–3 tbsp Kirsch, to glaze

Here the peaches are gently poached for a few minutes before assembling the cobbler, which helps to break them down on cooking. Really ripe, juicy peaches will need no such help.

PEACH COBBLER

 SERVES 6–8   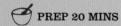 PREP 20 MINS   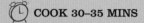 COOK 30–35 MINS

EQUIPMENT
shallow ovenproof dish

INGREDIENTS

FOR THE FILLING
50g (1¾oz) caster sugar
8 ripe peaches, peeled, stoned, and quartered
1 tsp cornflour
juice of ½ lemon

FOR THE COBBLER TOPPING
(For visual step by step instructions see cobbler dough pp118–119)
225g (8oz) self-raising flour
2 tsp baking powder
75g (2½oz) caster sugar
a pinch of salt
½–¾ tsp ground cinnamon, to taste
75g (2½oz) unsalted butter
1 egg
100ml (3fl oz) buttermilk
1 tbsp soft light brown sugar

1 Preheat the oven to 190°C (375°F/Gas 5). For the filling, heat the sugar and 3–4 tablespoons water in a large, heavy-based saucepan. Once the sugar has dissolved, add the quartered peaches, cover, and cook over a medium heat for 2–3 minutes.

2 Mix the cornflour with the lemon juice to make a paste, then add it to the peaches. Continue to cook uncovered, over a low heat until the liquid thickens around the peaches. Transfer the peaches and syrup to the ovenproof dish.

3 To make the cobbler topping, sift the flour, baking powder, sugar, salt, and cinnamon into a large bowl. Rub in the butter with your fingertips until the mixture resembles fine breadcrumbs. Whisk together the egg and buttermilk in a separate bowl. Add the liquid to the dry ingredients and bring together to form a soft, sticky dough.

4 Drop heaped tablespoons of the dough over the surface of the fruit, leaving a little space between them. Sprinkle with the brown sugar. Bake for 25–30 minutes until golden and bubbling. It is ready when a skewer inserted into the centre of the topping comes out clean. Set aside to cool for 5 minutes before serving with ice cream, custard, or cream.

Choose perfectly ripe peaches to make this classic American pie. In the United States, cornflour is often used to thicken the juices that the fruit yields up on cooking, but plain flour can also be used.

PEACH PIE

 **SERVES 8**

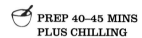 **PREP 40–45 MINS PLUS CHILLING**

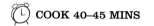 **COOK 40–45 MINS**

 **FREEZE UP TO 1 MONTH**

EQUIPMENT
23cm (9in) round pie tin

INGREDIENTS

FOR THE PASTRY
(For visual step by step instructions see shortcrust pastry p104)
250g (9oz) plain flour,
plus extra for dusting
½ tsp salt
125g (4½oz) lard or white
vegetable fat, chilled
75g (2½oz) unsalted butter, chilled
1 egg, lightly beaten
with ½ tsp salt, to glaze

FOR THE FILLING
4–5 ripe peaches
30g (1oz) plain flour
150g (5½oz) granulated sugar
salt
1–2 tbsp lemon juice, to taste

1 To make the pastry, sift the flour and salt into a bowl. Dice the lard and butter, and rub into the flour with your fingertips until the mixture resembles breadcrumbs. Sprinkle with 3 tablespoons water and bring together to form a soft dough. Wrap in cling film and chill in the refrigerator for 30 minutes.

2 Preheat the oven to 200°C (400°F/Gas 6). Put a baking tray inside to heat. Roll out two-thirds of the pastry on a floured surface and use to line the tin, making sure it overlaps the sides. Press the dough into the dish and chill for 15 minutes.

3 Immerse the peaches in boiling water for 10 seconds, then transfer to a bowl of cold water. Halve the peaches, remove the stones, and peel off the skins. Cut into 1cm (½in) slices and put it in a large bowl.

4 Sprinkle the peaches with the flour, sugar, a pinch of salt, and lemon juice, to taste. Carefully stir the peaches until they are coated, then transfer them to the pastry case, in the pie tin, with their juices.

5 Roll out the remaining dough into a rectangle. Cut out 8 strips, each 1cm (½in) wide and arrange them in a lattice-like pattern on top of the pie, then trim the pastry. Lightly beat the egg and ½ teaspoon salt together in a small bowl, and use to glaze the pie.

6 Bake for 40–45 minutes until the pastry is golden brown, and the peaches are soft and bubbling. Serve warm. The pie can be kept in an airtight container for 2 days, but it is really best eaten on the day it is baked.

When peaches are plentiful, this Almond and Peach Tart is a fabulous dessert for entertaining. Making your own frangipane is easy, and you can vary the soft fruits you use according to the season.

ALMOND AND PEACH TART

 SERVES 8   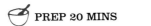 PREP 20 MINS   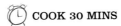 COOK 30 MINS

1 Preheat the oven to 200°C (400°F/Gas 6) and put a baking tray inside to heat up. Roll out the pastry on a lightly floured surface to about 5mm (¼in) thick, then use it to line the tart tin. Trim away any excess pastry and set the pastry case aside.

2 To make the filling, place the butter and sugar in a large bowl and whisk with an electric hand whisk until creamy, then beat in the eggs. Mix in the ground almonds and flour until well combined, then smooth the mixture into the pastry case.

3 Press the peach halves cut-side down into the almond mixture. Sit the tin on the hot baking tray, then bake for 30 minutes, or until the almond mixture is golden brown and cooked through. Serve cold or warm, dusted with icing sugar.

EQUIPMENT
12 x 36cm (5 x 14½in) tart tin

INGREDIENTS

FOR THE PASTRY
250g (7oz) ready-made shortcrust pastry
  (or to make your own, see p105)
flour, for dusting
icing sugar, for dusting

FOR THE FILLING
100g (3½oz) butter, at room temperature
100g (3½oz) caster sugar
2 large eggs
100g (3½oz) ground almonds
25g (scant 1oz) plain flour
4 peaches, halved and stoned

This beautiful fruit tart looks like the kind of thing that's only found in the best pâtisserie shop. However, with some good ingredients and a little patience, it is simple to re-create at home.

EXOTIC FRUIT TART

 **SERVES 8**

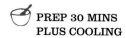 **PREP 30 MINS PLUS COOLING**

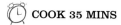 **COOK 35 MINS**

EQUIPMENT
24cm (9½in) loose-bottomed fluted tart tin, baking beans

INGREDIENTS

FOR THE PASTRY
270g (9½oz) ready-made filo pastry (6 x 26 x 44cm/10 x 17in sheets)
45g (1½oz) unsalted butter, melted

FOR THE FILLING
100g (3½oz) dark chocolate with ginger
300ml (10fl oz) double cream
250g (9oz) mascarpone cheese
200g (7oz) raspberries
1–2 tbsp raspberry liqueur
3 pieces stem ginger preserved in syrup, drained and finely chopped
1 tbsp stem ginger syrup, plus extra for drizzling
150g (5½oz) fresh pineapple slices
1 kiwi fruit, sliced
60g (2oz) fresh mango pieces

1 Preheat the oven to 200°C (400°F/Gas 6). Place a sheet of filo pastry in the tart tin with the edges hanging over the sides. Brush it generously with melted butter and place another sheet of pastry across the first, so they form a cross shape in the bottom. Brush with more butter. Repeat the pastry layers, until all the pastry is used up and the bottom of the tin is completely covered. Roughly trim the edges, so they are overhanging by about 1cm (½in).

2 Place the tin on a baking sheet, line with baking parchment, and fill with baking beans. Bake for 20 minutes, then remove the beans and paper and bake for a further 5 minutes, or until the pastry is cooked and golden brown. Set aside to cool in the tin, then remove from the tin and place on a serving plate.

3 For the filling, melt the chocolate in a heatproof bowl over a saucepan of simmering water. Spoon the melted chocolate into the pastry case and spread it over the bottom in an even layer with the back of a spoon. Whip the cream in a large bowl and stir in the mascarpone. Add half the raspberries and crush them with the back of a spoon. Stir in the liqueur to taste, chopped ginger, and syrup.

4 Just before serving, spoon the raspberry and ginger cream into the pastry case. Arrange the pineapple slices around the edge of the tart, followed by the kiwi slices, and then the mango pieces. Place a raspberry in the centre of the tart and in any spaces between the fruit, in a symmetrical pattern. Drizzle a little ginger syrup over the fruit, to serve.

For a tropical twist on a classic Tarte Tatin, try substituting the apples for slices of mango. These delicious tartlets make a quick dessert for entertaining, especially when mangoes are in season.

CARAMELIZED MANGO TARTLETS

 MAKES 6   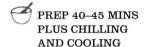 PREP 40–45 MINS PLUS CHILLING AND COOLING   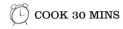 COOK 30 MINS

1 To make the pastry, combine the yolks and vanilla. In a food processor, pulse the flour, sugar, and salt for 5 seconds. Add the butter and pulse until the mixture resembles coarse breadcrumbs. Add the egg yolks, and work until the mixture resembles peas. If dry, work in 1–2 tablespoons water. On a floured surface, knead the dough until smooth. Chill for 30 minutes.

2 Gently heat the sugar and 125ml (4fl oz) water in a saucepan until dissolved. Boil, without stirring, until the mixture starts to turn golden around the edge. Reduce the heat and cook, swirling the pan once or twice so the syrup colours evenly, until the caramel is medium golden. Immediately plunge the pan into a bowl of cold water. Pour one-sixth of the caramel into the bottom of the baking dishes, tilting the dishes to coat with a thin layer. Set aside to cool.

3 Peel and cut each mango lengthways on both sides of the stone. Cut the remaining flesh away from each stone in 2 long slices, and set aside. Discard the stones. Cut each of the large pieces of mango into 3 diagonal slices. Arrange 3 slices, cut-side up, on top of the caramel in the dishes.

4 Preheat the oven to 200°C (400°F/Gas 6). On a floured surface, shape the dough into a cylinder about 30cm (12in) long and cut it into 6 equal pieces. Shape each piece into a ball and roll them out to 6 x 12cm (5in) circles. Drape the circles over the dishes and tuck the edge down around the mango slices. Chill for 15 minutes. Bake for 20–25 minutes until golden.

5 Purée the reserved mango in a food processor. Stir in the lime juice, taste, and add more icing sugar or juice. Chill and serve with the tartlets out of their dishes.

EQUIPMENT
6 x 10cm (4in) baking dishes

INGREDIENTS

FOR THE PASTRY
(For visual step by step instructions see sweet shortcrust pastry p105)
3 egg yolks
½ tsp vanilla extract
215g (7½oz) plain flour, plus extra for dusting
60g (2oz) caster sugar
¼ tsp salt
90g (3oz) unsalted butter, cut into pieces

FOR THE FILLING
200g (7oz) caster sugar
4 mangoes, total weight about 1.5kg (3lb 3oz)
juice of ½ lime, or to taste
1–2 tbsp icing sugar (optional)

This classic French tart is filled with a delicate custard and juicy apricots. Canned apricots are often more reliable than fresh ones, but if you have some ripe apricots do use them instead.

APRICOT TART

 SERVES 6–8   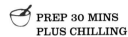 PREP 30 MINS PLUS CHILLING   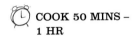 COOK 50 MINS – 1 HR    FREEZE PASTRY CASE, UP TO 3 MONTHS

1 To make the pastry, rub the flour, sugar, and butter together by hand, or in a food processor, until the mixture resembles fine breadcrumbs. Add the egg yolk and bring the mixture together to form a soft dough. Add a little more water if needed. Wrap and chill for 30 minutes. Preheat the oven to 180°C (350°F/Gas 4).

2 Roll out the pastry on a floured surface to 3mm (⅛in) thick and use to line the tart tin, leaving an overhang of at least 1cm (½in). Trim off any excess pastry that hangs down further than this. Prick the bottom with a fork, brush with the egg white to seal, line the pastry case with a piece of silicone or greaseproof paper, and fill with baking beans. Place the case on a baking tray and bake for 20 minutes. Remove the beans and paper, and bake for a further 5 minutes, if the centre looks uncooked. Trim off any ragged edges from the pastry case while still warm.

3 Whisk the cream, sugar, eggs, egg yolk, and vanilla together in a large bowl. Lay the apricots, face down, evenly over the bottom of the cooked tart case. Place the tart case on a baking tray and pour the cream mixture carefully over the fruit. Bake for 30–35 minutes until lightly golden and just set. Set the tart aside to cool to room temperature before dusting with icing sugar and serving with fresh cream.

EQUIPMENT
22cm (9in) loose-bottomed tart tin, baking beans

INGREDIENTS

FOR THE PASTRY
(For visual step by step instructions see sweet shortcrust pastry p105)
175g (6oz) plain flour,
plus extra for dusting
25g (scant 1oz) caster sugar
100g (3½oz) unsalted butter,
at room temperature, cut into pieces
1 egg yolk, beaten with 2 tbsp cold water,
plus 1 egg white, for brushing

FOR THE FILLING
200ml (7fl oz) double cream
50g (1¾oz) caster sugar
2 eggs, plus 1 egg yolk
½ tsp vanilla extract
400g tin apricot halves, drained
icing sugar, for dusting

Heady with the aroma of warming spices, these fruity parcels are best eaten warm, or at room temperature. Dust them with some cinnamon-laced icing sugar before serving with vanilla ice cream.

FILO APRICOT TURNOVERS

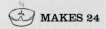 MAKES 24   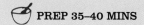 PREP 35–40 MINS   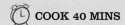 COOK 40 MINS   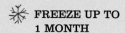 FREEZE UP TO 1 MONTH

EQUIPMENT
baking tray

INGREDIENTS

FOR THE FILLING
1 lemon
500g (1lb 2oz) apricots, stoned, halved, and cut into 4–5 pieces
200g (7oz) caster sugar
1 tsp ground cinnamon
a pinch of ground nutmeg
a pinch of ground cloves

FOR THE PASTRY
500g (1lb 2oz) ready-made filo sheets
175g (6oz) unsalted butter

1 For the filling, grate the zest from half of the lemon. In a medium saucepan, combine the apricots, lemon zest, 150g (5½oz) sugar, cinnamon, nutmeg, and cloves. Add 2 tablespoons water and cook gently for 20–25 minutes, stirring occasionally, until the mixture thickens to the consistency of jam. Transfer to a bowl and set aside to cool. Preheat the oven to 200°C (400°F/Gas 6).

2 Lay a tea towel on the work surface and sprinkle it lightly with water. Unroll the filo pastry and cut them lengthways in half. Cover them with a second damp towel. Melt the butter in a small pan. Take one half sheet of filo and and lightly brush half of it lengthways with butter. Fold the other half on top.

3 Brush the strip of dough with more melted butter. Spoon 1–2 teaspoons of the cooled apricot filling onto it, about 2.5cm (1in) from one end. Fold a corner of the filo strip over the filling to meet the other edge of filo, forming a triangle. Continue folding the strip over and over to form a triangle with the filling inside. Set the triangle with the final edge underneath, and cover with a dampened tea towel.

4 Continue making the filo triangles. Brush the top of each triangle with the rest of the melted butter and sprinkle with the remaining sugar. Bake for 12–15 minutes until golden brown and flaky. Transfer the turnovers to the rack to cool slightly, and serve warm or at room temperature. The filo turnovers can be prepared up to 2 days in advance and kept in the refrigerator. Bake just before serving.

This traditional German tart shares a common base of flavours with the great British classic, Bakewell Tart. The tart can be stored in an airtight container for up to 2 days; the flavour will mellow.

ALMOND AND RASPBERRY LATTICE TART

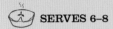 SERVES 6–8   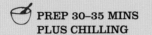 PREP 30–35 MINS PLUS CHILLING   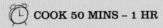 COOK 50 MINS – 1 HR

1 Sift the flour into a bowl. Mix in the spices and nuts, and make a well. Mix the butter, yolk, 100g (3½oz) sugar, salt, zest, and juice with your fingertips, add to the well, and work in the flour until breadcrumbs form. Shape into a ball, knead, wrap, and chill for 1–2 hours.

2 Cook the rest of the sugar and berries in a saucepan for 10–12 minutes until thick. Cool. Press half of the fruit through a sieve. Stir in the remaining pulp. Grease the tin. Preheat the oven to 190°C (375°F/Gas 5).

3 Roll out two-thirds of the dough on a floured surface into a 28cm (11in) circle and line the tin. Trim any excess pastry and add the filling in the case. Roll the remaining pastry to a 15 x 30cm (6 x 12in) rectangle for the lattice top (see below). Bake for 15 minutes, reduce to 180°C (350°F, Gas 4), and bake for 25–30 minutes. Cool and dust with icing sugar to serve.

EQUIPMENT
23cm (9in) loose-bottomed tart tin, fluted pastry wheel (optional)

INGREDIENTS

FOR THE PASTRY
125g (4½oz) plain flour,
  plus extra for dusting
a pinch of cloves and ⅛tsp ground cinnamon
175g (6oz) ground almonds
125g (4½oz) butter, plus extra for greasing
1 egg yolk
225g (8oz) caster sugar
¼ tsp salt
grated zest of 1 lemon and juice of ½ lemon

FOR THE FILLING
375g (13oz) raspberries

For the lattice top

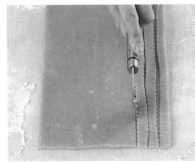

1 Using a fluted wheel, for a decorative edge, cut the dough into 12 x 1cm (12 x ½in) strips.

2 Arrange half the strips from left to right over the tart, 2.5cm (1in) apart. Turn the tart 45°.

3 Put strips diagonally over. Trim, re-roll trimmings, cut 4 strips, fix to edge, and chill for 15 minutes.

This dainty tart is perfect for afternoon tea. The usual custard filling is replaced by a mixture of cream cheese and soured cream – a perfect foil for the sharp sweetness of the raspberries.

RASPBERRY CREAM CHEESE TART

 SERVES 8   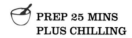 PREP 25 MINS
                                        PLUS CHILLING   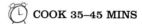 COOK 35–45 MINS

EQUIPMENT
23cm (9in) loose-bottomed
tart tin, baking beans

INGREDIENTS

FOR THE PASTRY
**(For visual step by step instructions
see sweet shortcrust pastry p105)**
175g (6oz) plain flour,
plus extra for dusting
85g (3oz) butter, diced
2 tbsp caster sugar
1 egg yolk

FOR THE FILLING
115g (4oz) cream cheese
60g (2oz) soured cream
60g (2oz) caster sugar
a pinch of grated nutmeg
3 eggs, beaten
zest of 1 lemon
350g (12oz) raspberries
icing sugar, for dusting

1 To make the pastry, place the flour, butter, and sugar in a food processor, and pulse until it resembles breadcrumbs. Alternatively, to make by hand, rub the butter into the flour with your fingertips until it resembles breadcrumbs, then stir in the sugar.

2 Add the egg yolk to the mixture and mix to a firm dough. Roll out the dough on a lightly floured surface and use to line the tin. Prick the bottom of the pastry with a fork and chill for 30 minutes. Preheat the oven to 200°C (400°F/Gas 6).

3 Line the pastry case with greaseproof paper and fill with baking beans. Bake for 10 minutes, then remove the paper and beans and bake for a further 10 minutes, or until pale golden. Remove from the oven and reduce the temperature to 180°C (350°F/Gas 4).

4 For the filling, beat together the cream cheese, soured cream, sugar, nutmeg, eggs, and lemon zest until well combined. Pour into the pastry case and scatter the raspberries over the surface. Bake for 25–30 minutes, or until just set. Set aside to cool before transferring to a serving plate. Serve warm or cold, dusted with icing sugar.

Fresh raspberries and dark chocolate are a classic combination and here they combine to make the ultimate in luxurious desserts. Try to use the best-quality dark chocolate that you can find.

RASPBERRY TART WITH CHOCOLATE CREAM

 SERVES 6–8   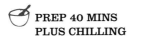 PREP 40 MINS PLUS CHILLING    COOK 20–25 MINS   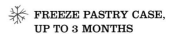 FREEZE PASTRY CASE, UP TO 3 MONTHS

1 To make the pastry, rub the flour, cocoa, and butter together with your fingertips until they resemble fine breadcrumbs. Stir in the sugar. Beat the egg yolk with the vanilla and add to the flour mixture, bringing it together to form a soft dough. Add a little water if it seems too stiff. Wrap and chill for 30 minutes.

2 Preheat the oven to 180°C (350°F/Gas 4). Roll out the pastry on a lightly floured surface to 3mm (⅛in) thick and use to line the tin. Leave an overlapping edge of 2cm (¾in), and trim the excess with scissors. Prick the bottom of the pastry with a fork, then line the pastry case with baking parchment and fill with baking beans. Place on a baking tray and bake for 20 minutes. Remove the beans and paper, and bake for a further 5 minutes. Trim the excess pastry.

3 For the filling, beat together the sugar, cornflour, eggs, and vanilla. Put the milk and 100g (3½oz) of the chocolate in a saucepan and bring to the boil, whisking constantly. Remove just as it starts to bubble. Pour the milk onto the egg mixture, whisking constantly. Return to the cleaned-out pan and bring to the boil, whisking. When it thickens, reduce the heat to its lowest and cook for 2–3 minutes, whisking. Turn into a bowl, cover with cling film, and cool.

4 Melt the remaining chocolate in a bowl set over a pan of simmering water, and brush the inside of the tart case. Leave aside to set. Beat the crème pâtissière with a wooden spoon, and spread over the case. Arrange the raspberries over, remove from the tin, and serve dusted with icing sugar. Best eaten the same day.

EQUIPMENT
22cm (9in) loose-bottomed tart tin, baking beans

INGREDIENTS

FOR THE PASTRY
(For visual step by step instructions see sweet shortcrust pastry p105)
130g (4½oz) plain flour, plus extra for dusting
20g (¾oz) cocoa powder
100g (3½oz) unsalted butter, chilled and diced
50g (1¾oz) caster sugar
1 egg yolk
½ tsp vanilla extract

FOR THE FILLING
100g (3½oz) caster sugar
50g (1¾oz) cornflour, sifted
2 eggs
1 tsp vanilla extract
450ml (15fl oz) whole milk
175g (6oz) good-quality dark chocolate, broken into pieces
400g (14oz) raspberries
icing sugar, for dusting

For a simple yet tasty alternative to a shortcrust pastry case, try making these biscuit-based crusts instead. Make a few extra and freeze the rest for an instant dessert another time.

RASPBERRY TARTLETS WITH CRÈME PÂTISSIÈRE

 MAKES 6

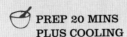 PREP 20 MINS PLUS COOLING

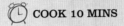 COOK 10 MINS

❄ FREEZE TART CASES, UP TO 2 MONTHS

1 Preheat the oven to 180°C (350°F/Gas 4). To make the base, crush the biscuits in a food processor, or by hand using a rolling pin, until they resemble fine breadcrumbs. Mix the biscuit crumbs, sugar, and melted butter, until the mixture resembles wet sand.

2 Divide the biscuit mixture between the tartlet tins and press it firmly into the bottom of each tin, allowing it to come up the sides as it spreads out. Bake for 10 minutes then set aside to cool. Once cooled, store the tart cases in the refrigerator until needed.

3 For the crème pâtissière, beat together the sugar, cornflour, eggs, and vanilla extract in a bowl. In a saucepan, bring the milk to the boil, and remove from the heat just as it starts to bubble up. Pour the hot milk onto the egg mixture, whisking constantly. Return the custard to the pan, and bring to the boil, whisking constantly to prevent lumps. As the custard heats it will thicken considerably. At this point reduce the heat to low and cook for a further 2–3 minutes.

4 Turn the thickened crème pâtissière out into a bowl, cover the surface of it with cling film (to prevent a skin forming), and set it aside to cool. Once it is cold, beat it well with a wooden spoon before use.

5 When you are ready to assemble the tartlets, spoon, or pipe, the crème patisserie into the cases. Top with raspberries, and dust with icing sugar to serve. The tart cases can be chilled for up to 3 days, and the crème patisserie for up to 2 days, well covered.

EQUIPMENT
6 x 10cm (4in) loose-bottomed tartlet tins

INGREDIENTS

FOR THE BISCUIT CASE
(For visual step by step instructions
  see biscuit case p120)
200g (7oz) digestive or Breton biscuits
50g (1¾oz) caster sugar
100g (3½oz) butter, melted and cooled

FOR THE FILLING
100g (3½oz) caster sugar
40g (1½oz) cornflour
2 eggs
1 tsp vanilla extract
400ml (14fl oz) whole milk
raspberries
icing sugar,
  for dusting

A great stand-by dessert, this Italian favourite is little more than a large jam tart decorated with a pastry top. Use whatever jam you have available, and try making individual ones for children.

CROSTATA DI MARMELLATA

 **SERVES 6–8**   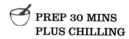 **PREP 30 MINS PLUS CHILLING**    **COOK 50 MINS**   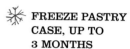 **FREEZE PASTRY CASE, UP TO 3 MONTHS**

EQUIPMENT
22cm (9in) loose-bottomed tart tin, baking beans

INGREDIENTS

FOR THE PASTRY
(For visual step by step instructions see sweet shortcrust pastry p105)
175g (6oz) plain flour,
plus extra for dusting
100g (3½oz) unsalted butter,
chilled and diced
50g (1¾oz) caster sugar
1 egg yolk, plus 1 egg, beaten, to glaze
2 tbsp milk, plus extra if needed
½ tsp vanilla extract

FOR THE FILLING
450g (1lb) good-quality raspberry, cherry, or apricot jam

1 To make the pastry, rub the flour and butter together with your fingertips until fine breadcrumbs form. Stir in the sugar. Beat the egg yolk with the milk and vanilla extract, and add it to the dry ingredients, bringing the mixture together to form a soft dough. Use an extra tablespoon of milk if the mixture seems a little dry. Wrap in cling film and chill for 30 minutes.

2 Preheat the oven to 180°C (350°F/Gas 4). Roll out the pastry on a well-floured surface to 3mm (⅛in) thick. If it begins to crumble, bring it together again with your hands and gently knead to get rid of any joins. Line the tin with the pastry, leaving an overlapping edge of 2cm (¾in) and trim away any excess pastry. Prick the bottom of the pastry with a fork, then roll up the excess and chill for later use.

3 Line the pastry case with baking parchment and fill with baking beans. Place it on a baking tray and bake for 20 minutes. Remove the beans and paper, and bake for a further 5 minutes if the centre still looks uncooked. Increase the heat to 200°C (400°F/Gas 6).

4 Spread the jam in a 1–2cm (½–¾in) layer over the pastry case. Roll out the remaining pastry into a square just larger than the tart and 3mm (⅛in) thick. Cut the pastry into 12 strips, each 1cm (½in) wide, and use these to top the tart in a lattice-like pattern.

5 Use beaten egg to secure the strips to the sides of the tart and to gently brush the lattice. Bake for 20–25 minutes until the lattice is cooked through and golden brown on top. Cool for 10 minutes before eating. Serve while still warm or at room temperature. The tart will keep in an airtight container for 2 days.

Strawberry shortbread is another favourite dessert, but by making the shortbread into a pastry the filling is better contained for a more elegant finish. Try this with raspberries when they are in season.

STRAWBERRIES AND CREAM SHORTBREAD TARTLETS

 MAKES 4   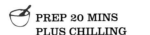 **PREP 20 MINS PLUS CHILLING**    **COOK 15–20 MINS**    **FREEZE UP TO 2 MONTHS**

1 To make the pastry, mix the flour, cornflour, and caster sugar together in a large bowl until well combined. Rub in the butter with your fingertips until the mixture resembles breadcrumbs, then bring the mixture together to form a soft dough. Wrap in cling film and chill for 30 minutes.

2 Preheat the oven to 170°C (325°F/Gas 3). Roll out the pastry on a well-floured surface to about 5mm (¼in) thick. This dough is very delicate so if you find it hard to roll out, divide it equally between the tartlet tins and use your fingers to press it into the bottom and sides of the tins to form the tartlet cases. Cut out 6 circles and use to line the bottom and the sides of the tartlet tins. Prick the bottom of the pastry with a fork and place them on a baking tray.

3 Bake the tartlet cases for 15–20 minutes until they start to brown at the edges. Remove them from the oven and set aside to cool completely before carefully removing them from the tins.

4 Fill the tartlet cases with the whipped double cream and top with the strawberry slices, layered over each other to cover the cream filling. Dust with icing sugar to serve within 30 minutes of assembling. The cooked pastry cases can be stored in an airtight container for up to 3 days. Theses tartlets are best eaten on the same day they are made.

EQUIPMENT
4 x 10cm (4in) loose-bottomed fluted tartlet tins

INGREDIENTS

FOR THE PASTRY
(For visual step by step instructions see p105)
100g (3½oz) plain flour, plus extra for dusting
25g (scant 1oz) cornflour
50g (1¾oz) caster sugar
100g (3½oz) butter, at room temperature

FOR THE FILLING
150ml (5fl oz) double cream (crème pâtissière can be used, see p260)
8–10 large ripe strawberries, thinly sliced, or raspberries can be used
icing sugar, for dusting

This sumptuous Strawberry Tart would take centre stage at any meal. Master the art of the delicate pastry case and the crème pâtissière, then use whatever soft fruits are in season.

STRAWBERRY TART

 SERVES 6–8

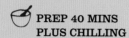 PREP 40 MINS PLUS CHILLING

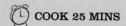 COOK 25 MINS

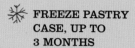 FREEZE PASTRY CASE, UP TO 3 MONTHS

EQUIPMENT
22cm (9in) loose-bottomed tart tin, baking beans

INGREDIENTS
FOR THE PASTRY
(For visual step by step instructions see sweet shortcrust pastry p105)
150g (5½oz) plain flour, plus extra for dusting
100g (3½oz) butter, chilled and diced
150g (5½oz) caster sugar
2 eggs, plus 1 egg yolk
½ tsp vanilla extract
6 tbsp redcurrant jelly, to glaze

FOR THE CRÈME PÂTISSIÈRE
50g (1¾oz) cornflour
1 tsp vanilla extract
400ml (14fl oz) whole milk
300g (10oz) strawberries, thickly sliced

1 For the pastry, rub the flour and butter together with your fingertips until the mixture resembles breadcrumbs. Stir in 50g (1¾oz) sugar. Beat the yolk and vanilla, and add to the flour. Bring together to form a dough. Wrap and chill for 30 minutes.

2 Preheat the oven to 180°C (350°F/Gas 4). Roll out the pastry on a floured surface to 3mm (⅛in) thick and use to line the tin, leaving an overlapping edge of 2cm (¾in). Trim away any excess pastry. Prick the bottom of the pastry, line with baking parchment, and fill with baking beans. Put on a baking tray and bake for 20 minutes. Remove the beans and paper and bake for a further 5 minutes. Trim off excess pastry. Melt the jelly with 1 tablespoon water and brush a little over the pastry case. Set aside to cool.

3 Make the crème pâtissière (see below), then spread over the pastry case. Top with strawberries. Reheat the jelly glaze, brush over the strawberries, then set.

Making crème pâtissière

1 Beat rest of sugar, cornflour, eggs, and vanilla. Bring milk to the boil; take off the heat just as it bubbles.

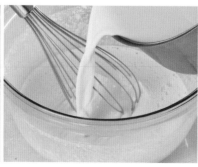

2 Pour the milk onto the egg mix, whisking. Return to the pan and boil over a medium heat, whisking.

3 When it thickens, reduce the heat to low, and cook for 2–3 minutes. Put in a bowl, cover, and cool, then beat.

This is a great recipe for the cook who is lucky enough to grow both of these in their garden. This homely double-crusted pie is best served with vanilla ice cream or thick, whipped cream.

RHUBARB AND STRAWBERRY PIE

 SERVES 6–8 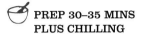 PREP 30–35 MINS PLUS CHILLING  COOK 50–55 MINS

1 To make the pastry, sift the flour and salt into a bowl. Add the shortening and cut it into the flour mixture with 2 round-bladed table knives or a pastry blender. Rub the shortening into the flour with your fingertips until the mixture forms coarse breadcrumbs. Sprinkle 6–7 tablespoons water over the mixture, 1 tablespoon at a time, and mix lightly with a fork. When the crumbs are moist enough to start sticking together, press the dough lightly into a ball, wrap it tightly, and chill for about 30 minutes, or until firm.

2 Combine the rhubarb, orange zest, sugar, salt, and flour in a bowl and stir to mix. Add the strawberries and toss until coated. Spoon the fruit mixture into the pastry-lined pie dish, doming the mixture slightly. Dot the pieces of butter all over the filling.

3 Brush the edge of the pastry case with water. Roll out the remaining dough on a floured surface into a 28cm (11in) circle. Drape the pastry over the filling, trim it to be even with the bottom crust, and, using your thumb and finger, press the edges together to seal.

4 Cut a steam vent in the centre of the pie. Brush with milk and sprinkle with the sugar. Chill for 15 minutes. Preheat the oven to 220°C (425°F/Gas 7) and put a baking tray inside to heat up.

5 Bake the pie on the baking tray for 20 minutes. Reduce the temperature to 180°C (350°F/Gas 4) and bake for a further 30–35 minutes until the crust is browned. Test the fruit with a skewer and if it needs longer but the top could burn, cover with foil. Transfer to a wire rack, and set aside to cool. The pastry can be made 2 days ahead and kept in the refrigerator.

EQUIPMENT
23cm (9in) shallow pie dish

INGREDIENTS

FOR THE PASTRY
330g (11oz) plain flour
½ tsp salt
150g (5½oz) white vegetable shortening
1 tbsp milk, to glaze

FOR THE FILLING
1kg (2¼lb) rhubarb, sliced
finely grated zest of 1 orange
250g (9oz) caster sugar,
   plus 1 tbsp to sprinkle
¼ tsp salt
30g (1oz) plain flour
375g (13oz) strawberries, hulled,
   and halved or quartered
15g (½oz) unsalted butter, diced

It's hard to beat the smooth, creamy vanilla flavour of custard matched with the sharp fruitiness of rhubarb. Here they come together in a very British tart that looks as good as it tastes.

RHUBARB AND CUSTARD TART

 **SERVES 6–8**

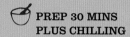 **PREP 30 MINS PLUS CHILLING**

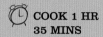 **COOK 1 HR 35 MINS**

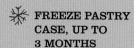 **FREEZE PASTRY CASE, UP TO 3 MONTHS**

EQUIPMENT
22cm (9in) loose-bottomed fluted tart tin, baking beans

INGREDIENTS

FOR THE PASTRY
(For visual step by step instructions see sweet shortcrust pastry p105)
175g (6oz) plain flour, plus extra for dusting
25g (scant 1oz) caster sugar
100g (3½oz) unsalted butter, at room temperature, cut into pieces
1 egg yolk, beaten with 2 tbsp cold water, plus leftover egg white for brushing

FOR THE FILLING
450g (1lb) rhubarb, prepared weight, cut into 2cm (¾in) chunks
75g (2½oz) caster sugar
200ml (7fl oz) double cream
2 eggs, plus 1 egg yolk
½ tsp vanilla extract
icing sugar, for dusting

1 To make the pastry, rub the flour, sugar, and butter together by hand, or in a food processor, until they resemble fine breadcrumbs. Add the egg yolk and bring the mixture together to form a soft dough. Add a little more water if necessary. Wrap and chill for 30 minutes.

2 Preheat the oven to 180°C (350°F/Gas 4). Toss the rhubarb with 25g (scant 1oz) of the sugar and roast in the oven, in a single layer, for 30 minutes. When cooked, remove the fruit and drain in a sieve, taking care not to break up the pieces.

3 Roll out the pastry on a floured surface to 3mm (⅛in) thick and use to line the tart tin, leaving an overhang of at least 1cm (½in). Trim off any excess pastry that hangs down further than this. Prick the bottom of the pastry with a fork, brush with the egg white to seal, line with a piece of silicone or greaseproof paper, and fill with baking beans. Place the case on a baking tray and bake for 20 minutes. Remove the beans and paper, and bake for a further 5 minutes, if the centre still looks uncooked. Trim off any ragged edges from the pastry case while it is still warm.

4 Whisk together the cream, the remaining 50g (1¾oz) of sugar, eggs, egg yolk, and vanilla extract. Spread the cooked rhubarb evenly over the bottom of the tart case. Place the tart case on a baking tray and pour the cream mixture carefully over the fruit.

5 Bake for 30–40 minutes until lightly golden and just set. Set aside to cool to room temperature before dusting with icing sugar and serving with fresh cream. Best eaten the same day. The cooked pastry case can be stored in an airtight container for up to 3 days.

Very similar to a classic British crumble, this Swedish dessert is simply a shallow layer of fruit topped with a delicious oaty crumble mix. The cornflour helps to thicken the fruit juices.

RHUBARB SMULPAJ

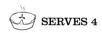 SERVES 4   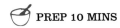 PREP 10 MINS    COOK 30 MINS   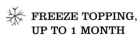 FREEZE TOPPING, UP TO 1 MONTH

EQUIPMENT
20cm (8in) round ovenproof dish

INGREDIENTS

FOR THE FILLING
300g (10oz) rhubarb, trimmed weight, chopped into 2cm (¾in) chunks
4 tbsp caster sugar
1 tsp cornflour

FOR THE CRUMBLE TOPPING
(For visual step by step instructions see crumble topping p121)
50g (1¾oz) plain flour
75g (2½oz) soft light brown sugar
75g (2½oz) unsalted butter, softened
75g (2½oz) oats
½ tsp ground cinnamon

1 Preheat the oven to 190°C (375°F/Gas 5). For the filling, put the chopped rhubarb, caster sugar, and cornflour in a large bowl and toss together, making sure that the fruit is well covered. Transfer the rhubarb into the ovenproof dish, packing the fruit down well.

2 For the crumble topping, mix the flour and soft light brown sugar together in a separate bowl. Add the butter and rub it in with your fingertips, making sure that there are a few pea-sized lumps of butter left. Stir in the oats and cinnamon, and mix together well.

3 Pile the crumble topping onto the rhubarb and spread it out, taking care not to pack it down too firmly. Place the ovenproof dish on a baking tray and bake for 30 minutes until the fruit is soft and the crumble is golden brown on top.

4 Set aside to rest for 5–10 minutes before serving hot or warm with thick cream. This is best eaten the day it is made, or stored overnight in the refrigerator.

Despite it's impressive appearance, a large millefeuilles is really just a good assembly job. Once you are confident with the basic pastry and construction, you can use whatever soft fruits are available.

SUMMER FRUIT MILLEFEUILLES

 SERVES 8   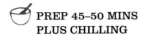 PREP 45–50 MINS
                                     PLUS CHILLING    COOK 25–30 MINS

1 Heat the milk in a saucepan over a medium heat until it just comes to the boil. Remove from the heat. Whisk the egg yolks and granulated sugar for 2–3 minutes until thick. Whisk in the flour and gradually whisk the milk into the egg mixture until smooth. Return to a clean pan. Bring to the boil, whisking until thickened. Reduce the heat to low and whisk again for 2 minutes. If lumps form, remove from the heat and whisk until smooth again. Set aside.

2 Preheat the oven to 200°C (400°F/Gas 6). Sprinkle a baking tray evenly with cold water. Roll out the pastry on a lightly floured surface to a rectangle larger than the baking tray and about 3mm (⅛in) thick. Roll the dough around a rolling pin, then unroll it onto the baking tray, letting the edges overhang. Press the dough down. Chill for about 15 minutes.

3 Prick the dough with a fork. Cover with baking parchment, then set a wire rack on top. Bake for 15–20 minutes until it just begins to brown. Gripping the tray and rack, invert the pastry. Slide the baking tray back under and bake for a further 10 minutes until both sides are browned. Remove from the oven and slide the pastry onto a chopping board. While still warm, trim the edges, then cut lengthways into 3 equal strips. Return to the wire rack and set aside to cool.

4 Whip the double cream until firm and fold into the pastry cream. Spread half the pastry cream filling over 1 pastry strip. Sprinkle with half the fruit. Repeat with another pastry strip to make 2 layers. Put the last pastry strip on top and press down gently. Sift the icing sugar thickly over the millefeuilles. The dish can be made ahead and chilled for up to 6 hours.

EQUIPMENT
baking tray

INGREDIENTS

FOR THE FILLING
375ml (13fl oz) milk
4 egg yolks
60g (2oz) granulated sugar
3 tbsp plain flour
250ml (9fl oz) double cream
400g (14oz) mixed summer fruits, such as strawberries, diced, and raspberries

FOR THE PASTRY
600g (1lb 5oz) ready-made puff pastry (or to make your own, see pp110–113)
flour, for dusting
icing sugar, for dusting

Once you have perfected the art of making a sweet pastry, you will always have dessert. For a quicker version, these little tartlet cases can be filled with whipped cream and whatever soft fruit is in season.

FRESH FRUIT TARTLETS

 MAKES 8   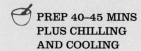 PREP 40–45 MINS PLUS CHILLING AND COOLING   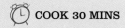 COOK 30 MINS   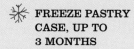 FREEZE PASTRY CASE, UP TO 3 MONTHS

EQUIPMENT
8 x 10cm (4in) tartlet tins

INGREDIENTS

FOR THE PASTRY
175g (6oz) plain flour, plus extra for dusting
4 egg yolks
90g (3oz) caster sugar
½ tsp salt
½ tsp vanilla extract
90g (3oz) unsalted butter, diced, plus extra for greasing

FOR THE FILLING
375ml (13fl oz) milk
1 vanilla pod, split, or 2 tsp vanilla extract
5 egg yolks
60g (2oz) caster sugar
30g (1oz) plain flour
500g (1lb 2oz) mixed fresh fruit, such as kiwi fruit, raspberries, grapes, peaches, peeled and sliced
175g (6oz) apricot jam or redcurrant jelly, to glaze

1 To make the pastry, sift the flour onto a work surface and make a well in the centre. Add the egg yolks, sugar, salt, vanilla, and butter. Work with your fingertips until mixed, then draw in the flour until breadcrumbs form. Press into a ball, and knead for 1–2 minutes until smooth. Wrap and chill for 30 minutes.

2 Bring the milk to the boil in a saucepan with the vanilla. Remove from the heat, cover, and leave for 10–15 minutes. Whisk the egg yolks, sugar, and flour together in a bowl. Beat in the hot milk. Return the mixture to the cleaned-out pan and cook gently, whisking, until the cream has thickened. Simmer over a low heat for 2 minutes. Transfer the pastry cream to a bowl and remove the vanilla pod (if using) or stir in the extract. Press cling film over the surface and cool.

3 Grease the tins. Roll out the pastry on a floured surface to 3mm (⅛in) thick. Group the tins with their edges nearly touching. Roll the dough round the rolling pin and drape it over the tins. Roll the rolling pin over the tops to remove excess pastry, then press the pastry into each tin. Set the tins on a baking tray and prick the pastry with a fork. Chill for 30 minutes.

4 Preheat the oven to 200°C (400°F/Gas 6). Line each tartlet case with foil, pressing it down well. Bake for 6–8 minutes, then remove the foil and bake for a further 5 minutes. Cool on a wire rack, then turn out.

5 Melt the jam with 2–3 tablespoons water in a small pan, and work it through a sieve, then use to brush the inside of each case. Half-fill each case with the pastry cream, smoothing the top. Arrange the fruit on top, and brush with jam. Chill in a container for 2 days.

When blueberries and peaches are in season, be sure to make this delicious summer dessert, which is perfect for any special occasion. It is good served with a spoonful of custard or double cream.

BLUEBERRY COBBLER

 SERVES 4   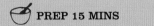 PREP 15 MINS   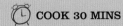 COOK 30 MINS

1 Preheat the oven to 190°C (375°F/Gas 5). Spread the blueberries and peaches over the bottom of the ovenproof dish, and sprinkle with lemon zest and sugar.

2 For the topping, sift the flour, baking powder, sugar, and salt into a bowl. Add the butter and work together with your fingertips until the mixture resembles breadcrumbs.

3 Break the egg into the buttermilk and beat well. Add to the dry ingredients and mix together to form a soft, sticky dough. Drop walnut-sized spoonfuls of the mixture over the top of the fruit, leaving a little space between them. Press them down lightly with your fingers, then sprinkle over the flaked almonds and 1 tablespoon of sugar.

4 Bake for 30 minutes, or until golden and bubbling, covering it loosely with foil if it is browning too quickly. It is done when a skewer pushed into the middle comes out clean. Cool briefly before serving.

EQUIPMENT
shallow ovenproof dish

INGREDIENTS

FOR THE FILLING
450g (1lb) blueberries
2 large peaches or 2 eating apples, sliced
grated zest of ½ lemon
2 tbsp caster sugar

FOR THE TOPPING
(For visual step by step instructions
   see cobbler topping pp118–119)
225g (8oz) self-raising flour
2 tsp baking powder
75g (2½oz) caster sugar,
   plus 1 tbsp for sprinkling
a pinch of salt
75g (2½oz) butter, chilled and diced
1 egg
100ml (3½fl oz) buttermilk
handful of flaked almonds

Here, the sweetness of the ripe blueberries is balanced by a tangy mix of soured cream and cream cheese. The perfect end to a dinner party, serve this tart with thick cream or a berry compote.

BLUEBERRY CREAM CHEESE TART

 SERVES 8   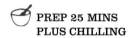 PREP 25 MINS
PLUS CHILLING   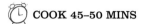 COOK 45–50 MINS

EQUIPMENT
23cm (9in) loose-bottomed
tart tin, baking beans

INGREDIENTS

FOR THE PASTRY
(For visual step by step instructions
see sweet shortcrust pastry p105)
175g (6oz) plain flour,
plus extra for dusting
85g (3oz) butter, diced
2 tbsp caster sugar
1 egg yolk

FOR THE FILLING
115g (4oz) cream cheese
60g (2oz) soured cream
60g (2oz) caster sugar
a pinch of grated nutmeg
3 eggs, beaten
zest of 1 lemon
350g (12oz) blueberries
icing sugar, for dusting

1 To make the pastry, rub the flour and butter together with your fingertips, or pulse in a food processor, until the mixture resembles breadcrumbs. Stir in the sugar, add the egg yolk, and mix to form a firm dough. Roll out the pastry on a lightly floured surface and use to line the tart tin. Prick the bottom with a fork. Wrap in cling film and chill for 30 minutes. Preheat the oven to 200°C (400°F/Gas 6).

2 Line the pastry case with greaseproof paper and fill with baking beans. Bake for 10 minutes, then remove the paper and beans, and bake for a further 10 minutes, or until pale golden. Remove from the oven, and reduce the heat to 180°C (350°F/Gas 4).

3 To make the filling, beat together the cream cheese, soured cream, sugar, nutmeg, eggs, and lemon zest until well combined. Pour into the pastry case and scatter the blueberries over the surface. Bake for 25–30 minutes until just set. Set aside to cool before transferring to a serving plate. Serve warm or cold, dusted with icing sugar. The tart case can be made several days in advance and kept in the refrigerator.

One of the best-known American desserts, this classic Cherry Pie is a great recipe to make when cherries are at their ripe, succulent best. Here cornflour helps to thicken the juices of the finished pie.

CHERRY PIE

 **SERVES 4–6**   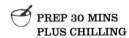 **PREP 30 MINS PLUS CHILLING**   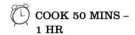 **COOK 50 MINS – 1 HR**    **FREEZE UP TO 1 MONTH**

EQUIPMENT
20cm (8in) metal pie dish with a lip

INGREDIENTS

FOR THE PASTRY
(For visual step by step instructions see sweet shortcrust pastry p105)
200g (7oz) plain flour,
plus extra for dusting
125g (4½oz) unsalted butter,
chilled and diced
50g (1¾oz) caster sugar
2 tbsp milk
1 egg, beaten, to glaze

FOR THE FILLING
50g (1¾oz) caster sugar
500g (1lb 2oz) fresh cherries, pitted
juice of 1 small or ½ large lemon
1 tbsp cornflour

1 To make the pastry, rub the flour and butter with your fingertips until the mixture resembles breadcrumbs. Stir in the sugar. Add the milk and mix to form a dough. Wrap in cling film and chill for 30 minutes. Preheat the oven to 180°C (350°F/Gas 4).

2 For the filling, melt the sugar in 3½ tablespoons of water in a saucepan. Once the sugar has dissolved, add the cherries and lemon juice. Bring to the boil, cover, reduce the heat, and simmer for 5 minutes. Mix the cornflour with 1 tablespoon of water to make a paste. Add it to the cherries and cook over a low heat until the mixture thickens. Set the cherries aside to cool.

3 Roll out the pastry on a floured surface to 3–5mm (⅛–¼in) thick. Lift it over the pie dish and line the bottom and the sides of the dish. Trim off the excess pastry, leaving an overhang of 2cm (¾in). Brush the edge with beaten egg.

4 Re-roll the excess pastry to make a circle just bigger than the dish. Fill the pastry case with the cherries, then place the remaining pastry carefully on top, pressing it firmly down around the edges to create a seal. Trim off the overhanging pastry with a sharp knife, and brush with beaten egg. Cut 2 small slits in the top of the pie to allow steam to escape.

5 Bake the pie for 45–50 minutes until the top is golden brown. Set aside to cool for 10–15 minutes but serve when still warm. The pie will keep in an airtight container for 1 day. The filling can be made 3 days ahead and refrigerated. The pastry can be made 1 day ahead and refrigerated.

You can make the dough for these individual tartlets using the old-fashioned method, or in a food processor. Either way, use cherries when they are at their juiciest for a truly luscious dessert.

CHERRY TARTLETS

 MAKES 8

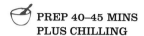 **PREP 40–45 MINS PLUS CHILLING**

 **COOK 20–25 MINS**

1 To make the pastry, sift the flour onto a work surface and make a well in the centre. Put the sugar, butter, vanilla, salt, and yolks into the well and work the ingredients with your fingertips until mixed. Work in the flour until coarse breadcrumbs form. Press the breadcrumbs firmly together to form a dough. On a floured surface, knead the dough for 1–2 minutes, then shape into a ball, wrap, and chill for 30 minutes.

2 Melt the butter for greasing, then use to brush 4 of the moulds. Roll out two-thirds of the dough on a floured surface to 3mm (⅛in) thick. Chill the remaining dough. Cut out 4 circles with the cutter; they should be large enough to line the moulds. Press 1 circle into the bottom and up the side of a mould to form a pastry shell. Repeat for the rest of the circles. Prick the bottom of each shell with a fork and chill for 15 minutes. Preheat the oven to 200°C (400°F/Gas 6). Put a baking tray in the oven. Line each of the pastry shells with a second mould and bake on the baking tray for 6–8 minutes. Remove the lining moulds, and reduce the heat to 190°C (375°F, Gas 5). Bake for 3–5 minutes. Unmould and cool each shell on a wire rack. Roll out the remaining dough, line the moulds, chill, and bake 4 more pastry shells in the same way.

3 Beat the cream cheese until soft. Add the vanilla, sugar, and lemon zest and beat for 2–3 minutes until light and fluffy. Pour the cream into a chilled bowl and whip until soft peaks form. Add the cream to the cream cheese mix and fold together until well mixed. Cover and chill. Heat the jelly and Kirsch in a small saucepan until melted, then use to brush the inside of each shell. Pipe the filling into the shells three-quarters full. Put the cherries in a circle on top and brush them with the remaining glaze.

EQUIPMENT
8 x 7.5cm (3in) diameter brioche moulds or tartlet tins, 10cm (4in) round pastry cutter, piping bag, star nozzle

INGREDIENTS

FOR THE PASTRY
215g (7oz) plain flour, plus extra for dusting
60g (2oz) caster sugar
90g (3oz) unsalted butter, softened, plus extra for greasing
2.5ml (½ tsp) vanilla extract
1.25ml (¼ tsp) salt
3 egg yolks

FOR THE FILLING
250g (9oz) cream cheese
2.5ml (½ tsp) vanilla extract
3 tsp sugar
grated zest of 1 lemon
125ml (4fl oz) double cream
375g (12oz) cherries, pitted

FOR THE GLAZE
75ml (2½fl oz) redcurrant jelly
15ml (1 tbsp) Kirsch

When fresh cherries are in season, take advantage of the plentiful supply to make this delicious dessert for any special occasion. Serve hot with lots of custard or a scoop of vanilla ice cream.

CHERRY CRUMBLE

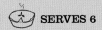 SERVES 6   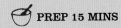 PREP 15 MINS   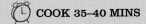 COOK 35–40 MINS    FREEZE UP TO 1 MONTH

EQUIPMENT
2 litre (3½ pint) ovenproof dish

INGREDIENTS

FOR THE CRUMBLE TOPPING
(For visual step by step instructions
see crumble topping p121)
125g (4½oz) plain flour
125g (4½oz) ground almonds
125g (4½oz) butter, diced
50g (1¾oz) caster sugar

FOR THE FILLING
550g (1¼lb) cherries, stoned
2 tbsp caster sugar
2 tbsp apple juice

1 Preheat the oven to 180°C (350°F/Gas 4). To make the crumble topping, put the flour and ground almonds in a large bowl, then rub in the butter with your fingertips until the mixture resembles rough breadcrumbs. Stir in the caster sugar.

2 Place the cherries in the ovenproof dish and scatter over the sugar and apple juice. Sprinkle the crumble mixture over the cherries and bake for 35–40 minutes, or until golden brown.

A classic strudel is given a modern twist by replacing the apples with a fresh cherry and walnut filling. Serve warm with creamy vanilla ice cream or a spoonful of thick, whipped cream or crème fraîche.

CHERRY STRUDEL

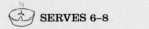 SERVES 6–8   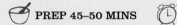 PREP 45–50 MINS   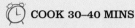 COOK 30–40 MINS

1 To make the pastry, sift the flour onto a work surface and make a well in the centre. Beat the egg with 125ml (4fl oz) water, lemon juice, and salt in a bowl, then pour into the well. Work the ingredients with your fingertips, gradually drawing in the flour. Knead in just enough flour so the dough forms a ball; it should be quite soft. On a floured surface, knead the dough for 10 minutes until shiny and smooth. Shape into a ball, cover with a bowl, and set aside to rest for 30 minutes.

2 Cover a work surface with an old, clean bed sheet. Lightly and evenly flour it. Roll out the dough to a very large square. Cover with damp tea towels for 15 minutes. Preheat the oven to 190°C (375°F/Gas 5). Grease a baking tray and melt the butter.

3 Make the strudel (see below). Brush the top of the strudel with the remaining melted butter and bake for 30–40 minutes until crisp. Leave for a few minutes before moving to a wire rack with a fish slice. Sprinkle with icing sugar and serve.

EQUIPMENT
baking tray

INGREDIENTS

FOR THE PASTRY
(For visual step by step instructions see strudel pastry pp114–115)
250g (9oz) plain flour,
  plus extra for dusting
1 egg
½ tsp lemon juice
a pinch of salt
125g (4½oz) unsalted butter,
  plus extra for greasing

FOR THE FILLING
500g (1lb 2oz) cherries, stoned
grated zest of 1 lemon
75g (2½oz) walnuts, coarsely chopped
100g (3½oz) soft light brown sugar
1 tsp ground cinnamon
icing sugar, to sprinkle

Constructing the strudel

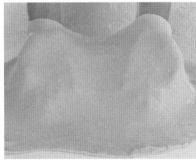

1 Stretch dough, starting at centre and working outwards until very thin. Brush with most of the butter.

2 Sprinkle the dough with the filling. Trim off the thicker edges, pulling them out and pinching them off.

3 Roll up the strudel using a bed sheet. Transfer to the baking tray and shape into a crescent or circle.

The classic American Cherry Pie is given a delicate, decorative lattice topping, making it just the thing to serve after a summer dinner party. Best served warm with vanilla ice cream.

CHERRY LATTICE PIE

 **SERVES 8**   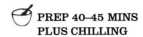 **PREP 40–45 MINS PLUS CHILLING**   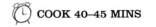 **COOK 40–45 MINS**    **FREEZE UP TO 1 MONTH**

EQUIPMENT
23cm (9in) pie dish

INGREDIENTS

FOR THE PASTRY
(For visual step by step instructions see sweet shortcrust pastry p105)
250g (9oz) plain flour, plus extra for dusting
1 tsp salt
125g (4½oz) lard or white vegetable fat, chilled and diced
75g (2½oz) unsalted butter, chilled and diced
1 egg, to glaze

FOR THE FILLING
500g (1lb 2oz) cherries, stoned
200g (7oz) caster sugar
45g (1½oz) plain flour
¼ tsp almond extract (optional)

1 To make the pastry, sift the flour and ½ teaspoon salt into a bowl. Rub the lard and butter into the flour with your fingertips until the mixture resembles breadcrumbs. Sprinkle with 3 tablespoons water, and mix until the dough forms a ball. Wrap in cling film and chill for 30 minutes.

2 Preheat the oven to 200°C (400°F/Gas 6), and put in a baking tray. Roll out two-thirds of the dough on a lightly floured surface and use to line the dish with some pastry hanging over the edge. Press the dough into the dish and chill for 15 minutes.

3 For the filling, place the cherries in a bowl and add the sugar, flour, and almond extract if using. Stir until well mixed, then spoon into the tin.

4 Roll out the remaining dough into a rectangle. Cut out 8 strips, each 1cm (½in) wide, and arrange them in a lattice-like pattern on top of the pie, then trim the pastry. Beat the egg with ½ teaspoon of salt, and use this to glaze the lattice. Secure the strips to the edge of the pie. Bake for 40–45 minutes until the pastry is golden brown. Serve at room temperature or chilled. The pie can be kept in an airtight container for 2 days, but is really best eaten on the day it is baked.

A true herald of summer, this Gooseberry Tart is nostalgia on a plate. The light, crisp pastry, just set custard, and sharp gooseberries work best when they are smothered with thick, cold cream.

GOOSEBERRY TART

 SERVES 6–8   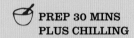 PREP 30 MINS PLUS CHILLING   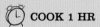 COOK 1 HR

EQUIPMENT
24cm (10in) loose-bottomed tart tin, baking beans

INGREDIENTS

FOR THE PASTRY
(For visual step by step instructions see sweet shortcrust pastry p105)
150g (5½oz) plain flour, plus extra for dusting
25g (scant 1oz) caster sugar
75g (2½oz) butter
1 egg yolk
or 250g (9oz) ready-made shortcrust pastry

FOR THE FILLING
400g (14oz) gooseberries
250ml (9fl oz) double cream
2 eggs
50g (1¾oz) caster sugar

1 To make the pastry, combine the flour, sugar, and butter and mix in a food processor to form fine breadcrumbs, or if making by hand, rub with your fingertips. Add the egg yolk and process or mix by hand, until the mixture forms a ball, adding a little cold water, a tablespoon at a time, if necessary. Wrap in cling film and chill for 30 minutes.

2 Preheat the oven to 180°C (350°F/Gas 4). Top and tail the gooseberries and set aside. To make the custard, whisk the cream, eggs, and sugar together in a bowl. Put the custard in the refrigerator.

3 Roll out the pastry on a lightly floured surface to a circle a little larger than the tart tin and use to line the tin. Line the pastry case with greaseproof paper and fill with baking beans. Bake for 15 minutes, then remove the beans and paper, and bake for a further 10 minutes until cooked through but still pale.

4 Remove the tin from the oven and put a single layer of gooseberries in the bottom of the pastry case. Pour the custard over and return it to the oven for a further 35 minutes until the custard is set and golden at the edges. Set aside to cool slightly before serving with thick cream or custard.

The unusual addition of rosemary is used in this tart to delicately flavour the pastry and the filling. Serve as part of a special occasion lunch with a scoop or two of vanilla ice cream or crème fraîche.

ORANGE AND ROSEMARY TART

 **SERVES 6–8**   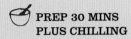 **PREP 30 MINS PLUS CHILLING**   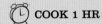 **COOK 1 HR**

1 Preheat the oven to 180°C (350°F/Gas 4). To make the pastry, place the flour, butter, and rosemary into a food processor, then pulse briefly until it resembles breadcrumbs. Alternatively, to make by hand, rub the butter into the flour and rosemary with your fingertips until the mixture resembles breadcrumbs. Add the sugar and egg, and briefly process, or bring together by hand, until the pastry forms a ball. If a ball does not form, add a little water. Wrap in cling film and chill in the refrigerator for 30 minutes.

2 Roll out the pastry on a lightly floured surface and use to line the tin. Line the pastry case with greaseproof paper and fill with baking beans. Bake for 10 minutes, then remove the paper and beans and bake for a further 10–15 minutes or until golden. Remove the tin from the oven and reduce the oven temperature to 160°C (325°F/Gas 3).

3 For the filling, place the orange juice and rosemary in a saucepan. Bring to the boil, then reduce the heat, and simmer until the liquid has thickened and reduced. Set aside to cool, then strain through a sieve, and discard the rosemary.

4 Whisk the strained juice, orange zest, sugar, eggs, and cream together until combined, then pour into the pastry case. Bake the tart for 35 minutes or until just set. Set aside to cool, then chill until required. Serve decorated with orange zest.

EQUIPMENT
20cm (8in) loose-bottomed tart tin, baking beans

INGREDIENTS

FOR THE PASTRY
(For visual step by step instructions see sweet shortcrust pastry p105)
225g (8oz) plain flour, plus extra for dusting
115g (4oz) unsalted butter, chilled
2 tbsp chopped rosemary
2 tbsp icing sugar
1 egg, lightly beaten

FOR THE FILLING
500ml (16fl oz) fresh orange juice
2 sprigs of rosemary
grated zest of 2 oranges
175g (6oz) caster sugar
4 eggs
120ml (4fl oz) double cream
orange zest, to decorate

A family favourite, the flavours of this pie are made to be together – sharp lemon and sweet vanilla meringue. Spread the meringue right to the edge of the pastry case to ensure it doesn't shrink on cooking.

LEMON MERINGUE PIE

 SERVES 8　　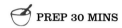 PREP 30 MINS　　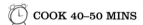 COOK 40–50 MINS

EQUIPMENT
23cm (9in) loose-bottomed
tart tin, baking beans

INGREDIENTS

FOR THE PASTRY
butter, for greasing
400g (14oz) ready-made sweet shortcrust
pastry (or to make your own see p105)
flour, for dusting

FOR THE FILLING
6 eggs, at room temperature, separated
3 tbsp cornflour
3 tbsp plain flour
400g (14oz) caster sugar
juice of 3 lemons
1 tbsp finely grated lemon zest
45g (1½oz) butter, diced
½ tsp cream of tartar
½ tsp vanilla extract

1 Preheat the oven to 200°C (400°F/Gas 6). Grease the tart tin. Roll out the pastry on a floured surface and use it to line the tin. Line the pastry case with baking parchment and fill with baking beans. Place on a baking tray and bake for 10–15 minutes until pale golden. Remove the paper and beans and bake for 3–5 minutes more until golden. Reduce the heat to 180°C (350°F/Gas 4). Set aside to cool slightly in the tin.

2 Lightly beat the egg yolks. Combine the cornflour, flour, and 225g (8oz) of the sugar in a saucepan. Slowly add 360ml (12fl oz) water and heat gently, stirring, until the sugar dissolves and there are no lumps. Increase the heat slightly and cook, stirring, for 3–5 minutes until the mixture starts to thicken.

3 Beat several spoonfuls of the hot mixture into the yolks. Pour the mixture back into the pan and slowly bring to the boil, stirring. Boil for 3 minutes, then stir in the lemon juice, zest, and butter. Boil for a further 2 minutes until the mix is thick and glossy, stirring and scraping down the sides of the pan as necessary. Remove from the heat and cover.

4 Whisk the egg whites in a large clean bowl until foamy. Sprinkle over the cream of tartar and whisk. Continue whisking, adding the remaining sugar, 1 tablespoon at a time. Add the vanilla with the last tablespoon of sugar, whisking until thick and glossy.

5 Place the pastry case on a baking tray, pour in the filling, then top with the meringue, spreading it so it covers the filling. Bake for 12–15 minutes until the meringue is golden. Cool on a wire rack before serving. The unfilled pastry case can be made 3 days ahead and stored in an airtight container.

This classic American pie benefits from using an easy biscuit crust, rather than a pastry one. Experiment with different biscuits, such as ginger snaps for a new twist on an old favourite.

KEY LIME PIE

 SERVES 8   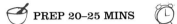 PREP 20–25 MINS    COOK 20–30 MINS

1 Preheat the oven to 180°C (350°F/Gas 4). To make the biscuit case, melt the butter in a saucepan over a low heat. Add the digestive biscuit crumbs and stir until well combined. Remove from the heat and tip the mixture into the tart tin, then use the base of a metal spoon to press it evenly and firmly all over the base and sides of the tin. Place on a baking tray and bake for 5–10 minutes.

2 Meanwhile, grate the zest of 3 of the limes into a bowl. Juice all 5 of the limes, and set aside.

3 Place the egg yolks into the bowl with the lime zest, and whisk until the egg has thickened. Pour in the condensed milk and continue whisking for 5 minutes if using an electric whisk, or for 6–7 minutes if whisking by hand. Add the lime juice, and whisk again until it is incorporated. Pour the mixture into the tin and bake for 15–20 minutes until set.

4 Remove the pie from the oven and set aside to cool completely. Serve the pie decorated with the lime slices and whipped cream.

EQUIPMENT
23cm (9in) loose-bottomed tart tin

INGREDIENTS

FOR THE BISCUIT CASE
**(For visual step by step instructions
   see biscuit case p120)**
100g (3½oz) butter
225g (8oz) digestive biscuits, crushed

FOR THE FILLING
**5 limes, plus 1 extra, cut into thin
   slices, to decorate**
3 large egg yolks
400g can condensed milk

When entertaining, there is nothing that seems to finish a meal quite as well as this classic French tart. The sharpness of the lemon filling encased in a rich pastry makes a fantastic end to any meal.

TARTE AU CITRON

 SERVES 8   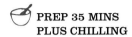 PREP 35 MINS
PLUS CHILLING    COOK 45 MINS

1 To make the pastry, place the flour, butter, and sugar into a food processor and pulse until it resembles breadcrumbs. Add the egg and process until the pastry draws together into a ball. To make the pastry by hand, rub the flour and butter together with your fingertips until the mixture resembles breadcrumbs. Stir in the sugar, then add the egg and bring the mixture together to form a soft dough.

2 Roll out the pastry on a lightly floured surface and use it to line the tart tin. Wrap in cling film and chill for at least 30 minutes.

3 To make the filling, beat the eggs and sugar together until combined. Beat in the lemon zest and juice, then whisk in the cream. Chill for 1 hour.

4 Preheat the oven to 190°C (375°F/Gas 5). Line the pastry case with greaseproof paper, fill with baking beans, and bake for 10 minutes. Remove the paper and beans, and bake for a further 5 minutes, or until the bottom is crisp.

5 Reduce the oven temperature to 140°C (275°F/Gas 1). Place the tart tin on a baking tray and pour in the lemon filling, being careful not to allow the filling to spill over the edges. Bake for 30 minutes, or until just set. Remove from the oven and set aside to cool. Dust with icing sugar, sprinkle with grated lemon zest, and serve with a spoonful of whipped cream.

EQUIPMENT
24cm (10in) loose-bottomed
tart tin, baking beans

INGREDIENTS

FOR THE PASTRY
**(For visual step by step instructions
   see sweet shortcrust pastry p105)**
175g (6oz) plain flour,
   plus extra for dusting
85g (3oz) butter, chilled
45g (1½oz) caster sugar
1 egg

FOR THE FILLING
5 eggs
200g (7oz) caster sugar
zest and juice of 4 lemons
250ml (9fl oz) double cream
icing sugar, for dusting
lemon zest, to sprinkle

For a perfect result, chill the bottom two layers until they firm up, but take care to remove the pie from the refrigerator 30 minutes before serving, and top with the bananas and cream at the last minute.

BANOFFEE PIE

 SERVES 6–8 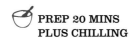 PREP 20 MINS PLUS CHILLING  COOK 5–10 MINS  FREEZE UP TO 2 MONTHS

EQUIPMENT
22cm (9in) round springform cake tin or loose-bottomed tart tin

INGREDIENTS

FOR THE BISCUIT CASE
(For visual step by step instructions see biscuit case p120)
250g (9oz) digestive biscuits
100g (3½oz) unsalted butter, melted and cooled

FOR THE CARAMEL
50g (1¾oz) unsalted butter
50g (1¾oz) soft light brown sugar
400g can condensed milk

FOR THE TOPPING
2 large, ripe bananas
250ml (9fl oz) double cream, whipped
a little dark chocolate, to decorate

1 Line the tart tin with baking parchment. To make the biscuit case, put the biscuits into a sturdy plastic bag, and use a rolling pin to crush them finely. Mix the biscuits with the melted butter, and tip them into the prepared tin. Press them down firmly to create a compressed, even layer. Cover and chill.

2 To make the caramel, melt the butter and sugar in a small, heavy saucepan over a medium heat. Add the condensed milk and bring to the boil. Reduce the heat and simmer for 2–3 minutes, stirring constantly. It will thicken and take on a light caramel colour. Pour the caramel over the biscuit case and leave to set.

3 Once set, remove the biscuit and caramel case from the tin and transfer to a serving plate. Peel and slice the bananas thinly into 5mm (¼in) discs, cut slightly on a diagonal, and use them to cover the surface of the caramel.

4 Spread the cream over the bananas using a spatula until smooth, then decorate with finely grated chocolate and larger chocolate curls made by grating the chocolate with a vegetable peeler. The pie will keep in an airtight container in the refrigerator for 2 days.

Using good-quality ready-made puff pastry is perfectly acceptable when time is short, but try to use one made purely with butter, for a better bake and flavour, rather than the margarine-based pastries.

BANANA SHUTTLES

 MAKES 6

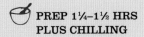 PREP 1¼–1½ HRS
PLUS CHILLING

 COOK 30–40 MINS

 FREEZE
UNCOOKED, UP TO
1 MONTH

1 Mix the sugar, cloves, and cinnamon together in a bowl. Pour the rum into another bowl. Peel the bananas and cut each in half. Dip in the rum then add to the sugar mixture and toss until coated.

2 Sprinkle a baking tray with water. Roll out the puff pastry on a lightly floured surface and trim it to a 30–37cm (12–15in) rectangle. Cut the pastry into twelve 7.5–12cm (3–5in) rectangles. Fold 6 of the rectangles in half lengthways, and make three 1cm (½in) cuts across the fold of each. Set the remaining rectangles on the baking tray, pressing lightly.

3 Cut each banana half into thin slices; then set the slices in the centre of each puff pastry rectangle, leaving a 1cm (½in) border around the edge. Brush the borders with water.

4 Line up and unfold the slashed rectangles over the filled bases. Press the edges with your fingers to seal. Trim one end of each rectangle to a blunt point, then scallop the edges of the shuttles with the back of a small knife. Chill the shuttles for 15 minutes.

5 Preheat the oven to 220°C (425°F/Gas 7). Bake for 15–20 minutes. Brush with the egg white and sprinkle over the remaining sugar. Bake for a further 10–15 minutes until crisp and golden. Carefully transfer to a wire rack and set aside to cool. Serve the shuttles warm or at room temperature. They can be frozen at the chilling stage.

EQUIPMENT
baking tray

INGREDIENTS

FOR THE FILLING
50g (1¾oz) caster sugar,
  plus 2 tbsp to sprinkle
¼ tsp cloves
¼ tsp cinnamon
3 tbsp dark rum
3 bananas

FOR THE PASTRY
600g (1lb 5oz) ready-made puff pastry
  (or to make your own, see pp110–113)
plain flour, for dusting
1 egg white, beaten, to glaze

This classic American pie is a sophisticated version of the childhood staple of bananas and cream. To save time, use a ready-made pastry case and custard, but it is well worth making your own.

BANANA CREAM PIE

 SERVES 8   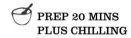 PREP 20 MINS
PLUS CHILLING    COOK 25–30 MINS

EQUIPMENT
23cm (9in) deep pie plate with a flat rim, baking beans

INGREDIENTS

FOR THE PASTRY
500g (1lb 2oz) ready-made shortcrust pastry (or to make your own, see p104)
plain flour, for dusting

FOR THE FILLING
4 large egg yolks
85g (3oz) caster sugar
4 tbsp cornflour
¼ tsp salt
450ml (15fl oz) full-fat milk
1 tsp vanilla extract
3 ripe bananas
½ tbsp lemon juice
360ml (12fl oz) double cream
3 tbsp icing sugar

1 Preheat the oven to 200°C (400°F/Gas 6). Roll out the pastry on a lightly floured surface to a 30cm (12in) circle, use to line the pie plate, and trim off the excess. Prick the bottom of the pastry with a fork.

2 Line the pastry with greaseproof paper, fill with baking beans, and place the plate on a baking tray. Bake for 15 minutes, or until the pastry looks pale golden. Lift off the paper and beans, and prick the bottom of the pastry again. Return to the oven and bake for a further 5–10 minutes, or until the pastry is golden and dry. Transfer the pie plate to a wire rack and set aside to cool completely.

3 Meanwhile, for the filling, beat the egg yolks, sugar, cornflour, and salt until the sugar dissolves and the mixture is pale yellow. Beat in the milk and vanilla. Transfer the mixture to a saucepan over a medium-high heat and bring to just below the boil, stirring until a smooth, thick custard forms. Reduce the heat and stir for 2 minutes. Strain through a fine sieve into a bowl and set aside to cool.

4 Peel and thinly slice the bananas and toss with the lemon juice. Spread them out in the pie case, then top with the custard. Cover the pie with cling film and chill for at least 2 hours.

5 Beat the cream until soft peaks form, then sift over the icing sugar, and continue beating until stiff. Spoon over the custard just before serving. The pastry case can be baked a day in advance and wrapped in foil.

variation

CHOCOLATE BANANA CREAM PIE
Add 2 tablespoons cocoa powder to the egg yolk mixture with the cornflour, and add 2 teaspoons cocoa powder to the cream with the icing sugar. To decorate, dust with cocoa, sprinkle over grated dark chocolate, or drizzle over melted dark chocolate.

A variation on the classic Tarte Tatin, use slightly underripe bananas for this upside down tart, as once the tart is turned out, you will want the banana slices to retain their shape for an impressive result.

CARAMEL BANANA TART

 SERVES 6    **PREP 15 MINS**   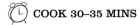 **COOK 30–35 MINS**

1 Preheat the oven to 200°C (400°F/Gas 6). Put the butter and syrup in a small, heavy-based saucepan and heat until the butter has melted and the mixture is smooth, then allow to boil for 1 minute. Pour into the tart dish or tin. Arrange the banana slices on top of the syrup mixture – this will be the top of the pudding when it's turned out. Place the dish or tin on a baking tray and bake for 10 minutes.

2 Meanwhile, roll out the pastry on a lightly floured surface to a circle about 23cm (9in) in diameter and 5mm (¼in) thick. Trim off any excess pastry.

3 Carefully remove the tart from the oven and place the pastry circle on top. Use the handle of a small knife to tuck the edge down into the tin, being very careful of the hot caramel, as it will burn.

4 Return the tart to the oven and bake for a further 20–25 minutes until the pastry is golden brown. Set aside for 5–10 minutes, then place a serving plate on top and turn the tart upside-down. Good served with vanilla ice cream.

EQUIPMENT
20cm (8in) tart dish or tin
(not loose-bottomed)

INGREDIENTS

FOR THE FILLING
75g (2½oz) butter
150g (5¼oz) golden syrup
4 medium bananas, peeled
 and sliced 1cm (½in) thick

FOR THE PASTRY
200g (7oz) ready-made puff pastry
 (or to make your own, see pp110–113)
plain flour, for dusting

These delicious, little, fried pastries are found all over Brazil, stuffed with both sweet and savoury fillings. A small amount of alcohol is used in the pastry, which could be omitted, if preferred.

BANANA AND CINNAMON PASTELS

 MAKES 10   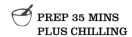 PREP 35 MINS
PLUS CHILLING   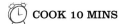 COOK 10 MINS

EQUIPMENT
medium, heavy-based saucepan

INGREDIENTS

FOR THE PASTRY
300g (10oz) plain flour,
plus extra for dusting
½ tsp salt
2 tbsp sunflower oil
1 tbsp Cachaça or vodka
1 tbsp white vinegar

FOR THE FILLING
1 large banana
2 tbsp muscovado sugar
1 tsp ground cinnamon
vegetable oil, for deep frying
icing sugar, for dusting

1 To make the pastry, mix the flour and salt in a bowl. Stir in the sunflower oil, Cachaça, and vinegar. Then gradually add 120ml (4fl oz) warm water, stirring well to form a smooth dough. On a well-floured surface, knead the dough very lightly. Wrap in cling film and chill for 1 hour.

2 For the filling, mash the banana in a small dish and stir in the sugar and cinnamon.

3 Divide the dough into 2 equal pieces. On a well-floured surface, roll out one piece of the dough to form a rectangle 18 x 30cm (7 x 12in). Cut the dough into 5 rectangles measuring 6 x 18cm (2½ x 7in). Put a little filling on one half of each rectangle, brush the edges with water, fold, and press firmly together, to seal, using the tines of a fork. Repeat to use up the remaining dough and filling.

4 Heat the vegetable oil in the saucepan to 180°C (350°F/Gas 4). Cook the pastels, 2 at a time, for about 1½–2 minutes until golden brown. Transfer the cooked pastels to a plate lined with kitchen paper, to drain. Serve hot, dusted with icing sugar.

When passionfruit are in plentiful supply, try baking this delicate tart. The sweet sharpness of the fruit really shines through, making it an unusual alternative to a classic lemon tart.

PASSIONFRUIT TART

 SERVES 6–8   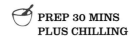 PREP 30 MINS
PLUS CHILLING    COOK 45–55 MINS   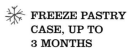 FREEZE PASTRY
CASE, UP TO
3 MONTHS

EQUIPMENT
22cm (8¾in) loose-bottomed fluted
tart tin, baking beans

INGREDIENTS

FOR THE PASTRY
(For visual step by step instructions
see sweet shortcrust pastry p105)
175g (6oz) plain flour,
plus extra for dusting
25g (scant 1oz) caster sugar
100g (3½oz) unsalted butter, softened
1 egg yolk

FOR THE FILLING
100ml (3½fl oz) passionfruit juice,
from 6–8 passionfruit
juice and grated rind of 1 lime
100g (3½oz) caster sugar
250ml (9fl oz) double cream
3 eggs, plus 1 egg yolk

1 To make the pastry, rub the flour, caster sugar, and butter together with your fingertips until the mixture resembles fine breadcrumbs. Beat the egg yolk together with 2 tablespoons of water and add it to the dry ingredients, bringing the mixture together to form a soft dough. Add a little more water if needed. Wrap in cling film and chill for 30 minutes.

2 Preheat the oven to 180°C (350°F/Gas 4). Roll out the pastry on a well-floured surface to 3mm (⅛in) thick and use to line the tart tin, leaving an overlapping edge of at least 1cm (½in). Trim away any excess. Prick the bottom, line with greaseproof paper, and fill with baking beans. Put the case on a baking tray and bake for 20 minutes. Remove the beans and paper and bake for a further 5 minutes if the centre still looks a little uncooked. Trim away any ragged edges from the pastry case while it is still warm.

3 For the filling, cut open the passionfruit and scrape the insides into a sieve. Use the back of a spoon to push as much juice through as possible, until just the black seeds are left in the sieve.

4 Whisk together the passionfruit juice, lime rind and juice, sugar, cream, eggs, and egg yolk until well combined. Pour the filling into a jug.

5 Place the pastry case on a baking tray and pour the filling into the case. The best way to do this is to rest the baking tray half on the oven shelf with the oven door open, then pour the filling in and slide the case into the oven. Bake for 25–30 minutes until just set. Set aside to cool for 30 minutes before serving. Best served on the day, but can be chilled overnight.

This impressive-looking tart uses almonds both in the frangipane and scattered on top to create layers of texture. Steeping the prunes in brandy is optional (otherwise use black tea), but highly recommended.

PRUNE AND ALMOND TART

 SERVES 8   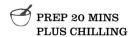 PREP 20 MINS
                                  PLUS CHILLING    COOK 50 MINS

1 To make the pastry, place the flour, sugar, and butter into a food processor and pulse until it resembles breadcrumbs. Add the egg, and process until the pastry forms a ball. To make by hand, rub the butter into the flour until it resembles breadcrumbs. Stir in the sugar, then add the egg. Bring it together into a dough using first a spoon and then your hands. Roll out on a floured surface and use to line the tart tin. Chill for 30 minutes.

2 Preheat the oven to 190°C (375°F/Gas 5). Line the pastry case with greaseproof paper and baking beans. Bake for 10 minutes, then remove the paper and beans, and bake for a further 5 minutes. Set the pastry case aside to cool on a wire rack.

3 Reduce the oven temperature to 180°C (350°F/Gas 4). For the filling, place the prunes in a saucepan, cover with water, and add the brandy. Simmer for 5 minutes, then remove from the heat and set aside. Place half the flaked almonds with the caster sugar in a food processor, and pulse until finely ground. Add the eggs, egg yolk, orange zest, almond extract, butter, and cream, and process until smooth.

4 Drain the prunes, and cut any large ones in half. Pour the almond cream into the tart, and arrange the prunes on top. Scatter the remaining flaked almonds on top, and bake for 30 minutes, or until just set. The tart can be made and chilled 2 days in advance.

EQUIPMENT
23cm (9in) loose-bottomed tart tin, baking beans

INGREDIENTS

FOR THE PASTRY
(For visual step by step instructions see sweet shortcrust pastry p105)
175g (6oz) plain flour, plus extra for dusting
1 tbsp sugar
85g (3oz) butter, chilled
1 small egg

FOR THE FILLING
200g (7oz) pitted prunes
2 tbsp brandy
100g (3½oz) flaked almonds, toasted
85g (3oz) caster sugar
2 eggs, plus 1 egg yolk
1 tbsp grated orange zest
a few drops of almond extract
30g (1oz) butter, softened
120ml (4fl oz) double cream

This rich, fruity strudel would make an ideal finale to a festive meal. Dusted with icing sugar and stuffed with dried fruit soaked in rum, it's the perfect alternative to Christmas pudding.

DRIED FRUIT STRUDEL

 SERVES 6–8　　 PREP 45–50 MINS　　 COOK 30–40 MINS　　 FREEZE UP TO 1 MONTH

EQUIPMENT
baking tray

INGREDIENTS

FOR THE FILLING
500g (1lb 2oz) mixed dried fruit
(apricots, prunes, dates, raisins, figs)
125ml (4½fl oz) dark rum
75g (2½oz) walnuts, coarsely chopped
100g (3½oz) soft light brown sugar
1 tsp ground cinnamon

FOR THE PASTRY
1 quantity strudel pastry (or to make your
own, see pp114–115), or 4 sheets
filo pastry, about 25 x 45cm (10 x 18in)
125g (4½oz) unsalted butter, melted,
plus extra for greasing
icing sugar, for dusting

1 Put the dried fruit into a saucepan with the rum and 125ml (4½fl oz) water. Place over a low heat for 5 minutes, stirring constantly. Remove from the heat and set aside to cool. The fruit will plump up. Preheat the oven to 190°C (375°F/Gas 5). Grease a baking tray.

2 If using filo, place a sheet on a clean surface and brush with a little melted butter. Lay another sheet on top and brush with melted butter. Repeat with the remaining pastry sheets.

3 Drain the dried fruit and sprinkle over the strudel or filo pastry, leaving a 2cm (¾in) border around the edge. Sprinkle over the chopped walnuts, soft light brown sugar, and cinnamon.

4 Roll the pastry, starting from one of the longer sides, and press the ends together tightly. Transfer the strudel to the baking tray and brush with a little more melted butter.

5 Bake for 30–40 minutes until crisp and golden brown. Set aside to cool before transferring to a wire rack with a fish slice. Dust with icing sugar and serve warm. The uncooked strudel can be stored in the refrigerator a few hours before baking. The cooked strudel can be warmed in the oven 1 day later.

A twist on the classic Mince Pie, here the filling is kept extra moist with the addition of finely diced banana. Freeze them in their trays, uncooked, to bake at the last minute during the festive season.

MINCE PIES

 MAKES 18 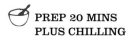 PREP 20 MINS PLUS CHILLING 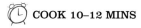 COOK 10–12 MINS  FREEZE UP TO 1 MONTH

1 Preheat the oven to 190°C (375°F/Gas 5). Grate the apple (including the skin), and place in a large bowl. Add the melted butter, sultanas, raisins, currants, mixed peel, nuts, lemon zest, mixed spice, brandy, and sugar, and mix. Peel and chop the banana into small dice, and add to the bowl. Mix well.

2 Roll out the pastry on a lightly floured surface to 2mm (⅛in) thick. Cut out 18 circles using the larger round cutter. Re-roll the pastry, and cut a further 18 smaller circles or shapes.

3 Line the patty tins with the larger pastry circles, and place a heaped teaspoon of mincemeat in each case. Top with the smaller circles or shapes. Chill for 10 minutes, and then bake for 10–12 minutes until the pastry is golden. Carefully remove from the tins, and set aside to cool on a wire rack. Dust with icing sugar. The pies can be baked up to 3 days in advance and stored in an airtight container.

EQUIPMENT
patty tins, 7.5cm (3in) and 6cm (2½in) round cutters

INGREDIENTS

FOR THE FILLING
1 small cooking apple
30g (1oz) butter, melted
85g (3oz) sultanas
85g (3oz) raisins
55g (1¾oz) currants
45g (1½oz) mixed peel, chopped
45g (1½oz) chopped almonds
   or hazelnuts
finely grated zest of 1 lemon
1 tsp mixed spice
1 tbsp brandy or whisky
30g (1oz) soft dark brown
   muscovado sugar
1 small banana

FOR THE PASTRY
500g (1lb 2oz) shortcrust pastry
   (or to make your own, see p104)
plain flour, for dusting
icing sugar, for dusting

CHOCOLATE PIES AND TARTS

A rich, dark chocolate tart such as this one is a wonderful way to finish a meal, but remember, a little goes a long way. Best served just-set and still warm from the oven, with thick, cold cream.

CHOCOLATE TART

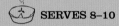 SERVES 8–10   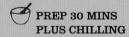 PREP 30 MINS PLUS CHILLING    COOK 35–40 MINS   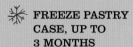 FREEZE PASTRY CASE, UP TO 3 MONTHS

EQUIPMENT
22cm (9in) loose-bottomed tart tin, baking beans

INGREDIENTS

FOR THE PASTRY
(For visual step by step instructions see sweet shortcrust pastry p105)
150g (5½oz) plain flour, plus extra for dusting
100g (3½oz) butter, chilled and diced
50g (1¾oz) caster sugar
3 eggs, plus 1 egg yolk
½ tsp vanilla extract

FOR THE FILLING
150g (5½oz) unsalted butter, diced
200g (7oz) dark chocolate, chopped
30g (1oz) caster sugar
100ml (3½fl oz) double cream

1 For the pastry, rub the flour and butter together in a large bowl with your fingertips until the mixture resembles breadcrumbs. Stir in the sugar. Beat the egg yolk and vanilla, add to the bowl, and bring together to form a dough; add water if dry. Wrap and chill for 30 minutes. Preheat the oven to 180°C (350°F/Gas 4).

2 Roll out the pastry on a floured surface to 3mm (⅛in) thick and use to line the tart tin, leaving an overlapping edge of 2cm (¾in). Trim off any excess pastry that hangs down further than this. Prick the bottom with a fork, line with baking parchment, and fill with baking beans. Place on a baking tray and bake for 20 minutes. Remove the beans and paper and return to the oven for another 5 minutes. Trim off excess pastry.

3 Prepare the chocolate filling (see below), and assemble the tart. Bake for 10–15 minutes until just set. Cool for 5 minutes and serve. The tart can be chilled for two days in an airtight container.

For the chocolate filling

1 Melt butter and chocolate in a bowl set over a pan of simmering water. Cool. Whisk eggs and sugar to mix.

2 Pour in the cooled chocolate mixture and whisk gently, but thoroughly, to combine.

3 Mix in the cream. Pour the filling into a jug. Put the tart case on a baking tray and pour in the filling.

This recipe will have your children begging for more, and most likely the adults too. This delicious pie is best if it is served still warm, with vanilla ice cream or a spoonful of whipped cream.

CHOCOLATE CHIP COOKIE PIE

 **SERVES 6**   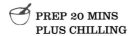 **PREP 20 MINS PLUS CHILLING**   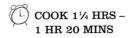 **COOK 1¼ HRS – 1 HR 20 MINS**   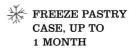 **FREEZE PASTRY CASE, UP TO 1 MONTH**

1 To make the pastry, rub the flour and butter together in a bowl with your fingertips until the mixture resembles fine breadcrumbs. Stir in the sugar. Add the egg yolk to the flour mixture and bring the mixture together to form a smooth dough, adding 1–2 teaspoons cold water if needed. Wrap in cling film and chill in the refrigerator for 30 minutes.

2 Preheat the oven to 180°C (350°F/Gas 4). Roll out the pastry on a floured surface to a circle large enough to line the tart tin. Place the pastry in the tin, pressing down well into the bottom and around the edges. Trim off any excess pastry, prick the bottom with a fork, and line with baking parchment. Place the tin on a baking tray and fill with baking beans. Bake for 20 minutes. Remove the beans and paper and bake for a further 5 minutes. Reduce the oven temperature to 160°C (325°F/Gas 3).

3 For the filling, place the eggs in a large bowl and, using an electric whisk, whisk for 2–3 minutes, or until they are foamy. Whisk in the flour and sugars. Add the butter and whisk until the mixture is smooth.

4 Sprinkle the chocolate chips over the bottom of the pastry case and spoon the filling over, in an even layer. Bake for 50–55 minutes until the filling is set. Set aside to cool on a wire rack.

EQUIPMENT
20cm (8in) loose-bottomed straight-sided tart tin, baking beans

INGREDIENTS

FOR THE PASTRY
(For visual step by step instructions see sweet shortcrust pastry p105)
150g (5½oz) plain flour, plus extra for dusting
100g (3½oz) unsalted butter
50g (1¾oz) caster sugar
1 egg yolk

FOR THE FILLING
2 eggs
50g (1¾oz) plain flour
75g (2½oz) caster sugar
75g (2½oz) soft dark brown sugar
125g (4½oz) butter, chilled and diced
50g (1¾oz) milk chocolate chips
50g (1¾oz) white chocolate chips

Using a good-quality, shop-bought crust is a great time saver for this truly decadent dessert. Use ripe, fresh raspberries and the best quality white and dark chocolate that you can find.

DOUBLE CHOCOLATE RASPBERRY TART

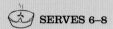 SERVES 6–8   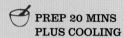 PREP 20 MINS PLUS COOLING   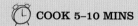 COOK 5–10 MINS   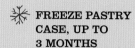 FREEZE PASTRY CASE, UP TO 3 MONTHS

EQUIPMENT
22cm (9in) loose-bottomed tart tin, baking beans

INGREDIENTS

FOR THE FILLING
100g (3½oz) good-quality white chocolate, broken into pieces
75g (2½oz) good-quality dark chocolate, broken into pieces
250ml (9fl oz) double cream
400g (14oz) raspberries
icing sugar, for dusting

FOR THE PASTRY
ready-made chocolate pastry case (or to make your own, see p105 and pp122–123)

1 Melt the white chocolate in a heatproof bowl, set over a saucepan of barely simmering water. Set the chocolate aside to cool.

2 Melt the dark chocolate in the same way, then use a pastry brush to paint the inside of the tart case with a layer of the chocolate. This will stop the pastry case going soggy once it is filled with the creamy filling. Set the pastry case aside until the chocolate has set.

3 Whip the cream stiffly. Fold the cooled white chocolate into the whipped cream. Crush half the raspberries and fold them through the cream mixture. Pile the filling into the pastry case evenly. Decorate with the remaining raspberries, dust with icing sugar, and serve. The tart will keep in an airtight container in the refrigerator for 2 days. The unfilled, cooked pastry case can be kept in an airtight container for 3 days.

Chocolate and pears are a classic combination, and here they come together to form these delicious tartlets, which are good served either hot or at room temperature with a scoop of vanilla ice cream.

CHOCOLATE AND PEAR TARTLETS

 MAKES 8   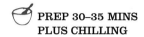 PREP 30–35 MINS    COOK 25–30 MINS
                                PLUS CHILLING

EQUIPMENT
8 x 10cm (3 x 4in) tartlet tins

INGREDIENTS

FOR THE PASTRY
175g (6oz) plain flour,
plus extra for dusting
60g (2oz) caster sugar
½ tsp salt
½ tsp vanilla extract
90g (3oz) unsalted butter, softened,
plus extra for greasing
3 egg yolks

FOR THE FILLING
150g (5½oz) plain chocolate,
finely chopped
1 egg
125ml (4fl oz) single cream
1 tbsp Kirsch (optional)
2 large, ripe pears
1–2 tbsp caster sugar, to sprinkle

1 To make the pastry, sift the flour onto a work surface and make a well in the centre. Put the sugar, salt, vanilla, and butter into the well and, with your fingertips, work the ingredients together until mixed. Work in the yolks, then work in the flour until the mixture resembles breadcrumbs. Press the dough into a ball and knead for 1–2 minutes until smooth. Shape into a ball, wrap, and chill for 30 minutes.

2 Melt the butter for greasing in a saucepan and use to brush the insides of the tartlet tins. Group 4 of the tartlet tins together, with their edges nearly touching. On a lightly floured surface, divide the dough in half, and roll 1 piece out to 3mm (⅛in) thick. Roll the dough loosely round the rolling pin, and drape it over the 4 tins to cover. Push the dough into the tins, then roll the rolling pin over the tops of the tins to cut off the excess pastry. Repeat with the 4 remaining tins and the second piece of dough.

3 Preheat the oven to 200°C (400°F/Gas 6). Put a baking tray into the oven. Sprinkle the finely chopped chocolate into each tartlet shell. Whisk the egg, cream, and Kirsch, if using, together until thoroughly mixed. For an extra-smooth custard, rub the mixture through a sieve. Spoon 2–3 tablespoons of the Kirsch custard over the chocolate in each shell.

4 Peel the pears, cut them in half, and remove the cores. Cut each pear half across into thin slices. Arrange the slices on the custard so that they overlap. Press them down lightly into the custard, then sprinkle each tartlet evenly with the sugar. Place the tins on a baking tray and bake for 10 minutes. Reduce the heat to 180°C (350°F/Gas 4) and bake for 15–20 minutes until set. Cool slightly, unmould, and serve.

The sweet Italian *pasta frolla* pastry is used here to contain a rich, truffled chocolate filling. Toasting the walnuts first intensifies their flavour and gives them added texture. Serve at room temperature.

CHOCOLATE WALNUT TRUFFLE TART

 SERVES 6–8   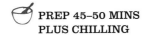 PREP 45–50 MINS PLUS CHILLING   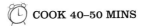 COOK 40–50 MINS

1 To make the pastry, sift the flour onto a work surface and make a well in the centre. Put the butter, sugar, salt, and egg into the well and mix. Mix in the flour, then rub with your fingertips until the mixture resembles breadcrumbs. Press into a ball. Knead for 1–2 minutes, wrap, and chill for 30 minutes.

2 Grease the tin. Roll out the dough on a floured surface into a 28cm (11in) circle and press it into the tin, sealing any cracks. Prick the bottom of the pastry with a fork and chill for 15 minutes.

3 Preheat the oven to 180°C (350°F/Gas 4). Spread out the nuts on a baking tray and toast for 5–10 minutes until lightly browned. Cool. Return the baking tray to the oven. Reserve 8 walnut halves. Grind the remaining nuts with the sugar in a food processor.

4 Beat the butter until creamy. Add the flour and walnut mix and beat for 2–3 minutes until fluffy. Add the yolks and egg, one at a time, beating after each addition. Mix in the chocolate and vanilla. Spread the filling over the pastry and smooth the top. Bake on the baking tray for 35–40 minutes. Cool on a wire rack.

5 Put the chocolate for the glaze in a bowl, set over a saucepan of simmering water. Stir until melted. Dip the reserved walnuts in the chocolate to coat, then set aside. Cut the butter into pieces and stir it into the chocolate. Add the Grand Marnier. Set aside to cool.

6 Remove the tart from the tin. Pour the glaze on the tart and spread it on top. Cool and set. Dust with cocoa and arrange the walnuts on top to serve.

EQUIPMENT
23cm (9in) springform cake tin

INGREDIENTS

FOR THE PASTRY
150g (5½oz) plain flour, plus extra for dusting
75g (2½oz) unsalted butter, softened, plus extra for greasing
50g (1¾oz) caster sugar
¼ tsp salt
1 egg

FOR THE FILLING
150g (5½oz) walnuts
100g (3½oz) caster sugar
150g (5½oz) unsalted butter
2 tsp plain flour
2 egg yolks, plus 1 whole egg
60g (2oz) good-quality dark chocolate, finely chopped
1 tsp vanilla extract

FOR THE CHOCOLATE GLAZE
175g (6oz) good-quality dark chocolate, broken into pieces
75g (2½oz) unsalted butter
2 tsp Grand Marnier
cocoa powder, sifted, for dusting

In this classic American recipe, a crunchy biscuit crust is filled with a light mousse and topped with thick whipped cream. Baking the biscuit crust briefly helps to hold the case together.

CHOCOLATE CHIFFON PIE

 SERVES 8

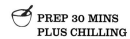 PREP 30 MINS PLUS CHILLING

 COOK 15 MINS

EQUIPMENT
23cm (9in) loose-bottomed tart tin

INGREDIENTS

FOR THE BISCUIT CASE
(For visual step by step instructions see biscuit case p120)
175g (6oz) ginger biscuits, coarsely broken into pieces
50g (1¾oz) caster sugar
75g (2½oz) butter, melted

FOR THE FILLING
50g (1¾oz) dark chocolate, chopped, plus extra to decorate
350ml (12fl oz) double cream, plus 200ml (7fl oz) to decorate
2 sheets leaf gelatine
3 egg yolks, plus 2 egg whites
140g (5oz) caster sugar
a pinch of salt
2 tbsp ginger syrup, plus 3 pieces stem ginger, from a jar of stem ginger in syrup
¼ tsp cream of tartar
2 tbsp sugar, to decorate

1 Preheat the oven to 190°C (375°F/Gas 5). To make the case, put the biscuits in a food processor and blitz until fine crumbs form. Add the sugar and pulse to mix. Pour in the butter and blitz until blended. Or, crush the biscuits in a plastic bag with a rolling pin, then mix in the sugar and butter. Press the crumbs over the bottom of the tin. Bake for 8–10 minutes until browned at the edge. Cool on a wire rack.

2 Melt the chocolate in 150ml (5fl oz) cream in a saucepan, without letting the cream boil, stirring until smooth. Remove from the heat. Add the gelatine and leave for several minutes, then stir until dissolved.

3 Meanwhile, using an electric mixer, beat the egg yolks with 100g (3½oz) of the caster sugar until the sugar dissolves and the mixture is thick and creamy. Add the salt, then slowly add the cream mixture and ginger syrup, beating for 1 minute until the mixture is well blended. Cover with cling film and chill for 15 minutes, or until firm.

4 Whisk the egg whites in a large bowl until soft peaks start to form. Sprinkle over the cream of tartar, then add the remaining sugar, 1 tablespoon at a time, whisking until stiff peaks form. Set aside. Beat the chocolate mixture for 2 minutes. Beat in a little of the egg white, then fold in the remainder. Spoon the chocolate mixture into the case and smooth the surface. Whip the cream for the decoration until thick. Sprinkle over the sugar and whip until stiff, then use to cover the pie. Grate the dark chocolate over and sprinkle the chopped ginger over. Chill for 2 hours before serving.

variation

CHOCOLATE COCONUT CHIFFON PIE
Replace the ginger biscuits with coconut biscuits or cookies, and the ginger syrup with 1 teaspoon coconut extract. Sprinkle 50g (1¾oz) toasted desiccated coconut over the finished pie, instead of the chocolate and ginger.

An all-time favourite, whip a little of the ginger syrup into double cream to serve. This tart will keep for a week in the refrigerator or in an airtight container in a cool place, if it lasts that long!

DOUBLE CHOCOLATE AND GINGER TRUFFLE TART

 SERVES 4–6   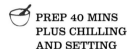 PREP 40 MINS PLUS CHILLING AND SETTING   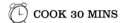 COOK 30 MINS

1 Preheat the oven to 180°C (350°F/Gas 4). Roll out the pastry to the thickness of a £1 coin, then use it to line the tart tin. Prick the bottom of the pastry with a fork, line with baking parchment, and fill with baking beans. Bake for 10–15 minutes until the sides are starting to brown lightly. Remove the beans and paper, cover the sides of the pastry with foil and bake for a further 10 minutes, or until the bottom is golden and sandy to the touch. Set aside to cool.

2 For the filling, melt 100g (3½oz) of the white chocolate in a small bowl over a saucepan of simmering water, stirring occasionally. Pour the melted white chocolate over the bottom of the pastry case. Set aside to set for about 15–20 minutes.

3 Melt the golden syrup and dark chocolate together in a medium bowl over a pan of simmering water, stirring occasionally. Set aside to cool slightly.

4 Put the cream into a large bowl, fold in the melted dark chocolate mixture, then add the chopped ginger and ginger syrup. Spoon the mixture into the pastry case. Chill in the refrigerator until set for 2–3 hours, or overnight. Roll the rolling pin over the top of the tin, pressing down to cut off the excess pastry.

5 To decorate, melt the remaining white chocolate as above, and use a spoon to drizzle the melted white chocolate over the tart to decorate (or use a piping bag with a small round nozzle). Chill again for 30 minutes–1 hour until the decorative white chocolate swirls have set, then serve.

EQUIPMENT
23cm (9in) loose-bottomed tart tin, baking beans, piping bag and small round nozzle (optional)

INGREDIENTS

FOR THE PASTRY
375g (13oz) ready-made shortcrust or sweet shortcrust pastry (or to make your own, see p104 or 105)

FOR THE FILLING
150g (5½ oz) white chocolate
3 tbsp golden syrup
200g (7oz) 70% dark chocolate
300ml (10fl oz) double cream
4 pieces stem ginger, finely chopped
3 tbsp syrup from the ginger jar

variation

CHOCOLATE AND PEANUT BUTTER TART:
Replace half the dark chocolate with 5 tablespoons crunchy or smooth peanut butter. Add the peanut butter to the bowl with the syrup and remaining dark chocolate. Omit the stem ginger and syrup from the cream.

These unusual little tartlets have to be tasted to be believed and will be a hit with adults and children alike. Serve warm or at room temperature with cream and eat on the day they are made.

BANANA AND NUTELLA CRUMBLE TARTLETS

 MAKES 6   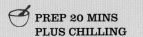 PREP 20 MINS PLUS CHILLING   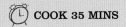 COOK 35 MINS   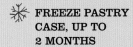 FREEZE PASTRY CASE, UP TO 2 MONTHS

1 To make the pastry, rub the flour, caster sugar, and butter together, by hand or in a food processor, until they resemble fine breadcrumbs. Add the egg yolk and bring the mixture together to form a soft dough; add a little water if needed. Wrap and chill for 30 minutes.

2 Preheat the oven to 180°C (350°F/Gas 4). Roll out the pastry on a floured surface to 3mm (⅛in) thick and use to line the tart tins, leaving an overlapping edge of 1cm (½in). Trim off any excess pastry that hangs down further than this. Prick the bottom with a fork, line with greaseproof paper, and fill with baking beans. Place on a baking tray and bake for 15 minutes. Remove the beans and paper and return to the oven for a further 5 minutes if the centres look uncooked. Trim off any ragged edges from the cases while still warm. Increase the temperature to 200°C (400°F/Gas 6).

3 For the filling, mix together the flour, soft light brown sugar, and coconut in a large bowl. Rub in the butter by hand, making sure that the mixture isn't too well mixed, and that there are some larger lumps of butter remaining.

4 Peel and slice the bananas into 1cm (½in) slices across on a diagonal slant, and use pieces to create a single layer on the bottom of the tart cases, breaking them to fit if needed. Spread 1 tablespoon Nutella over the banana to cover. Divide the crumble mix between the tarts and loosely spread it over, taking care not to pack it down. Bake for 15 minutes until the crumble has started to brown.

EQUIPMENT
6 x 10cm (4in) loose-bottomed fluted tart tins, baking beans

INGREDIENTS

FOR THE PASTRY
(For visual step by step instructions see sweet shortcrust pastry p105)
175g (6oz) plain flour, plus extra for dusting
25g (scant 1oz) caster sugar
100g (3½oz) unsalted butter, softened
1 egg yolk, beaten with 2 tbsp cold water

FOR THE FILLING
25g (scant 1oz) plain flour
25g (scant 1oz) soft light brown sugar
10g (¼oz) desiccated coconut
25g (scant 1oz) butter, softened
2–3 bananas, not too ripe
4 tbsp Nutella

The rich chocolate filling used here contrasts beautifully with a delicate sweet pastry made of finely ground almonds. If short on time, use ready-ground almonds. The tart can be made a day ahead and chilled.

CHOCOLATE PIE WITH A CRUNCHY CRUST

 SERVES 8　　　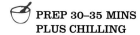 PREP 30–35 MINS PLUS CHILLING　　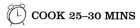 COOK 25–30 MINS

EQUIPMENT
25cm (10in) loose-bottomed tart tin

INGREDIENTS

FOR THE TART CASE
60g (2oz) caster sugar
175g (6oz) blanched almonds
1 egg white
butter, for greasing
plain flour, for dusting

FOR THE FILLING
270g (9oz) plain chocolate, finely chopped
375ml (12fl oz) double cream
2 eggs, plus 1 egg yolk

1 For the case, grind the sugar and blanched almonds finely in a food processor. Whisk the egg white in a medium bowl just until it is frothy. Add the ground almond and sugar mixture to the beaten egg white and stir with a wooden spoon to form a stiff paste. Shape it into a ball, wrap in cling film and chill for 30 minutes.

2 Melt the butter in a small saucepan and use to brush the tart tin. On a lightly floured surface, gently pound out the crust mixture with a rolling pin until flattened. Transfer the crust mixture to the tin and press the mixture into the bottom, then push it well up the side. Chill for 15 minutes.

3 Preheat the oven to 180°C (350°F/Gas 4). Put a baking tray into the oven. Put the shell on the tray and bake for 8–10 minutes until lightly browned. Slide the shell off the baking tray, onto the wire rack and cool in the tin. Leave the oven on.

4 Put the chocolate into a bowl. Bring the cream just to the boil in a pan, then pour over the chocolate and whisk until the chocolate has melted. Set aside to cool to tepid. Put the eggs and yolk into another bowl and whisk until mixed. Whisk the tepid chocolate mix into the eggs just to combine. Pour the filling into the shell. Put the tart on the baking tray and bake for 15–20 minutes until the filling begins to set, but is still soft in the centre. Cool slightly on a wire rack, then remove from the tin onto the wire rack to cool.

These delicate little creamy tartlets are perfect for a special afternoon tea or a garden party piled high with luscious summer fruits. Use the best-quality white chocolate that you can find.

WHITE CHOCOLATE AND MASCARPONE TARTS

 MAKES 6   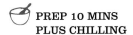 **PREP 10 MINS PLUS CHILLING**   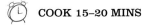 **COOK 15–20 MINS**

1 Preheat the oven to 200°C (400°F/Gas 6). To make the pastry, place the flour, butter, and sugar into a food processor and pulse until the mixture resembles breadcrumbs. To make by hand, rub the butter into the flour with your fingertips until the mixture resembles breadcrumbs. Mix in the sugar. Add the egg and process or bring together with your hands until the pastry draws together in a ball. Roll out the pastry on a lightly floured surface and use to line the tart tins. Chill the tins in the refrigerator for 30 minutes.

2 Line the pastry cases with greaseproof paper and fill with baking beans. Bake for 10 minutes, then remove the paper and beans, and bake for a further 5 minutes. Set aside to cool.

3 To make the filling, place the white chocolate and 125g (4½oz) of the mascarpone cheese into a heatproof bowl set over a saucepan of simmering water, and stir until melted. Add the remaining mascarpone to the bowl, whisk briskly until it is smooth, then whisk in the double cream.

4 Pour the mixture into the pastry cases and chill for 3 hours, or until softly set. To serve, arrange the berries on top of the tart, and decorate with mint leaves and a sprinkle of icing sugar.

EQUIPMENT
6 x 10cm (4in) loose-bottomed tart tins, baking beans

INGREDIENTS

FOR THE PASTRY
(For visual step by step instructions see sweet shortcrust pastry p105)
250g (9oz) plain flour, plus extra for dusting
125g (4½oz) butter, chilled
3 tbsp caster sugar
1 large egg

FOR THE FILLING
200g (7oz) white chocolate, broken into pieces
450g (1lb) mascarpone cheese
150ml (5fl oz) double cream
200g (7oz) strawberries, hulled
200g (7oz) raspberries
mint leaves, to decorate
icing sugar, sifted, to decorate

A chocolate-lover's delight, this very sweet traditional American dessert will be a crowd-pleaser whatever the occasion. Serve the pie in small slices as it is extremely rich, so a little will go a long way.

MISSISSIPPI MUD PIE

 SERVES 8–10   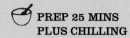 PREP 25 MINS PLUS CHILLING   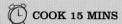 COOK 15 MINS

EQUIPMENT
23cm (9in) springform tin

INGREDIENTS

FOR THE FILLING
200g (7oz) marshmallows
4 tbsp milk
350g (12oz) milk chocolate, roughly broken
400ml (14fl oz) whipping cream, lightly whipped
mini marshmallows and chocolate flakes, to decorate

FOR THE BISCUIT CASE
(For visual step by step instructions see biscuit case p120)
75g (2½oz) unsalted butter, plus extra for greasing
250g (9oz) digestive biscuits, crushed to a fine crumb

1 Grease and line the bottom of the tin with baking parchment. Place the marshmallows and milk in a small saucepan over a low heat to melt the marshmallows, stirring occasionally. Set aside to cool.

2 Melt the chocolate in a large heatproof bowl over a pan of simmering water. Remove the bowl from the heat and set aside to cool.

3 Melt the butter in a small pan and mix in the crushed biscuits. Turn into the prepared tin and press down with the back of a metal tablespoon.

4 Pour the cooled marshmallow mixture into the cooled melted chocolate and stir well. Fold in the whipped cream until well combined and pour the mixture over the biscuit base. Smooth and chill for 2–3 hours until ready to serve.

5 To serve, place the pie on a serving plate and remove the tin. Decorate with mini marshmallows and chocolate flakes before serving.

A delicious chocolate variation of a classic Millefeuilles, this is a great entertaining dessert. The pastry and filling can be made the day before, and assembled at the last minute.

CHOCOLATE MILLEFEUILLES

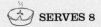 **SERVES 8**   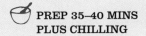 **PREP 35–40 MINS PLUS CHILLING**    **COOK 25–30 MINS**

1 Heat the milk in a saucepan over a medium heat until it just comes to the boil. Remove from the heat and whisk the egg yolks and granulated sugar for 2–3 minutes until thick. Whisk in the flour. Gradually whisk the milk into the egg mix until smooth and return to a clean pan. Bring to the boil, whisking, until thick. Reduce the heat to low and whisk for 2 minutes. Set aside to cool, then stir in the rum. Transfer to a bowl, cover with a cling film, and chill for 1 hour.

2 Stir the brandy into the double cream, cover with cling film, and chill for 1 hour. Preheat the oven to 200°C (400°F/Gas 6). Sprinkle a baking tray with water.

3 Roll out the pastry to a rectangle larger than the baking tray. Transfer to the tray, letting the edges overhang. Press the dough down. Chill for 15 minutes. Prick all over with a fork. Cover with parchment, then set a wire rack on top. Bake for 15–20 minutes until it just begins to brown. Gripping the tray and rack, invert the pastry, slide the baking tray back under and bake for 10 minutes until both sides are browned. Remove from the oven and slide the pastry onto a chopping board. Trim the edges while still warm, then cut lengthways into 3 equal strips. Set aside to cool.

4 Whip the double cream until stiff. Stir it into the pastry cream with two-thirds of the dark chocolate. Cover and chill. Spread the remaining melted chocolate over one of the pastry strips to cover it. Set aside to set. Put another pastry strip on a plate, spread with half the cream, top with the remaining strip, and spread with cream. Cover with the chocolate-coated strip. Put the white chocolate into one corner of a plastic bag. Twist the bag to enclose the chocolate and snip off the tip of the corner. Pipe chocolate over the millefeuilles.

EQUIPMENT
baking tray

INGREDIENTS

FOR THE FILLING
375ml (13fl oz) milk
4 egg yolks
60g (2oz) granulated sugar
3 tbsp plain flour, sifted
2 tbsp dark rum
2 tbsp brandy
375ml (13fl oz) double cream
50g (1¾oz) dark chocolate,
  melted and cooled
30g (1oz) white chocolate,
  melted and cooled

FOR THE PASTRY
600g (1lb 5oz) ready-made puff pastry
  (or to make your own, see pp110–113)

The pastry used in this tart is called *pasta frolla*, the classic Italian sweet pastry. The gentle hint of orange zest in the crust sets off the rich, dark chocolate and orange filling. Serve with whipped cream.

HAZELNUT, CHOCOLATE, AND ORANGE TART

 SERVES 6–8   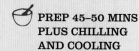 PREP 45–50 MINS PLUS CHILLING AND COOLING   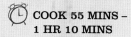 COOK 55 MINS – 1 HR 10 MINS

EQUIPMENT
23cm (9in) springform tin

INGREDIENTS

FOR THE PASTRY
150g (5½oz) plain flour, plus extra for dusting
75g (2½oz) unsalted butter, softened, plus extra for brushing
50g (1¾oz) caster sugar
½ tsp salt
grated zest of 1 orange
1 egg

FOR THE FILLING
pared zest of 2 oranges, cut into very fine julienne strips
125g (4½oz) hazelnuts
150g (5½oz) caster sugar
150g (5½oz) unsalted butter
2 tsp plain flour
2 egg yolks, plus 1 egg
60g (2oz) plain chocolate, chopped into chunks

FOR THE CHOCOLATE GLAZE
75g (2½oz) unsalted butter, cut into small pieces
125g (4½oz) plain chocolate, melted
2 tsp Grand Marnier

1 For the pastry, sift the flour onto a surface and make a well in the centre. Add the remaining ingredients and mix. Work the flour until breadcrumbs form. Press the dough into a ball. On a floured surface, knead until smooth, wrap, and chill for 30 minutes.

2 Brush the tin with melted butter. Roll the pastry out on a lightly floured surface to a 28cm (11in) circle and use to line the tin. Trim off excess pastry. Prick the bottom with a fork and chill for 15 minutes.

3 Bring a saucepan of water to the boil, add the zest, reduce the heat, and simmer for 2 minutes. Drain. Preheat the oven to 180°C (350°F/Gas 4). Toast the nuts for 5–15 minutes until browned. Rub the nuts in a tea towel while still hot to remove the skins. Cool.

4 Put one-third of the sugar into a pan, add 60ml (2fl oz) water, and heat gently until dissolved. Add the zest and simmer for 8–10 minutes until the water has evaporated and the strips are tender. Transfer the zest to baking parchment and cool slightly. Chop two-thirds.

5 Heat a baking tray. Grind the remaining sugar and nuts in a food processor. Beat the butter until creamy. Add the flour and nuts and beat until light and fluffy. Add the yolks and egg, one at a time, beating after each addition. Mix in the chocolate and chopped zest. Spread over the case and level. Bake on the baking tray for 35–40 minutes. Cool. Stir the butter into the warm chocolate in 2–3 batches. Add the Grand Marnier and cool to tepid. Spread the glaze over the top of the tart and decorate with candied zest.

This impressive tart is perfect to serve at a dinner party or special event, yet is easily assembled from storecupboard essentials. Use a ready-baked sweet tart case to make it even quicker.

BITTER CHOCOLATE, APRICOT, AND ALMOND TART

 SERVES 6–8   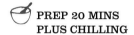 PREP 20 MINS PLUS CHILLING   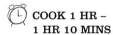 COOK 1 HR – 1 HR 10 MINS

1 To make the pastry, combine the flour, sugar, and butter and mix in a food processor to form fine breadcrumbs, or if making by hand, rub with your fingertips. Add the egg yolk and process or mix by hand, until the mixture forms a ball, adding a little cold water, a tablespoon at a time, if necessary. Wrap in cling film and chill for 30 minutes.

2 Roll out the pastry on a lightly floured surface to a circle a little larger than the tart tin and use to line the tin. Line the pastry case with greaseproof paper and fill with baking beans. Bake for 15 minutes, then remove the beans and paper, and bake for a further 10 minutes until cooked through but still pale.

3 Put the well-drained apricots cut-side down in the pastry case and scatter over the chocolate chunks.

4 For the filling, cream the butter with the sugar in a large bowl, using an electric whisk, until light and fluffy. Slowly beat in the eggs, one at a time, taking care not to curdle the mixture.

5 Fold in the almond and crumb mixture, then spoon it over the chocolate and apricots, and smooth down lightly. Bake for 40 minutes or until the tart is firm and golden. Serve warm.

EQUIPMENT
23cm (9in) tart tin, baking beans

INGREDIENTS

FOR THE PASTRY
(For visual step by step instructions see sweet shortcrust pastry p105)
150g (5½oz) plain flour, plus extra for dusting
25g (scant 1oz) caster sugar
75g (2½oz) butter
1 egg yolk
or 250g (9oz) ready-made shortcrust pastry

FOR THE FILLING
400g tin apricot halves, well drained
100g (3½oz) dark chocolate, broken into chunks
115g (4oz) butter
110g (4oz) caster sugar
2 large eggs
75g (2½oz) ground almonds, mixed with 75g (2½oz) Madeira cake crumbs

OTHER SWEET
PIES AND TARTS

An ice-cream pie is the perfect dessert to serve in hot weather. Use good-quality chocolate ice cream and your favourite types of nuts for the ultimate sweet treat. Serve chilled.

ROCKY ROAD ICE-CREAM PIE

 **SERVES 8**   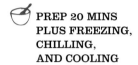 **PREP 20 MINS PLUS FREEZING, CHILLING, AND COOLING**   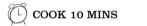 **COOK 10 MINS**   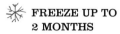 **FREEZE UP TO 2 MONTHS**

EQUIPMENT
22cm (9in) loose-bottomed, fluted tart tin

INGREDIENTS

FOR THE BISCUIT CASE
(For visual step by step instructions see biscuit case p120)
250g (9oz) digestive or Breton biscuits
60g (2oz) caster sugar
125g (4½oz) unsalted butter, melted and cooled

FOR THE FILLING
1 litre good quality chocolate ice cream
30g (1oz) mini marshmallows
50g (1¾oz) pecans, roughly chopped
50g (1¾oz) blanched almonds, roughly chopped

1 Preheat the oven to 180°C (350°F/Gas 4). To make the biscuit case, crush the biscuits by hand, or in a food processor until they resemble fine breadcrumbs. Mix the biscuit crumbs with the sugar, and the melted butter until the mixture resembles wet sand.

2 Pour the biscuit mixture into the tart tin, and press it firmly into the bottom and sides of the tin. Make sure the mixture is as packed as possible, and that there is a good side to the case (it should go, at least, 3cm/1¼in up the sides of the tin). Bake the tart case for 10 minutes, then set aside to cool. Once cold, store the tart case in the refrigerator until needed.

3 For the filling, take the ice cream out of the freezer at least 15 minutes before needed, to allow it to soften in the refrigerator. Scoop the ice cream into a food processor with a large spoon. Don't just tip the whole block in as it will be too difficult to break down quickly. Process the ice cream until it is thick and creamy, but entirely smooth. Quickly scrape it into a large bowl, and fold in the mini marshmallows and chopped nuts. Pour the mixture into the prepared case and freeze for 1 hour, or until firm.

4 To serve the ice-cream pie, remove it from the freezer and leave it in the refrigerator for about 20–30 minutes to soften before serving.

This is as far away from the shop-bought varieties as you can imagine. The crisp butter-based pastry and home-made frangipane ensures a truly sophisticated result when served warm with cream.

BAKEWELL TART

 SERVES 6–8

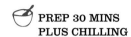 PREP 30 MINS
PLUS CHILLING

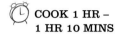 COOK 1 HR –
1 HR 10 MINS

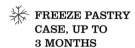 FREEZE PASTRY
CASE, UP TO
3 MONTHS

EQUIPMENT
22cm (9in) loose-bottomed tart tin,
baking beans

INGREDIENTS

FOR THE PASTRY
(For visual step by step instructions
see sweet shortcrust pastry p105)
150g (5½ oz) plain flour, sifted,
plus extra for dusting
100g (3½ oz) unsalted butter,
chilled and diced
50g (1¾ oz) caster sugar
finely grated zest of ½ lemon
1 egg yolk
½ tsp vanilla extract

FOR THE FILLING
125g (4½ oz) unsalted butter, softened
125g (4½ oz) caster sugar
3 large eggs
½ tsp almond extract
125g (4½ oz) ground almonds
150g (5½ oz) good-quality raspberry jam
25g (scant 1oz) flaked almonds
icing sugar, for dusting

1 To make the pastry, rub the flour and butter together with your fingertips until the mixture resembles breadcrumbs. Stir in the sugar and lemon zest. Beat the egg yolk with the vanilla and mix into the crumbs, bringing the mixture together to form a soft dough; add a little water, if needed. Wrap in cling film and chill for 30 minutes.

2 Preheat the oven to 180°C (350°F/Gas 4). Roll the dough out on a floured surface to about 3mm (⅛in) thick and use to line the tin, leaving an overlapping edge of at least 2cm (¾in). Prick the bottom over with a fork. Line the pastry case with baking parchment and fill with baking beans. Place it on a baking tray and bake for 20 minutes. Remove the beans and the paper, and bake for a further 5 minutes, if the centre still looks a little uncooked.

3 For the filling, cream the butter and sugar together in a bowl until pale and fluffy. Beat in the eggs and almond extract until well combined. Fold in the ground almonds to form a thick paste.

4 Spread the jam evenly over the base of the cooked tart case. Tip the frangipane over the jam layer and use a palette knife to spread it out evenly. Scatter the flaked almonds over the top.

5 Bake for 40 minutes until golden brown. Set aside to cool for 5 minutes, then trim the excess pastry from the edges and set the tart aside to cool before dusting with icing sugar to serve. The baked tart will keep in an airtight container for up to 2 days. The unfilled pastry case can be prepared in advance and stored in an airtight container for up to 3 days.

There are only a few ingredients in this simple dessert, so make sure they are the best quality. The pastry slices can be made in advance and stored for up to 2 days, to be filled at the last minute.

VANILLA MILLEFEUILLES SLICES

 MAKES 6   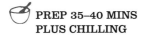 PREP 35–40 MINS
PLUS CHILLING    COOK 35–40 MINS

1 Heat the milk in a saucepan until it just comes to the boil. Remove from the heat. Whisk the egg yolks and granulated sugar for 2–3 minutes until thick. Whisk in the flour. Gradually whisk the milk into the egg mix until smooth. Return to a clean pan. Bring to the boil, whisking until thickened. Reduce the heat to low and whisk for 2 minutes. If lumps form in the pastry cream, remove from the heat and whisk until smooth. Cool, then stir in the rum. Transfer to a bowl, cover with cling film, and chill for 1 hour.

2 Whip the double cream until stiff peaks form. Fold it into the pastry cream and chill. Preheat the oven to 200°C (400°F/Gas 6). Sprinkle the baking tray with water. Roll out the pastry to a rectangle larger than the tray and transfer to the tray, letting the edges overhang. Press down and chill for 15 minutes.

3 Prick the dough with a fork. Cover with baking parchment, then set a wire rack on top. Bake for 15–20 minutes until just brown. Gripping the tray and rack, invert the pastry and bake for 10 minutes until both sides are browned. While still warm, cut it into 5 x 10cm (2 x 4in) rectangles, in multiples of 3.

4 Mix the icing sugar with 1–1½ tablespoons water, then 2 tablespoons of the icing with the cocoa. Place the chocolate icing in the piping bag. Take one-third of the pastry pieces and spread with white icing, then pipe horizontal lines across it with chocolate icing. Drag a skewer through the lines vertically to produce a striped effect; dry. Spread a layer of jam over remaining pastry pieces. Spread a 1cm (½in) layer of pastry cream on top of the jam; trim the edges. Take a piece of pastry with jam and pastry cream, and place another on top. Press down before topping with a third iced pastry piece.

EQUIPMENT
baking tray, small piping bag
with thin nozzle

INGREDIENTS

FOR THE FILLING
375ml (13fl oz) milk
4 egg yolks
60g (2oz) granulated sugar
3 tbsp plain flour, sifted
2 tbsp dark rum
250ml (9fl oz) double cream
½ jar smooth strawberry
    or raspberry jam

FOR THE PASTRY
600g (1lb 5oz) puff pastry
    (or to make your own, see pp110–113)
100g (3½oz) icing sugar
1 tsp cocoa powder

This traditional Italian tart is really a variation on a cheesecake baked in a shortcrust pastry base. Use very fresh ricotta for a perfect result and the best-quality vanilla extract you can afford.

CROSTATA DI RICOTTA

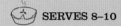 SERVES 8–10   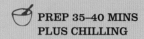 PREP 35–40 MINS PLUS CHILLING   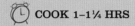 COOK 1–1¼ HRS

EQUIPMENT
23–25cm (9–10in) round springform cake tin

INGREDIENTS

FOR THE PASTRY
250g (9oz) plain flour, plus extra for dusting
finely grated zest of 1 lemon
50g (1¾oz) caster sugar
175g (6oz) unsalted butter, softened, plus extra for greasing
4 egg yolks, plus 1 egg, beaten, to glaze
a pinch of salt

FOR THE FILLING
1.25kg (2¾lb) ricotta cheese
100g (3½oz) caster sugar
1 tbsp plain flour
a pinch of salt
finely grated zest of 1 orange
2 tbsp chopped candied orange peel
1 tsp vanilla extract
45g (1½oz) sultanas
30g (1oz) flaked almonds
4 egg yolks

1 To make the pastry, sift the flour onto a work surface and make a well in the centre. Put the lemon zest, sugar, butter, egg yolks, and salt into the well and work together with your fingertips until mixed. Draw in the flour and press the dough into a ball. On a floured surface, knead the dough for 1–2 minutes until smooth. Shape into a ball, wrap in cling film, and chill for 30 minutes.

2 Grease the tin. Roll out three-quarters of the dough on a floured surface to make a 35–37cm (14–15in) circle and use to line the tin. Trim the excess pastry. Chill, with the dough and trimmings, for 15 minutes.

3 Place the ricotta in a bowl and beat in the sugar, flour, and salt. Add the orange zest, candied peel, vanilla, sultanas, almonds, and egg yolks and beat to combine. Spoon the filling into the pastry case. Tap the tin on the surface to remove any bubbles. Smooth the top of the filling with the back of a wooden spoon.

4 Press the trimmings into the remaining dough and roll out on a floured surface to a 25cm (10in) circle. Cut it into strips, about 1cm (½in) wide, and place them on the top in a criss-cross fashion. Trim off the hanging ends. Moisten the ends of the strips with the beaten egg, then seal them to the edge. Brush the lattice with egg and chill for 15–30 minutes until firm.

5 Preheat the oven to 180°C (350°F/Gas 4), and put a baking sheet inside to heat up. Place the tart on the baking sheet and bake for 1–1¼ hours until firm and golden brown. Set aside to cool in its tin until warm, then remove the sides of the tin and cool completely. The crostata can be made 1 day ahead and kept chilled.

Using ground hazelnuts in the pastry for this tart makes it quite delicate and hard to handle. However, the results are worth it, and the rich flavours of this dessert make it a decidedly adult affair.

MOCHA TART WITH A HAZELNUT CRUST

 SERVES 8   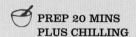 PREP 20 MINS PLUS CHILLING   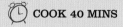 COOK 40 MINS   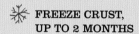 FREEZE CRUST, UP TO 2 MONTHS

1 To make the pastry, pulse the hazelnuts and caster sugar in a food processor to a fine powder. Tip it into a large bowl and mix well with the flour. Rub in the butter with your fingertips until the mixture resembles loose breadcrumbs. Add the egg yolk and bring the mixture together to form a soft dough. Wrap in cling film and chill for 30 minutes.

2 Preheat the oven to 170°C (325°F/Gas 3). Roll the pastry out on a well-floured surface to 7mm (¼in) thick and use to line the tart tin. Trim away excess pastry, leaving a 1cm (½in) overhang. Prick the bottom of the pastry with a fork, line the tart with greaseproof paper, and fill with baking beans. Bake for 15 minutes. Remove the beans and paper and bake for a further 5 minutes until the base is lightly cooked. Trim any excess pastry from around the edges.

3 Place the chocolate and the butter in a heatproof bowl and melt it over a saucepan of simmering water. The level of the water should not touch the bottom of the bowl. Set aside to cool. In a large bowl or food processor, whisk together the eggs and caster sugar until they are light, thick, and frothy.

4 Fold the cooled chocolate mixture into the eggs, then fold in the cooled coffee mixture, mixing well. Pour the filling into the crust and bake for 15–20 minutes until the centre is just set. Remove and set aside for 20 minutes before serving warm or at room temperature with cream. The baked pastry case can be stored in a container for up to 2 days. Best eaten the same day, but can be chilled overnight.

EQUIPMENT
22cm (9in) loose-bottomed fluted tart tin, baking beans

INGREDIENTS

FOR THE PASTRY
(For visual step by step instructions see sweet shortcrust pastry p105)
50g (1¾oz) hazelnuts, skinned
25g (scant 1oz) caster sugar
150g (5½oz) plain flour, plus extra for dusting
75g (2½oz) butter, at room temperature
1 egg yolk

FOR THE FILLING
200g (7oz) good-quality dark chocolate, broken up
100g (3½oz) unsalted butter, diced
3 eggs
50g (1¾oz) caster sugar
1 tbsp strong coffee powder dissolved in 3 tbsp boiling water and cooled, espresso powder can be used for a stronger coffee taste

Traditionally, this classic British recipe was made using fresh curds – a by-product of cheese-making. Nowadays, you will have to make them from scratch, but it is a simple yet pleasing procedure.

YORKSHIRE CURD TART

 **SERVES 6–8**   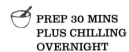 **PREP 30 MINS PLUS CHILLING OVERNIGHT**   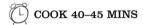 **COOK 40–45 MINS**

EQUIPMENT
22cm (9in) loose-bottomed tart tin

INGREDIENTS

FOR THE CURD CHEESE
1.2 litres (2 pints) whole milk
4 tbsp lemon juice

FOR THE PASTRY
(For visual step by step instructions see sweet shortcrust pastry p105)
150g (5½oz) plain flour, plus extra for dusting
100g (3½oz) unsalted butter
50g (1¾oz) caster sugar
1 egg yolk

FOR THE FILLING
75g (2½oz) butter, at room temperature
75g (2½oz) caster sugar
1 egg
zest of 1 lemon
½ tsp freshly grated nutmeg
45g (1½oz) currants
45g (1½oz) raisins

1 Prepare the curd for the filling a day in advance. Heat the milk in a medium saucepan until just boiling. Remove from the heat, stir in the lemon juice, and set aside to cool for an hour, stirring occasionally. Line a sieve or colander with a clean muslin, or tea towel, and place over a large bowl. Pour the milk mixture into the tea towel and chill overnight.

2 To make the pastry, rub the flour and butter together in a bowl with your fingertips until the mixture resembles fine breadcrumbs. Stir in the sugar. Add the egg yolk to the flour mixture and bring it together to form a smooth dough; add 1–2 tablespoons cold water if needed. Wrap and chill for 30 minutes.

3 For the filling, place the butter and sugar in a large bowl and cream them together, using an electric whisk, until pale and fluffy. Add the egg and whisk until combined. Spoon in the curd cheese (from the tea towel), lemon zest, and nutmeg. Stir well and set aside.

4 Preheat the oven to 180°C (350°F/Gas 4). Roll out the pastry on a floured surface to a circle large enough to line the tart tin. Place the pastry in the tin, pressing down well into the bottom and around the edges. Trim off any excess pastry and prick the bottom with a fork. Place the tin on a baking tray.

5 Evenly scatter the currants and raisins over the pastry. Spoon the cheese mixture over the fruit and spread it out in an even layer. Bake for 25–30 minutes until the filling is golden brown. Cool in the tin for 30 minutes before serving warm or chilled.

A great British sweet tart, here a traditional Treacle Tart recipe is given a more sophisticated touch with the addition of cream and eggs to the filling. Serve warm with thick cream.

TREACLE TART

 SERVES 4–6   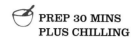 PREP 30 MINS PLUS CHILLING   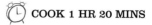 COOK 1 HR 20 MINS

1 To make the pastry, rub the flour and butter together with your fingertips until the mixture resembles breadcrumbs. Stir in the sugar. Beat together the egg yolk and vanilla. Add them to the bowl and bring the mixture together to form a soft dough; add a little water if needed. Wrap and chill for 30 minutes. Preheat the oven to 180°C (350°F/Gas 4).

2 Roll out the dough on a well-floured surface to 3mm (⅛in) thick and use to line the tin, leaving an overlapping edge of at least 2cm (¾in). Prick the bottom of the pastry with a fork, line with baking parchment and fill with baking beans. Place the pastry case on a baking tray and bake for 20 minutes. Remove the beans and paper, and return to the oven for a further 5 minutes if the centre still looks uncooked. Reduce the heat to 170°C (340°F/Gas 3½).

3 For the filling, measure out the golden syrup into a large measuring jug. Measure the cream on top of it (the density of the syrup will keep the two separate, making measuring easy). Add the eggs and orange zest, and whiz together, with a hand-held blender, until well combined. Alternatively, transfer to a bowl and whisk. Gently fold in the brioche crumbs.

4 Place the tart case on a baking tray and put on an oven rack. Pour the filling into the case and carefully slide the rack back into the oven. Bake for 30 minutes until just set, but before the filling starts to bubble up. Trim the pastry edge with a small, sharp knife while still warm, then set aside to cool in its tin for at least 15 minutes before turning out. Serve warm with thick cream or ice cream.

EQUIPMENT
22cm (9in) loose-bottomed tart tin, baking beans

INGREDIENTS

FOR THE PASTRY
(For visual step by step instructions see sweet shortcrust pastry p105)
150g (5½oz) plain flour, plus extra for dusting
100g (3½oz) unsalted butter, chilled and diced
50g (1¾oz) caster sugar
1 egg yolk
½ tsp vanilla extract

FOR THE FILLING
200ml (7fl oz) golden syrup
200ml (7fl oz) double cream
2 eggs
finely grated zest of 1 orange
100g (3½oz) brioche or croissant crumbs

This pie heralds from the Pennsylvania region of the USA. It uses a lot of molasses, and supposedly got its name from the fact that it was so sweet, you had to "shoo" the flies from gathering around it!

SHOO FLY PIE

 SERVES 6–8   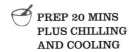 PREP 20 MINS PLUS CHILLING AND COOLING   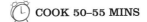 COOK 50–55 MINS   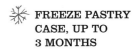 FREEZE PASTRY CASE, UP TO 3 MONTHS

EQUIPMENT
22cm (9in) loose-bottomed tart tin, baking beans

INGREDIENTS

FOR THE PASTRY
(For visual step by step instructions see sweet shortcrust pastry p105)
175g (6oz) plain flour, plus extra for dusting
25g (scant 1oz) caster sugar
100g (3½oz) unsalted butter, at room temperature, cut into pieces
1 egg yolk, beaten with 2 tbsp cold water

FOR THE FILLING
150g (5½oz) plain flour
100g (3½oz) soft light brown sugar
1 tsp mixed spice
50g (1¾oz) unsalted butter, softened
150g (5½oz) molasses or black treacle
½ tsp bicarbonate of soda
1 egg

1 To make the pastry, rub the flour, sugar, and butter together with your fingertips until the mixture resembles fine breadcrumbs. Add the egg yolk and bring the mixture together to form a soft dough; add a little water if needed. Wrap and chill for 30 minutes.

2 Preheat the oven to 180°C (350°F/Gas 4). Roll out the pastry on a floured surface to 3mm (⅛in) thick and use to line the tart tin, leaving an overlapping edge of at least 1cm (½in). Trim off any excess pastry. Prick the bottom with a fork, line with a piece of greaseproof paper, and fill with baking beans. Place the case on a baking tray and bake for 20 minutes. Remove the beans and paper, and bake for a further 5 minutes if the centre still looks a little uncooked. Trim off any ragged edges from the pastry case while it is still warm. Increase the heat to 190°C (375°F/Gas 5).

3 For the filling, mix the flour, soft light brown sugar, and mixed spice together by hand, or in a food processor. Rub in the butter until the mixture resembles fine breadcrumbs. Weigh out the molasses or black treacle in a large bowl. Mix 100ml (3½fl oz) boiling water with the bicarbonate of soda and whisk it into the molasses until dissolved. Set aside to cool.

4 When the pastry case is ready, whisk the egg into the cooled molasses mixture. Set aside 4 heaped tablespoons of the crumb mixture, and whisk the rest into the molasses. Place the tart case on a baking tray and carefully pour in the filling. Scatter the remaining crumbs over the top and bake for 30 minutes until it is puffed up and just set. Serve warm or at room temperature with thick cream or vanilla ice cream. Best eaten the day it is made.

A simple tart, this classic custard filling is flavoured with a hint of nutmeg. To prevent overcooking, remove from the oven while the centre is gently wobbling, as it will continue to set.

CUSTARD TART

 SERVES 8   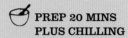 PREP 20 MINS PLUS CHILLING   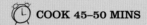 COOK 45–50 MINS   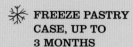 FREEZE PASTRY CASE, UP TO 3 MONTHS

EQUIPMENT
22cm (9in) loose-bottomed tart tin, baking beans

INGREDIENTS

FOR THE PASTRY
(For visual step by step instructions see sweet shortcrust pastry p105)
170g (6oz) plain flour, plus extra for dusting
100g (3½oz) butter, chilled and diced
50g (1¾oz) caster sugar
2 egg yolks
1 tsp vanilla extract

FOR THE FILLING
225ml (7½fl oz) milk
150ml (5fl oz) double cream
30g (1oz) caster sugar
¼ tsp freshly grated nutmeg
2 eggs

1 To make the pastry, mix the flour and butter together with your fingertips until the mixture resembles fine breadcrumbs. Stir in the sugar. Beat the 2 egg yolks with ½ teaspoon vanilla, add them to the bowl, and bring the mixture together to form a soft dough. Wrap in cling film and chill for 30 minutes.

2 Preheat the oven to 180°C (350°F/Gas 4). Roll the dough out on a floured surface to 3mm (⅛in) thick and use to line the tin, leaving an overlapping edge of at least 2cm (¾in). Prick the bottom of the pastry with a fork, line with baking parchment, and fill with baking beans. Bake for 20 minutes. Remove the beans and paper and bake for a further 5 minutes. Trim off excess pastry. Reduce the heat to 170°C (340°F/Gas 3½).

3 Make the custard filling (see below). Place the tart case on a baking tray. Pour the filling into the case and bake for 20–25 minutes until just set but still with a slight wobble in the centre. Set aside to cool.

For the custard filling

1 Put the milk and the cream in a heavy saucepan and bring gently to the boil over a medium heat.

2 Meanwhile, whisk 2 eggs, sugar, remaining vanilla, and nutmeg together in a heatproof bowl.

3 Once the milk and cream have come to the boil, pour them over the egg mixture, whisking constantly.

This classic French tart is a deep-dish custard tart, which is best served chilled. Using a loose-bottomed cake tin gives the requisite depth, and the low baking temperature helps the custard to set.

FLAN NATURE

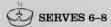 SERVES 6–8   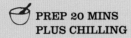 PREP 20 MINS PLUS CHILLING   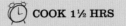 COOK 1½ HRS   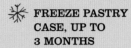 FREEZE PASTRY CASE, UP TO 3 MONTHS

1 To make the pastry, rub the flour, caster sugar, and butter together with your fingertips until the mixture resembles fine breadcrumbs. Beat the egg yolk and vanilla together, and add it to the dry ingredients, bringing the mixture together to form a soft dough; adding a little water if needed. Wrap in cling film and chill in the refrigerator for 30 minutes.

2 Preheat the oven to 170°C (340°F/Gas 3½). Roll out the pastry on a well-floured surface to 3mm (⅛in) thick and use to line the cake tin, leaving an overlapping edge of 2cm (¾in). Trim off any excess pastry that hangs down further than this. Line the case with a piece of greaseproof paper and fill with baking beans. Place the case on a baking tray and bake for 25 minutes. Remove the beans and paper and return to the oven for a further 5 minutes if the centre still looks a little uncooked. Reduce the oven temperature to 150°C (300°F/Gas 2).

3 For the filling, whisk the flour, sugar, eggs, butter, and vanilla together in a bowl to a thick, smooth paste. Whisk in the milk and pour into a jug. Rest the baking tray with the pastry case on the edge of the middle oven shelf. Holding it with one hand, pour the filling carefully into the tart case with the other, then gently push the tart onto the oven shelf and bake for 50 minutes–1 hour until the tart is just set, but has not puffed up at all. The surface should be golden brown. At this point, trim off the excess pastry from the sides.

4 Set the tart aside to cool completely in its tin before eating. The pastry case can be prepared up to 3 days before and stored in an airtight container.

EQUIPMENT
18cm (7in) loose-bottomed cake tin, 4cm (1½in) deep, baking beans

INGREDIENTS

FOR THE PASTRY
(For visual step by step instructions see sweet shortcrust pastry p105)
150g (5½oz) plain flour, plus extra for dusting
50g (1¾oz) caster sugar
100g (3½oz) unsalted butter, softened
1 egg yolk
½ tsp vanilla extract

FOR THE FILLING
100g (3½oz) plain flour
125g (4½oz) caster sugar
3 eggs
50g (1¾oz) unsalted butter, melted and cooled
½ tsp vanilla extract
500ml (6fl oz) milk

One of the most celebrated pastries to come out of Portugal, these ambrosial custard tarts are well worth the effort of baking at home. Rolling the pastry is quite tricky at first, but it is easily mastered.

PASTEIS DE NATA

 MAKES 16    PREP 30 MINS   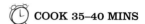 COOK 35–40 MINS

EQUIPMENT
16-hole muffin tray

INGREDIENTS

FOR THE PASTRY
500g (1lb 2oz) ready-made puff pastry
(or to make your own, see pp110–113)
plain flour, for dusting

FOR THE FILLING
500ml (16fl oz) milk
1 cinnamon stick
1 large piece lemon zest
4 egg yolks
100g (3½oz) caster sugar
30g (1oz) plain flour
1 tbsp cornflour

1 Preheat the oven to 220°C (425°F/Gas 7). Roll out the puff pastry on a floured surface to a 40 x 30cm (16 x 12in) rectangle. Roll up the pastry from the long end nearest you to make a log and trim the ends. Cut the pastry into 16 equal-sized slices.

2 Take a piece of rolled pastry and tuck the loose end underneath it. Lay it down and lightly roll into a thin circle, about 10cm (4in) in diameter, turning it over only once to ensure a natural curve to the finished pastry. You will be left with a pastry that resembles a shallow bowl. Press it into a muffin tray with your thumb, ensuring it is well-shaped to the tray. Lightly prick the bottom and chill while you make the filling.

3 Heat the milk, cinnamon stick, and lemon zest in a heavy saucepan. Remove when the milk starts to boil. Whisk the egg yolks, sugar, flour, and cornflour together in a bowl until it forms a thick paste. Remove the cinnamon stick and lemon zest from the hot milk, and pour the milk gradually over the egg yolk mixture, whisking constantly. Return the custard to the cleaned-out pan and place over a medium heat, whisking constantly, until it thickens. Remove from the heat.

4 Fill each pastry case, two-thirds full, with the custard and bake at the top of the oven for 20–25 minutes until the custards are puffed and blackened in places. Set aside to cool. The custards will deflate slightly, but this is normal. Set aside for at least 10–15 minutes before eating warm or cold. The tarts will keep in an airtight container for 1 day. The custard and the pastry cases can be prepared ahead and stored separately in the refrigerator overnight before using.

Traditionally prepared in France for Epiphany, on 6th January, to celebrate the arrival of the three kings, a rich buttery puff pastry is filled with frangipane and baked until golden brown.

GALETTE DES ROIS

 SERVES 6–8   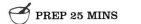 PREP 25 MINS    COOK 30 MINS    FREEZE UP TO 2 MONTHS

1 Preheat the oven to 200°C (400°F/Gas 6). Cream the sugar and butter together in a bowl with an electric whisk. Beat in the egg and blend well. Mix in the ground almonds, almond extract, and rum, brandy, or milk, to make a thick paste.

2 Roll out the pastry on a well-floured surface to a 50 x 25cm (20 x 10in) rectangle. The measurements do not have to be exact, but the pastry should be 3–5mm (⅛–¼in) thick. Fold the pastry in half and use a 25cm (10in) dinner plate, or similar, to cut out 2 discs.

3 Lay 1 disc out on the baking tray. Use a little beaten egg to brush around the edge of the disc. Spoon the frangipane filling on the pastry disc, spreading it out smoothly to within 1cm (½in) of the edge. Put the other pastry disc on top of the filling, and use your fingers or the back of a fork to press down and seal the 2 discs together.

4 Use a small, sharp knife to score a series of thin slivers on the top of the pastry, in a spiral design, being careful not to allow them to meet in the centre or the pastry will pull apart when cooking. If you are feeling artistic, cut the edges of the pastry into a scalloped edge before cooking.

5 Brush the top of the pastry with the beaten egg, and bake at the top of the oven for 30 minutes until golden brown and puffed up. Set aside to cool for 5 minutes on its tray before removing to a wire rack. Serve either warm or cold. The galette will keep in an airtight container for 3 days. The frangipane can be prepared 3 days ahead and stored in the refrigerator.

EQUIPMENT
baking tray

INGREDIENTS

FOR THE FILLING
100g (3½oz) caster sugar
100g (3½oz) unsalted butter, softened
1 egg, plus 1 extra, beaten, to glaze
100g (3½oz) ground almonds
1 tsp almond extract
1 tbsp brandy, rum, or milk

FOR THE PASTRY
500g (1lb 2oz) ready-made puff pastry
   (or to make your own, see pp110–113)
plain flour, for dusting

These crisp, crunchy filo cases are full of just-set delicately spiced custard, and are the perfect way to end a Middle Eastern feast. These little tartlets are best eaten on the day they are made.

CARDAMOM CUSTARD FILO TARTLETS

 MAKES 6    PREP 15 MINS   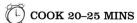 COOK 20–25 MINS

EQUIPMENT
6-hole deep (6cm/2½in) muffin tin

INGREDIENTS

FOR THE FILLING
225ml (7½fl oz) full-fat milk
150ml (5fl oz) double cream
6 cardamom pods, crushed
plain flour, for dusting
2 eggs
30g (1oz) caster sugar
icing sugar, for dusting

FOR THE PASTRY
3 sheets ready-made filo pastry
25g (scant 1oz) unsalted butter, melted

1 Preheat the oven to 190°C (375°F/Gas 5). Heat the milk, cream, and cardamom pods in a heavy-based saucepan to boiling point. Turn off the heat and leave the cardamom to infuse.

2 On a well-floured surface, lay out 1 sheet of the filo pastry, covering the rest in a clean, damp tea towel. Brush the surface of the pastry with a little melted butter, and cover with a second layer. Brush the second layer with more melted butter and cover with a third layer. Cut the pastry into 6 equal pieces.

3 Brush the insides of the muffin tin with a little melted butter. Take a piece of the layered filo and use it to line the muffin mould, pushing it into the sides. The pastry should be ruffled and stick up over the edges in places. Do this with all 6 pieces of pastry. Repeat the layering process with the remaining sheets of pastry until you have 6 filo cases. Brush the pastry edges with any remaining butter and cover the tin with the damp tea towel.

4 For the custard, reheat the milk mixture gently over a medium heat, but do not allow it to boil. Whisk together the eggs and caster sugar in a large bowl. Pour the milk mixture into the whisked eggs and cream through a sieve to remove the cardamom. Whisk the mixture together and transfer it to a jug.

5 Pour the custard into the tart cases and bake for 15–20 minutes until the pastry is crisp at the edges and the custard is just set in the middle. Set the tarts aside to cool in their tins for 10 minutes before removing to cool completely on a wire rack. Dust the tartlets with a little icing sugar before serving.

This rich Middle Eastern confection is baked until crisp, then drenched in a honey syrup for the ultimate after-dinner treat with a strong coffee. Any leftovers can be stored in an airtight container.

BAKLAVA

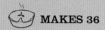 **MAKES 36**   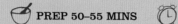 **PREP 50–55 MINS**   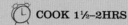 **COOK 1½–2HRS**

EQUIPMENT
30 x 40cm (12 x 16in) baking tray with deep sides, sugar thermometer (optional)

INGREDIENTS

FOR THE FILLING
250g (9oz) unsalted pistachio nuts, shelled and coarsely chopped
250g (9oz) walnut pieces, coarsely chopped
50g (1¾oz) caster sugar
2 tsp ground cinnamon
a large pinch of ground cloves

FOR THE PASTRY
500g (1lb 2oz) filo pastry
250g (9oz) unsalted butter, melted

FOR THE SYRUP
200g (7oz) caster sugar
250ml (9fl oz) honey
juice of 1 lemon
3 tbsp orange flower water

1 Set aside 3–4 tablespoons of the pistachios. Put the remainder in a bowl with the walnuts, sugar, cinnamon, and cloves and stir to mix.

2 Preheat the oven to 180°C (350°F/Gas 4). Unroll the filo onto a damp tea towel and cover with a second damp towel. Brush the baking tray with butter. Take a sheet of filo and use to line the tin, folding over one end to fit. Brush the filo with butter, and press it into the corners and sides of the tin. Lay another sheet on top, brush with butter, and press into the tin. Continue layering, buttering each sheet, until one-third has been used. Scatter half the filling over the top.

3 Layer another third of the filo sheets as before, then sprinkle the remaining filling over. Layer the remaining sheets in the same way. Trim away excess. Brush with butter and pour any remaining butter on top. Cut diagonal lines, 1cm (½in) deep, in the filo to mark out 4cm (1½in) diamond shapes. Bake on a low shelf for 1¼–1½ hours until golden. A skewer inserted in the centre for 30 seconds should come out clean.

4 To make the syrup, heat the sugar and 250ml (9fl oz) water in a pan until dissolved. Stir in the honey. Boil for 25 minutes without stirring, until the syrup reaches the soft ball stage, 115°C (239°F) on a thermometer. Or, remove from the heat and dip a teaspoon in the syrup. Cool slightly then take some between your finger and thumb; a soft ball should form. Cool to lukewarm. Add the lemon juice and orange flower water.

5 Remove from the oven and pour the syrup over the pastries. Cut along the marked lines, almost to the bottom. Cool, then cut through the marked lines. Sprinkle the pastries with the pistachios. The pastries can be made 5 days before serving.

Originating from the southern United States where pecans are widely grown, a little of this traditional pie goes a very long way. It is best served warm with crème fraîche or whipped cream.

PECAN PIE

 SERVES 6–8

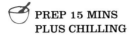 PREP 15 MINS PLUS CHILLING

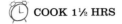 COOK 1½ HRS

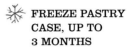 FREEZE PASTRY CASE, UP TO 3 MONTHS

1 To make the pastry, rub the flour and butter together with your fingertips until the mixture resembles fine breadcrumbs. Stir in the sugar. Beat the egg yolk with the vanilla extract and mix them into the dry ingredients, bringing the mixture together to form a soft dough; add a little water to bring the dough together, if necessary. Wrap in cling film and chill in the refrigerator for 30 minutes.

2 Preheat the oven to 180°C (350°F/Gas 4). Roll out the pastry on a well-floured surface to 3mm (⅛in) thick and use it to line the tin, leaving an overlapping edge of at least 2cm (¾in). Prick the bottom all over with a fork, line with baking parchment, and fill with baking beans. Place on a baking tray and bake for 20 minutes. Remove the beans and paper, and bake for a further 5 minutes, if the centre looks uncooked.

3 Pour the maple syrup into a pan, and add the butter, sugar, vanilla extract, and salt. Place the pan over a low heat and stir constantly until the butter has melted and the sugar dissolved.

4 Set the mixture aside to cool until it feels just tepid, then beat in the eggs, one at a time. Stir in the pecans, then pour the mixture into the pastry case.

5 Bake for 40–50 minutes until just set. Cover with foil if it is browning too quickly. Remove the pie, transfer it to a wire rack, and set aside to cool for 15–20 minutes. Remove from the tin and serve warm or leave it on the wire rack to cool completely. The pie will keep in an airtight container for 2 days. The unfilled pastry case can be prepared ahead and stored in an airtight container for up to 3 days.

EQUIPMENT
22cm (9in) loose-bottomed tart tin, baking beans

INGREDIENTS

FOR THE PASTRY
(For visual step by step instructions see sweet shortcrust pastry p105)
150g (5½oz) plain flour, plus extra for dusting
100g (3½oz) unsalted butter, chilled and diced
50g (1¾oz) caster sugar
1 egg yolk
½ tsp vanilla extract

FOR THE FILLING
150ml (5fl oz) maple syrup
60g (2oz) butter
175g (6oz) soft light brown sugar
a few drops of vanilla extract
a pinch of salt
3 eggs
200g (7oz) pecan nuts

Recipes using these seeds are popular all over Eastern Europe, and this German tart is a fantastic showcase for a classic combination of tangy curd cheese and poppy seeds. Serve either warm or cold.

SILESIAN POPPY SEED TART

 **SERVES 8**   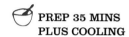 **PREP 35 MINS PLUS COOLING**    **COOK 1½ HRS**

EQUIPMENT
22cm (9in) loose-bottomed fluted tart tin

INGREDIENTS

FOR THE PASTRY
(For visual step by step instructions see sweet shortcrust pastry p105)
250g (9oz) plain flour
2 tsp baking powder
125g (4½oz) caster sugar
2–3 drops vanilla extract
a pinch of salt
1 egg
125g (4½oz) butter, softened, plus extra for greasing

FOR THE FILLING
1 litre (1¾ pints) milk
150g (5½ oz) butter
200g (7oz) semolina
200g (7oz) poppy seeds
175g (60oz) caster sugar
1 tsp vanilla extract
2 eggs
100g (3½oz) curd cheese
50g (1¾oz) ground almonds
50g (1¾oz) raisins
1 pear, peeled, cored, and grated
icing sugar, for dusting

1 To make the pastry, sift the flour and baking powder into a large bowl. Add the sugar, vanilla, salt, egg, butter, and a little water and mix together to make a dough, roll into a ball, and set aside.

2 Place the milk and butter in a saucepan and bring to the boil. Gradually stir in the semolina and poppy seeds. Simmer over a low heat for 20 minutes, stirring occasionally, then remove from the heat and set aside to cool for 10 minutes.

3 Preheat the oven to 180°C (350°F/Gas 4) and grease the bottom of the tin. Roll out half of the dough and fit it into the bottom of the tin. Roll out the remaining dough into a long strip and press it to the side of the tin to form an edge 3cm (1¼in) high.

4 Stir together the sugar, vanilla extract, eggs, curd cheese, almonds, and raisins into the cooled poppy seed and semolina mixture. Stir in the pear. Pour the mixture evenly into the pastry base, and bake for 1 hour.

5 Place the tin on a wire rack to cool, loosen the edge of the tart with a knife, and remove the ring. Dust with icing sugar before serving.

Some walnut tart recipes use halved walnuts to decorate the top, but try this alternative. Half a walnut can be difficult to tackle with a fork, so grinding them gives a smooth texture that's easier to handle.

WALNUT TART

 SERVES 8

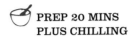 **PREP 20 MINS PLUS CHILLING**

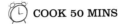 **COOK 50 MINS**

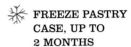 **FREEZE PASTRY CASE, UP TO 2 MONTHS**

1 To make the pastry, rub the flour, sugar, and butter together with your fingertips until the mixture resembles fine breadcrumbs. Beat the egg yolk together with 2 tablespoons of cold water and add it to the dry ingredients, bringing the mixture together to form a soft dough. Add a little more water if the pastry seems dry. Wrap the pastry in cling film and chill for 30 minutes to make it easier to handle when rolling out.

2 Preheat the oven to 180°C (350°F/Gas 4). Roll out the pastry on a well-floured surface to 5mm (¼in) thick and use to line the tart tin, leaving an overlapping edge of at least 1cm (½in). Trim any excess pastry using a pair of scissors. Prick the bottom of the pastry with a fork, line with greaseproof paper, and fill with baking beans. Place the tin on a baking tray and bake for 20 minutes. Remove the beans and the paper, and bake for a further 5 minutes if the centre looks uncooked. Trim off any ragged edges while it is still warm.

3 For the filling, whiz the shelled walnuts and sugar together in a food processor to a fairly fine texture. Whisk together the eggs, cream, and vanilla extract, then whisk in the nut and sugar mixture. Pour the filling into the pastry case and bake for 20–25 minutes until the filling has just set.

4 Remove and set aside for at least 10 minutes before serving warm or at room temperature with thick cream. The cooked pastry case can be stored in an airtight container for up to 3 days.

EQUIPMENT
22cm (9in) loose-bottomed fluted tart tin, baking beans

INGREDIENTS

FOR THE PASTRY
(For visual step by step instructions see sweet shortcrust pastry p105)
175g (6oz) plain flour,
  plus extra for dusting
25g (scant 1oz) caster sugar
100g (3½oz) unsalted butter, softened
1 egg yolk

FOR THE FILLING
200g (7oz) walnuts, shelled
125g (4½oz) caster sugar
2 eggs
200ml (7fl oz) single cream
½ tsp vanilla extract

This large, decorative Millefeuilles is a perfect way to end a Christmas meal. When ready to serve, carefully cut the pastry into even portions so as not to disrupt its delicate structure.

CHESTNUT MILLEFEUILLES

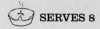 SERVES 8   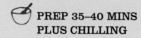 PREP 35–40 MINS
PLUS CHILLING   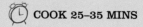 COOK 25–35 MINS

EQUIPMENT
baking tray

INGREDIENTS

FOR THE FILLING
375ml (13fl oz) milk
4 egg yolks
60g (2oz) granulated sugar
3 tbsp plain flour, sifted
2 tbsp dark rum
250ml (9fl oz) double cream
500g (1lb 2oz) marrons glacés,
coarsely crumbled
45g (1½oz) icing sugar,
plus extra if needed

FOR THE PASTRY
600g (1lb 5oz) ready-made puff pastry
(or to make your own, see pp110–113)

1 Heat the milk in a saucepan until it just boils. Whisk the yolks and granulated sugar for 2–3 minutes until thick. Whisk in the flour, then gradually whisk in the milk until smooth. Return to a clean pan, bring to the boil, whisking, until thick. Reduce the heat to low and whisk for 2 minutes. Cool, then stir in the rum. Transfer to a bowl, cover, and chill for 1 hour.

2 Preheat the oven to 200°C (400°F/Gas 6). Sprinkle a baking tray with water. Roll out the pastry to a rectangle a little larger than the tray, 3mm (⅛in) thick and put it on the tray. Let the edges overhang. Press the dough down. Chill for 15 minutes, then prick with a fork. Cover with parchment. Set a wire rack on top. Bake for 15–20 minutes. Grip the tray and rack, invert the pastry. Slide tray back under pastry and bake for 10 minutes. Prepare the pastry layers (see below). Whip the cream until fairly firm, then fold into the pastry cream. Spread half the cream over 1 pastry strip and sprinkle with half the chestnuts. Repeat to make 2 layers then top with the last strip. Sift over icing sugar.

Preparing the pastry layers

1 Remove the pastry from the oven and carefully slide the pastry onto a chopping board.

2 While still warm, trim round the edges with a large, sharp knife to neaten.

3 Cut the trimmed sheet lengthways into 3 equal strips. Set the pastry aside to cool.

This Baklava has a crisp yet chewy texture. Serve this delicious treat at teatime or after dinner with a cup of tea or coffee. If you can't find Chilean honey, any variety of runny honey will do.

MIXED NUT BAKLAVA WITH HONEY AND ORANGE

 SERVES 10   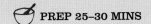 PREP 25-30 MINS    COOK 1 HR

1 Preheat the oven to 180°C (350°F/Gas 4). Chop the nuts in a food processor until coarse, then stir in the cinnamon and set aside.

2 Brush the baking tin with melted butter to prevent it from drying.

3 Start layering sheets of filo into the prepared tin, brushing each one with a little of the melted butter before placing the next neatly on top of the last layer. After 6 layers, scatter on half of the nut mixture. Repeat, then add a final 6 layers. Brush the top with melted butter and trim off any overlapping pastry. Cut the pastry into 4–5cm (1½–2in) diamonds, making sure that the knife cuts all the way through the pastry layers to the bottom of the tin.

4 Bake for 40–45 minutes until golden and crisp. Reduce the heat to 160°C (325°F/Gas 3) if the pastry is browning quickly.

5 To make the syrup, place the caster sugar, honey, cinnamon, orange zest, and cloves with 300ml (10fl oz) water in a saucepan and bring to a simmer. Simmer, stirring occasionally, for 15 minutes, or until the liquid has reduced by a third. Set aside to cool.

6 Remove the pastry from the oven and spoon half the syrup on top. Leave for 5 minutes, then spoon over the remaining syrup. Set aside to cool completely before removing the pieces from the tin with a palette knife. Store in the tin. The baklava will keep for 3–4 days, but will get increasingly soggy.

EQUIPMENT
24 x 24cm (9½ x 9½in) baking tin

INGREDIENTS

FOR THE FILLING
150g (5½oz) Brazil nuts
150g (5½oz) cashew nuts
1½ tsp ground cinnamon

FOR THE PASTRY
150g (5½oz) butter, melted,
  plus extra for greasing
18 sheets of 25 x 24cm (10 x 9½in)
  ready-made filo pastry

FOR THE SYRUP
350g (12oz) unrefined caster sugar
125ml (4fl oz) Chilean honey
1 tsp ground cinnamon
grated zest of ½ orange
1 tsp whole cloves

Iranian nibbed pistachios are the best type of nuts to use for this tart, as they give a vivid, bright green colour to the finished dish. They are expensive, so normal shelled and skinned pistachios can be used.

PISTACHIO AND ORANGE FLOWER TART

 SERVES 6–8   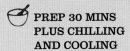 PREP 30 MINS PLUS CHILLING AND COOLING   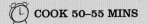 COOK 50–55 MINS   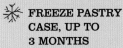 FREEZE PASTRY CASE, UP TO 3 MONTHS

1 To make the pastry, rub the flour, sugar, and butter together with your fingertips until the mixture resembles fine breadcrumbs. Add the egg yolk and bring the mixture together to form a soft dough. If the dough is too dry, add a little water. Wrap the dough in cling film and chill for 30 minutes.

2 Preheat the oven to 180°C (350°F/Gas 4). Roll out the pastry on a floured surface to 3mm (⅛in) thick and use to line the tart tin, leaving an overlapping edge of at least 1cm (½in). Trim off any excess pastry that hangs down further than this. Prick the bottom of the pastry with a fork, line with greaseproof paper, and fill with baking beans. Place the case on a baking tray and bake for 20 minutes. Remove the beans and paper, and return to the oven for a further 5 minutes if the centre still looks a little uncooked. Trim off any ragged edges from the pastry case while it is still warm.

3 To make the filling, first melt the butter and set aside to cool. Next, finely grind the pistachios in a food processor. Whisk together the eggs, sugar, orange flower water, and honey. Whisk in the cooled, melted butter, then fold in the ground pistachios. Place the tart case on a baking tray and carefully pour the filling in. Bake immediately (or it may separate) for 25–30 minutes until the centre has just set, but the top is not browning.

4 Set the tart aside to cool for 15 minutes, then dust with icing sugar and serve warm, or at room temperature, with whipped cream flavoured with a little orange flower water. Best eaten on the day it is made.

EQUIPMENT
22cm (9in) loose-bottomed fluted tart tin, baking beans

INGREDIENTS

FOR THE PASTRY
(For visual step by step instructions
   see sweet shortcrust pastry p105)
175g (6oz) plain flour,
   plus extra for dusting
25g (scant 1oz) caster sugar
100g (3½oz) unsalted butter, softened
1 egg yolk, beaten with
   2 tbsp cold water

FOR THE FILLING
75g (2½oz) unsalted butter
200g (7oz) nibbed pistachios
   (these give the best colour,
   although others can be used)
4 eggs
100g (3½oz) caster sugar
½ tbsp orange flower water
2 tbsp runny honey
icing sugar, for dusting

Otherwise known as "Grandmother's Tart", this classic Italian recipe is made using the freshest of ricotta and little else. This tart is fantastic served still warm from the oven drizzled with honey.

TORTA DELLA NONNA

 **SERVES 6**

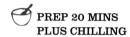 **PREP 20 MINS PLUS CHILLING**

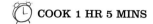 **COOK 1 HR 5 MINS**

 **FREEZE PASTRY CASE, UP TO 1 MONTH**

EQUIPMENT
20cm (8in) loose-bottomed deep tart tin, baking beans

INGREDIENTS

FOR THE PASTRY
(For visual step by step instructions see sweet shortcrust pastry p105)
150g (5½oz) plain flour, plus extra for dusting
100g (3½oz) unsalted butter, diced
50g (1¾oz) caster sugar
1 egg yolk
½ tsp vanilla extract

FOR THE FILLING
400g (14oz) ricotta cheese
2 large eggs
zest and juice of 1 lemon
75g (2½oz) icing sugar, sifted, plus extra for dusting
1 tsp almond extract
70g (1¼oz) toasted pine nuts
30g (1oz) toasted sliced almonds

1 To make the pastry, rub the flour and butter together in a bowl with your fingertips until the mixture resembles breadcrumbs. Stir in the sugar. Add the egg yolk and vanilla to the flour mixture and bring together to form a smooth dough, adding 1–2 teaspoons cold water if needed. Wrap and chill for 30 minutes.

2 For the filling, place the ricotta and eggs in a large bowl and whisk until smooth. Stir in the lemon zest and juice, icing sugar, and almond extract. Set aside. Preheat the oven to 180°C (350°F/Gas 4).

3 Roll out the pastry on a floured surface to a circle large enough to line the tart tin. Place the pastry in the tin, pressing it down well into the bottom and around the edges. Trim off any excess pastry, prick the bottom with a fork, and line with baking parchment. Place the tin on a baking tray and fill with baking beans. Bake for 20 minutes. Remove the beans and paper and bake for a further 5–10 minutes to crisp.

4 Evenly scatter the pine nuts over the pastry base. Spoon the cheese mixture in, spread it out in an even layer, and sprinkle the almonds over the top. Bake the tart for 30–35 minutes until the filling is just set. Transfer to a wire rack and set aside to cool for 15 minutes. Serve dusted with icing sugar.

This rich almond tart is lovely served with a glass of dessert wine at the end of a meal. A sweet and sour mixture of marmalade and orange juice is used to glaze the tart before baking.

ALMOND AND ORANGE TART

 SERVES 8   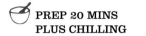 PREP 20 MINS
PLUS CHILLING    COOK 45–55 MINS

1 To make the pastry, put the ground almonds, flour, and sugar into a food processor and pulse briefly to mix. Add the butter, and pulse until the mixture resembles breadcrumbs. Add the orange zest and egg yolk through the feeder funnel and process briefly to a smooth dough. Chill for 15 minutes.

2 For the almond filling, process the blanched almonds in a food processor, until coarsely ground. Add the citrus zests and juices with the amaretto, and process briefly to mix. Pour into a bowl and set aside.

3 Place the butter and sugar in a food processor and process. Add the eggs, one at a time, processing briefly to combine. Add this mix to the almond mixture, stir well, and set aside.

4 Roll out the pastry on a floured surface and use to line the tart tin. If the pastry is difficult to handle, roll it out between 2 sheets of cling film. Chill in the refrigerator for 30 minutes.

5 Preheat the oven to 180°C (350°F/Gas 4). Line the pastry case with greaseproof paper and baking beans, and bake for 10 minutes. Remove the paper and beans and bake for a further 5 minutes. Set the pastry case aside to cool on a wire rack.

6 For the topping, warm the marmalade in a small saucepan with 1 tablespoon water and the orange juice, stirring until melted. Spread evenly over the bottom of the tart. Spoon the almond mixture on top. Bake for 30–40 minutes until the filling is golden. Set the tart aside to cool in the tin for 15 minutes, then carefully remove to a large serving plate. Dust the top with icing sugar and serve warm.

EQUIPMENT
25cm (10in) loose-bottomed
fluted tart tin, baking beans

INGREDIENTS

FOR THE PASTRY
30g (1oz) ground almonds
175g (6oz) plain flour,
    plus extra for dusting
1 tbsp icing sugar
85g (3oz) butter, softened
grated zest of 1 orange
1 egg yolk

FOR THE FILLING
200g (7oz) blanched almonds
grated zest and juice of 1 orange
grated zest and juice of 1 lemon
2 tbsp amaretto liqueur
200g (7oz) butter
100g (3½oz) icing sugar
4 eggs

FOR THE TOPPING
175g (6oz) thin cut marmalade
squeeze of orange juice
icing sugar, for dusting

Pear and ginger is a fabulous combination, and using a mixture of ginger biscuits, stem ginger, and ginger syrup adds layers of flavour to this classic pie. Make sure the ice cream is soft enough to scoop.

PEAR AND GINGER ICE-CREAM PIE

 **SERVES 8**

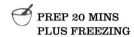 **PREP 20 MINS PLUS FREEZING**

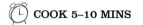 **COOK 5–10 MINS**

 **FREEZE UP TO 1 MONTH**

EQUIPMENT
23cm (9in) round springform tin

INGREDIENTS

FOR THE BISCUIT CASE
(For visual step by step instructions
see biscuit case p120)
75g (2½oz) unsalted butter
plus extra for greasing
250g (9oz) ginger biscuits, crushed

FOR THE TOPPING
1 litre tub good-quality vanilla ice cream
5 pieces stem ginger preserved
in syrup, drained
2 tbsp stem ginger syrup,
plus extra for drizzling
415g can pear halves in natural juice,
drained and finely chopped

1 Grease and line the bottom of the tin with baking parchment. Take the ice cream out of the freezer to allow it to soften.

2 To make the biscuit case, melt the butter in a saucepan and mix in the crushed biscuits. Turn the mixture into the prepared tin and press down with the back of a metal tablespoon.

3 For the topping, scoop the softened ice cream, the stem ginger pieces, and stem ginger syrup into a food processor. Process until the ice cream is thick and creamy, but smooth. Stir in the chopped pears, by hand. Pour the mixture into the prepared tin and freeze the pie for at least 2 hours, or until completely frozen.

4 To serve the ice-cream pie, remove it from the freezer and place it on a serving plate. Chill it in the refrigerator for 30 minutes, then unclip the tin and remove the sides. Drizzle a little ginger syrup over the top of the pie and slice to serve.

This dessert came about when I wanted to cook something to finish an Asian dinner party. Not being big on Asian desserts, I adapted my classic Tart au Citron recipe with truly delicious results.

LIME AND COCONUT TART

 **SERVES 8**   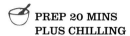 **PREP 20 MINS PLUS CHILLING**   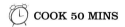 **COOK 50 MINS**   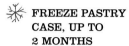 **FREEZE PASTRY CASE, UP TO 2 MONTHS**

1 To make the pastry, rub the flour, sugar, and butter together with your fingertips until the mixture resembles fine breadcrumbs. Beat the egg yolk with 2 tablespoons of water and add it to the dry ingredients, bringing the mixture together to form a soft dough. Add a little more water if the pastry seems dry. Wrap in cling film and chill in the refrigerator for 30 minutes.

2 Preheat the oven to 180°C (350°F/Gas 4). Roll out the pastry on a well-floured surface to 5mm (¼in) thick. Line the tart tin, leaving an overlapping edge of at least 1cm (½in). Trim away any excess. Prick the bottom of the pastry with a fork, line with silicone or greaseproof paper, and fill with baking beans. Place the tin on a baking tray and bake for 20 minutes. Remove the beans and paper and bake for a further 5 minutes if the centre still looks a little uncooked. Trim off any ragged edges from the pastry case while still warm.

3 Meanwhile, prepare the filling. Whisk together all the ingredients for the filling in a large bowl until well amalgamated. Pour the cream mixture into a jug and set aside until the bubbles on the surface go down.

4 When the pastry case has finished baking, pull the baking tray with the pastry case on it halfway out of the oven. Holding it carefully with one hand (while it is resting securely on the oven shelf) pour the cream into the case then slide the case back into the oven and bake for 20–25 minutes until the centre has barely set. Set aside to cool completely before serving, dusted with icing sugar. The cooked pastry case can be stored, well wrapped, for up to 3 days. Best eaten the same day.

EQUIPMENT
22cm (9in) loose-bottomed fluted tart tin, baking beans

INGREDIENTS

**FOR THE PASTRY
(For visual step by step instructions see sweet shortcrust pastry p105)**
175g (6oz) plain flour, plus extra for dusting
25g (scant 1oz) caster sugar
100g (3½oz) unsalted butter, softened
1 egg yolk
icing sugar, for dusting

FOR THE FILLING
200ml (7fl oz) thick coconut milk or coconut cream
225g (8oz) caster sugar
5 eggs
grated zest of 2 limes
juice of 4 limes

Rich, buttery shortcrust tartlets can be baked in bulk and frozen for future use. Just crisp them up in a hot oven for a few minutes before filling, here with a deliciously thick coconut cream.

COCONUT CREAM TARTLETS

 MAKES 4   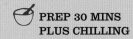 **PREP 30 MINS PLUS CHILLING**   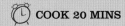 **COOK 20 MINS**

EQUIPMENT
4 x 12cm (5in) loose-bottomed fluted tart tins

INGREDIENTS

FOR THE PASTRY
(For visual step by step instructions see sweet shortcrust pastry p105)
150g (5½oz) plain flour, plus extra for dusting 100g (3½oz) unsalted butter, diced, plus extra for greasing
50g (1¾oz) caster sugar
1 egg yolk
½ tsp vanilla extract

FOR THE FILLING
400ml tin coconut milk
240ml (8½fl oz) whole milk
4 egg yolks
50g (1¾oz) caster sugar
4 tbsp cornflour
1 tsp vanilla extract
4 tbsp desiccated coconut

1 Preheat the oven to 200°C (400°F/Gas 6). Lightly grease the tart tins. To make the pastry, rub the flour and butter together in a bowl with your fingertips until the mixture resembles fine breadcrumbs. Stir in the sugar. Add the egg yolk and vanilla to the flour mixture and bring together to form a smooth dough, adding 1–2 tablespoons cold water if needed. Wrap in cling film and chill for 30 minutes.

2 For the filling, heat the coconut milk and whole milk in a small non-stick saucepan, until just boiling. Whisk the egg yolks, sugar, cornflour, and vanilla together in a heatproof medium bowl or large jug. Gradually pour in the hot milk mixture, whisking constantly. Pour the coconut custard back into the pan and stir, with a wooden spoon, over a medium heat, until it thickens. Remove the pan, cover the coconut custard with greaseproof paper, and set aside to cool.

3 Divide the pastry equally into 4 parts. Roll out one-quarter of the dough on a well-floured surface to a circle large enough to line one of the tins. Place the pastry in the tin and trim the edges. Prick the bottom with a fork and place on a baking tray. Repeat using the remaining pastry. Chill for 30 minutes.

4 Line each tartlet case with foil, pressing it down well. Bake for 5 minutes, then remove the foil, and bake for a further 5 minutes. Set aside to cool.

5 In a small, dry frying pan, lightly toast the coconut over a medium heat, shaking the pan occasionally. Remove the pastry cases from the tins. An hour before serving, spoon the cooled coconut custard into the pastry cases and chill for 1 hour. Sprinkle with the toasted coconut to serve.

This version of the classic American dessert produces a delicate, just-set pie. Gently flavoured with the warm tones of cinnamon and mixed spice, it is best served warm with whipped cream.

PECAN AND MAPLE PUMPKIN PIE

 **SERVES 6–8**   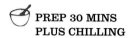 **PREP 30 MINS PLUS CHILLING**   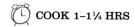 **COOK 1–1¼ HRS**   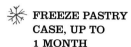 **FREEZE PASTRY CASE, UP TO 1 MONTH**

EQUIPMENT
22cm (9in) loose-bottomed tart tin, baking beans

INGREDIENTS

FOR THE PASTRY
(For visual step by step instructions see sweet shortcrust pastry p105)
150g (5½oz) plain flour, plus extra for dusting
100g (3½oz) unsalted butter, chilled and diced
50g (1¾oz) caster sugar
1 egg yolk
½ tsp vanilla extract

FOR THE FILLING
75g (2½oz) pecan nuts, roughly chopped
3 eggs
100g (3½oz) soft light brown sugar
2 tsp ground cinnamon
1 tsp mixed spice
4 tbsp maple syrup
400ml (14fl oz) double cream
425g tin processed pumpkin, or 400g (14oz) roasted and puréed pumpkin

1 To make the pastry, rub the flour and butter in a large bowl together with your fingertips until the mixture resembles breadcrumbs. Stir in the sugar. Beat together the egg yolk and vanilla, then add to the flour mixture and bring the mixture together to form a soft dough, adding a little water if needed. Wrap in cling film and chill for 30 minutes.

2 Preheat the oven to 180°C (350°F/Gas 4). Roll out the pastry on a floured surface to 3mm (⅛in) thick and use to line the tin, leaving an overlapping edge of at least 2cm (¾in). Prick the bottom with a fork, line with baking parchment and fill with baking beans. Place the case on a baking tray and bake for 20 minutes. Remove the beans and paper and bake for a further 5 minutes if the centre is uncooked. Sprinkle the pecan nuts over the bottom of the pastry case.

3 Whisk the eggs, soft light brown sugar, half the cinnamon, the mixed spice, half the maple syrup, and half the cream together in a large bowl. When they are well blended, beat in the pumpkin to make a smooth filling. Partially pull out an oven rack from the oven, and place the pastry case on it. Pour the filling into the case and slide the rack back into the oven. Bake for 45–50 minutes until the filling is quite set, but before it begins to bubble up at the edges. Trim off the pastry edge while still warm, then set the pie aside to cool in its tin for 15 minutes before turning out.

4 Lightly whip the remaining cream until soft peaks start to form, stir in the remaining ground cinnamon and maple syrup, and serve with the pie. The pie can be chilled in an airtight container for 2 days.

Another American classic and a close relative of the pumpkin pie, here a rich, sweet shortcrust is used for a truly crisp crust. This is a deliciously festive dessert, perfect for the holiday season.

SWEET POTATO PIE

 SERVES 6   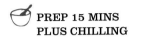 PREP 15 MINS PLUS CHILLING   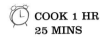 COOK 1 HR 25 MINS    FREEZE UP TO 1 MONTH

1 To make the pastry, rub the flour and butter together in a bowl with your fingertips until the mixture resembles fine breadcrumbs. Stir in the sugar. Add the egg yolk and vanilla to the flour mixture and bring together to form a smooth dough, adding 1–2 teaspoons cold water, if needed. Wrap in cling film and chill in the refrigerator for 30 minutes.

2 For the filling, cook the sweet potato chunks in a saucepan of boiling water for 15 minutes, or until tender. Drain, return to the pan, and mash. Stir in the butter, muscovado sugar, cream, egg, and spices. Beat well to combine, then set aside.

3 Preheat the oven to 180°C (350°F/Gas 4). Roll out the pastry on a floured surface to a circle large enough to line the tart tin. Place the pastry in the tin, pressing down well into the bottom and around the edges. Trim off any excess pastry, prick the bottom with a fork, and line with baking parchment. Place the tin on a baking tray and fill with baking beans. Bake for 20 minutes. Remove the beans and paper and bake for a further 5 minutes if the centre is uncooked.

4 Spoon the filling into the pastry case and level with the back of a spoon. Bake for 40–45 minutes until the filling is set. Remove from the oven, set aside to cool a little, then dust with icing sugar to serve.

EQUIPMENT
20cm (8in) loose-bottomed tart tin, baking beans

INGREDIENTS

FOR THE PASTRY
(For visual step by step instructions see sweet shortcrust pastry p105)
150g (5½oz) plain flour, plus extra for dusting
100g (3½oz) unsalted butter
50g (1¾oz) caster sugar
1 egg yolk
½ tsp vanilla extract

FOR THE FILLING
400g (14oz) sweet potato, peeled and chopped into small chunks
85g (3oz) unsalted butter
100g (3½oz) muscovado sugar
3 tbsp single cream
1 egg
½ tsp ground nutmeg
½ tsp ground cinnamon
icing sugar, for dusting

These delicate fried pastries are a classic all over Greece, where they are served still warm and scattered with icing sugar. Here orange flower water is used to flavour the filling, but rose water can be used.

BOUREKIA

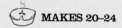 MAKES 20–24   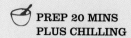 PREP 20 MINS PLUS CHILLING   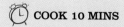 COOK 10 MINS   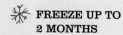 FREEZE UP TO 2 MONTHS

EQUIPMENT
8cm (3in) round cutter

INGREDIENTS

FOR THE PASTRY
(For visual step by step
instructions see p105)
200g (7oz) plain flour,
plus extra for dusting
100g (3½oz) unsalted butter,
at room temperature
1 tsp orange flower water (optional)
1 egg, beaten, to glaze

FOR THE FILLING
150g (5½oz) ricotta cheese
½ tsp ground cinnamon
grated rind of 1 orange
1 tbsp caster sugar
1 tsp orange flower water (optional)
750ml (1¼ pints) sunflower oil,
for frying
icing sugar, for dusting

1 To make the pastry, rub the flour and butter together in a large bowl with your fingertips until the mixture resembles loose breadcrumbs. Add the orange flower water, if using, and 4 tablespoons cold water and bring the mixture together to form a dough. Wrap well in cling film and chill for 30 minutes.

2 For the filling, mix the ricotta, cinnamon, orange rind, caster sugar, and orange flower water, if using, together in a large bowl and set aside.

3 Roll out the pastry on a floured surface to as thin as you can without it becoming too fragile, and cut out 20–24 rounds with the cutter; use a fluted one for a pretty finish. With a pastry brush, brush the edges of the pastry discs with the beaten egg. Place a teaspoon of the filling in the centre of each disc. Pick the disc up carefully and hold it in one hand, then fold 2 opposite edges up over the filling and pinch them together where they meet to seal, making sure that the filling does not spill out. Set aside and make the remaining pastries in the same way.

4 Pour enough sunflower oil into a large, deep frying pan to a depth of 3cm 1¼in). Heat the oil. To see if the oil is hot enough for frying dip the edge of one of the pastries into the oil. If it sizzles it is ready. Now gently lower a few pastries at a time into the oil and cook over a medium heat for 2–3 minutes, turning occasionally, until they are golden brown and puffed up.

5 Remove the cooked pastries from the oil and set them aside to cool a little on some kitchen paper while you cook the rest. Serve while still hot, dusted liberally with icing sugar. They can be stored overnight in an airtight container.

A great way to use up leftover mincemeat, here I have taken
inspiration from the Greek Bourekia to make this simple dessert.
They are best served hot with good-quality vanilla ice cream.

DEEP-FRIED MINCEMEAT RAVIOLI

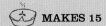 **MAKES 15**   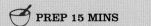 **PREP 15 MINS**   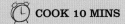 **COOK 10 MINS**   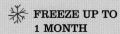 **FREEZE UP TO 1 MONTH**

1 On a well-floured surface, unroll the pastry sheet
and measure it. Roll it out or trim, as necessary,
to form a 25 x 30cm (10 x 12in) rectangle. Using a
sharp knife, cut the pastry into 30 x 5cm (2in) squares.
Put 1 teaspoon mincemeat onto half the squares. Brush
the edges of the mincemeat-topped squares with water
and cover each with a pastry square. Using the tines
of a fork, press the edges firmly together to seal.

2 Heat the vegetable oil to 180°C (350°F) in the
saucepan. Cook the ravioli, 3 at a time, for about
1½–2 minutes until golden brown. Transfer the cooked
ravioli to a plate lined with kitchen paper to drain.
Serve hot, dusted with icing sugar.

EQUIPMENT
medium heavy saucepan

INGREDIENTS

FOR THE PASTRY
plain flour, for dusting
320g (10¾oz) sheet ready-rolled
  puff pastry (or to make your own,
  see pp110–113)

FOR THE FILLING
115g (4oz) mincemeat
vegetable oil, for deep frying
sieved icing sugar, for dusting

INDEX

AUTHOR

Caroline Bretherton is a mother of two who really knows her baking. She has worked in the food industry for the last 17 years. A love of cooking led her to start her own catering company, which soon led to the establishment of an eatery in the heart of London's Notting Hill – Manna Café. She has worked extensively in television, presenting a wide range of food programmes, and in print media, contributing to, among others, *The Times* as their family food writer. She has written two books published by DK – *The Allotment Cookbook Through the Year* and the gloriously clear and precise baking tome *Step-by-Step Baking*. Caroline lives in North Carolina, USA with her husband and two sons.

ACKNOWLEDGMENTS

Caroline Bretherton would like to thank:
Peggy Vance, Dawn Henderson, and Alison Shaw at Dorling Kindersley for all their help and encouragement. Borra Garson and all at Deborah McKenna for their work on my behalf. Jane Bamforth for her much valued help and recipe contribution and my family, who again have eaten their way through far too many pies for their own good!

Dorling Kindersley would like to thank:
Art Directors for Photoshoot: Nicky Collings, Katherine Mead
Food stylists: Jane Lawrie, Rosie Reynolds
Props stylist: Wei Tang
Recipe testers: Anna Burges-Lumsden, Jan Fullwood, Katy Greenwood, Anne Harnan, Emma Lahaye, Ann Reynolds
Image retouching: Tom Morse, Steve Crozier, and Opus Multi Media Services PVT. Ltd
Proofreader: Claire Tennant-Scull
Indexer: Hilary Bird

Thanks also to Anne Fisher, Zaurin Thoidingjam, and Era Chawla for design assistance.